EVERYONE'S GUIDE TO DISTANCE RUNNING

Everyone's Guide to
DISTANCE RUNNING

NORRIE WILLIAMSON

MAINSTREAM
PUBLISHING

EDINBURGH AND LONDON

First published in 1993 by Oxford University Press Southern Africa

First published in Great Britain in 1998 by
MAINSTREAM PUBLISHING COMPANY (EDINBURGH) LTD
7 Albany Street
Edinburgh EH1 3UG

ISBN 1 84018 065 X

A catalogue record for this book is available from the British Library

Typeset in Times and Optane
Printed and bound in Great Britain by The Bath Press Ltd, Bath

CONTENTS

FOREWORD

by Professor Tim Noakes

I first came to know Norrie Williamson during 1984 when he single-handedly organised, managed, coached and even participated as a member of the winning team in the inaugural London to Paris Triathlon. I learned then that Norrie has not only superior athletic ability but also a real talent for organisation, a tireless enthusiasm for work and attention to detail, and an unquenchable desire for knowledge. On that trip, nothing escaped his attention. The team's ultimate success was largely due to his personal efforts both as an athlete and as the organising force necessary to cope with the very major logistical problems posed by that unique event.

Although he began principally as an ultradistance runner, Norrie's proficiency at and experience in cycling, swimming and canoeing have allowed him to compete at high level in both swimming and canoeing triathlons. It is this broad, possibly unique, competitive experience that forms the basis for his sporting wisdom. When that experience is combined with his other special personal characteristics, most especially his genuine enthusiasm for his sports, his inquisitiveness and his desire to communicate his knowledge, it is natural that something unusual should result. The reward of that concentrated effort is this book, which must be required reading for all who have even the most modest competitive running goals. The book is written for all runners of whatever ability. It highlights the real problems and the important decisions that each runner must make at some stage in his or her running career.

It has been said that there are already too many running books. Why, then, do we need another? The answer is that too often these books convey knowledge but no wisdom. It takes something extra to write a book of wisdom which will materially influence its readers. This is one such book. Norrie Williamson has condensed a lifetime of running experience into a meaningful and valuable message. Runners will do well to consider the wisdom that he has imparted.

ABOUT THE AUTHOR

Before accepting the advice of anyone in sport, it is necessary to be able to evaluate the creditability of the source. After all, you are going to lay the fate of your next peak sporting performance in his or her hands. You need to know that the advice is not the result of some theoretical conceptualisation undertaken by someone who has never left the status of armchair sports observer.

This description could certainly never be applied to the author. By virtue of an ever-inquisitive mind and substantial dedication to training, competition and participation, Norrie Williamson has reached a level of achievement in a number of sports that would easily satisfy many sports participants. His initial love in sport was rugby, which he played for a number of Scottish league first teams, earning caps for the North and Midlands District XV and Scottish Colleges. He opted to take up road running in 1981 and developed a particular aptitude for ultradistance events, in which he has recorded many successes. These include: winner of a 1,000km race, 1983; winner of a track 100-miler, 1982, 1984, 1986, 1988; winner of a 200km race, 1985; winner of a 100km race, 1988; winner of a 100 mile road race, 1989; winner of the 50 mile South Downs cross-country race, 1989.

Norrie has also completed the Western States 100 mile trail race in the USA and numerous 42km and 56km ultras; he has a best of 6:07 and 27th place in the gruelling Comrades Marathon (55 miles), which has a field of over 13,000 runners; he has completed over 100 ultra events, including 30 of 100 miles or longer; and he holds the record for the longest distance ever run on a treadmill in 24 hours (over 161km in 18 hours).

In 1993 Norrie was selected by the British Athletic Federation to run in the European 24-hour Challenge, and he ran for Scotland in 100km teams in 1994, 1995, 1996 and 1998. In more recent years he has also participated in track and cross-country races in an attempt to improve his speed.

Not content with participation, he has moved into the area of coaching and has advised many runners since 1985 through a series of columns in newspapers and magazines. In addition he has been nominated as provincial coaching co-ordinator and national team coach for the Technikon cross-country team. *Everyone's Guide to Distance Running* was first published in South Africa in 1989 and became a best seller. It was revised in 1992.

Since 1983 Norrie has also been involved in triathlons, earning national colours and competing in prestigious international events such as the Hawaii Ironman World Championship and the London to Paris Triathlon in 1984 and 1985. He has earned gold medals in many ultratriathlons. He has also been the president of the South African Triathlon Federation and was vice-president of the International Triathlon Federation from 1984 to 1986.

His triathlon experience led naturally to participation in specialist events such as 3.5km surf swims, 160km canoe marathons and 160km cycle races, yielding a wealth of experience in these individual sports.

Norrie's quest for competition and peak performance has prompted in him an unusual attention to detail, and this has resulted in a more than passing interest in the physiological aspects of sport. His training as a structural and civil engineer and experience as a lecturer have given him the ability to communicate complicated concepts in a way readily understood by the average person.

It is clear that the reader can accept with confidence the author's advice, secure in the knowledge that the wisdom has been derived from trials, tests, successes and failures on the field of play.

Ask yourself: why reinvent the wheel when the work has been done for you?

PREFACE

Running has been around as long as the human species. From the hunter who ran in search of the next meal, to the foot courier delivering messages, to the Olympic athlete, runners have been challenged by distance and speed from the very beginning. It stands to reason, then, that there have been many theories proposed and many books written on running, its benefits and methods of improvement; but what is interesting is the way in which many concepts are developed, adopted, doubted, then discarded, only to be revised and adopted again. As runners proceed down the various paths of the sport, they gain much experience of what works for them, but frequently they find themselves being presented with conflicting theories or reinventing the wheel. If only we could be forewarned. I suspect this is the reason that most of the books on running have been written.

The search for a solution to any problem is instigated by the question 'Why?' and for the development of my enquiring mind I have my parents and the Scottish education system to thank. Questioning is an inherent part of my professional career as a structural engineer and a habit I tried to promote in my students as a lecturer. I believe that the skill of questioning is one that will see them well down the road of life, since it is something that can be applied in nearly every situation we face. It is an attitude of questioning that resulted in this book. This is only one of the many things for which I have to thank my parents, and indeed, they have been extremely supportive and motivational in everything I try to do.

Probably the greatest influence on my involvement in running has been Professor Tim Noakes. It is my opinion that we have not given this man sufficient recognition for his work, which is among the best, if indeed not the best, in his field. Although we have not always been in agreement, his impact on my thinking has been substantial, and for that and his friendship I thank him. I also owe a great debt to Bruce Fordyce.

Ultra running as a sport becomes vastly more expensive than the average club race or marathon. The cost of getting to events, providing seconds, the food and drink requirements and the cost of equipment all add up, and without the assistance of sponsors I would not have been able to undertake many of the challenges or develop the experience that I have. Although not wanting to place the trust and assistance any sponsor has given me above any other, I would like to acknowledge the friendship and loyalty of Nils and Till Hannermann (of GW Leppin) and Norman Daniels. I became their first sponsored runner/triathlete in 1983 and they have stuck with me since then and have been a constant source of encouragement and friendship.

I made my debut in the world of writing with *The Daily News*, to which I first submitted a series of coaching columns for Comrades runners. It is as a result of these, and more so thanks to the editing of Hugh Crawford, Mike Tarr and the other characters in the sports department, that others suggested to me that I should write a book.

Many of my experiences and lessons have been gained through people I have run with – people with old, proven theories or new, innovative ones, runners and triathletes I have attempted to coach and hopefully helped. I hesitate to list these people for fear of missing anyone out, but this book in many ways is a compilation of their thoughts, which deserve recognition. I would like to mention Kenny Craig, Dave Park, Dave Box, Philip Kuhn, Mike Hogg, Gary Seaman, Jack Usdin, Wally Steel, Brian Roff and the Mazda runners, George Thomson, Frank Marrins, Graham 'Jockstrap' Law, Jean de Wet, Manfred Fuchs, Lindy Bradshaw, Helen Lucre, Tony and Ann Clewlow, Keith, Sharon and Lauren Emmerich, and Beverley and the late Dave McCarney – another man whom I believe sport has not properly honoured for his administrative and competitive contribution. Many of these people have been close and very supportive friends when things have not been going well; for that I cannot be thankful enough.

I must also mention Andy Booth, my 'non-running' Duzi partner and always willing second, without whom I would never have made the times I have in many ultras and triathlons, and William 'Big Bill' Jamieson, who was unwittingly an inspiration to me in the early years, and became a friend and one of the prime motivators behind the book. Moreover, his faith was such that he took it on as a joint venture, willingly shouldering the risk of the first edition. It was the success of that project that resulted in this edition.

Particular thanks must also go to Vicky, who spent endless hours turning my 'Scottish' into English! My thanks go to all the staff of PenPrint for their assistance and effort in putting the original book together.

There are many administrators connected with our sport. Some are innovative and have a strong empathy for the athletes whom they represent, particularly in the early years. I have to thank such administrators for their backing early in my running career.

In everyone's life there is always a mixture of good and bad. The good we cherish, the bad we can best try to learn from, and hope that time will take the painful edges off the memories. Even in these experiences, we are brought into contact with people we trust and respect, people who inspire, support, care and console, and overall we are better for the experience and for their company. Like you I have had my share of the bad, but am grateful for having shared these experiences with close friends and family. These are things that time and distance cannot steal away, and for that I am thankful to Leigh, Vernon, Copper, Elizabeth, Stewart, Gail and Jenny.

Inspiration can be fleeting; commitment and support are long-term. They are vehicles which carry us through the troughs and up to the joyous crests. This is a road to be shared with understanding and one I would not wish to travel alone. The encouragement, loyalty and companionship shared with my wife, Karin, has flattened the troughs, and raised the crests. I am very grateful that we have been able to run this road together.

This book could not have been possible without all these experiences and these friends. To them I offer my sincere gratitude and dedicate this book.

1

AN INTRODUCTION TO DISTANCE RUNNING

CHAPTER ONE

INTRODUCTION

In 1986 I was asked to write a series of articles for *The Daily News* in South Africa as a guide to training for the Comrades Marathon. There had been many clinics and articles written on the subject before, but this series differed in being aimed specifically at the average runner.

Everyone who has ever donned a pair of running shoes in South Africa has dreamt of winning the 55-mile Comrades, but this is a privilege reserved for the select few. The main attribute required to win Comrades, as the scientists constantly remind us, is inherited talent. This is so much the case that Professor Tim Noakes has calculated that even if Bruce Fordyce stayed in bed from January to May without training, he could probably run the 55 miles in under seven hours and collect a silver medal!

To win Comrades, or any top-notch distance race, though, Bruce and the other top competitors have to undertake very heavy training and their total commitment to the race is absolutely essential if they are to perform to their full ability on the day. Such is their dedication that many of them make sacrifices in their work, family and social life. For the five months before the race their top priority is Comrades; all else takes second place.

This does not mean that the other 14,000 plus competitors cannot succeed in the race. However, the majority of runners are not in a position to give the marathon top priority in their lives, nor would they want to. Most recognise that even with the most perfect training conditions they would be unable to compete with the Fordyces, Pages or De La Mottes of this world.

The same principle applies to any of the major city marathons or other prestige events. In each case there are a few élite, highly talented athletes going in search of the spoils. There are then thousands of others in the field who run without any thoughts of climbing onto the winner's podium – but who do have the capability of 'winning' within the limitations and targets they have set themselves.

The majority of entrants are unable to fit in much more than 55 miles (90km) of running a week, and that is often only for a couple of weeks' peak training during the build-up. Many find that their best intentions are destroyed by a last-minute business lunch or a meeting that goes on too long, or by a family commitment that cannot be broken.

However, every entrant wants to complete every race he enters to the best of his ability within the limitations that his lifestyle allows. The aim of this book is to put into perspective the training and approach to distance (and ultradistance) running that will allow the runner to achieve these aims.

This book purposely addresses races from 5km to the marathon and beyond, to 100km, 100 miles and multi-day events. Not everyone is fast, so their ability to challenge time is limited. Thankfully those who aren't fast tend to have an ability to go that bit further. This provides another challenge – that of distance. I and others take heart from the saying 'The race is not always to the fleet of foot, but to he who goes the distance'. There are two challenges: time and distance. A few can do both; most runners can set themselves targets in one or the other.

In order to appreciate and have confidence in the approach adopted in the book, it is perhaps useful to give a bit of further background to my own sporting experiences. My first sporting love was rugby, a game that is still very high in my regard. I was introduced to rugby at the tender age of ten at the Royal High School in Edinburgh. As was the way at that age, the forwards were 'selected' on the basis of size, and since I led the table in the bulk stakes I was put in the hooking berth. I became noted for my ability to flatten any loose scrum; the only problem was waiting long enough for me to arrive! I vividly remember spending 80 minutes chasing the game around the field, glad of set scrums and lineouts as opportunities to rejoin the game with the other 29 players.

I had a three-year break from rugby between the ages of 16 and 19, after which I returned to play in the former pupils' club. In 1973 many of the Royal High former pupils' first team decided to drop out of the annual New Year's Day fixture against Gala Rugby Club. This was not only because of the Scots' flair for New Year celebrations, but also because Gala were the top club in the country, providing about seven of the Scotland team, whereas Royal High had experienced a disastrous start to the season.

Although I could identify with the first reason, I always enjoyed the challenge of the game and felt that those players who called off were in fact making it harder for their teammates. As a result of this mass defection, however, I was given a chance to play in the second team and, more through naivety than skill, had a blinder of a game which ensured my first-team selection for the rest of the season. My promotion from fifth team to first team so fast must have caused some to suspect that it was part of a business deal!

I really enjoyed playing top-league club rugby and in that off-season I realised that if I was to keep my place I would have to ensure that I was fit. Although my hooking ability was good, I still carried more than a few extra pounds around the field with me. The story of my life to that date had been that I was always a safe bet for the last place in any race or training sprint. I decided this would now change, and the first step was to kick the 30 cigarettes I was smoking each day.

I suppose that this was when I first started running, but, to be fair, my 'long runs' in those days were all of one to two miles. On one of the early runs I managed to 'conquer' a hill by running to the top, but cigarette-induced breathlessness prevented even a walk down the other side.

From then to 21 February 1981 I was rugby-committed. Through keeping fitter than many of my rivals, I consistently played first-team rugby and even made the North and Midlands District team and the Scottish Colleges team. The date of 21 February was important because that was the day I flew to South Africa, but such was my love for the game that I wouldn't leave until after the Scotland v. England international at Twickenham. We played the British Army team on the Saturday morning, watched the international in the afternoon and left a snow-covered Heathrow Airport the following day.

Although my running for rugby training had seldom gone over ten miles, I did enter one marathon in the UK just for the challenge. In that 1980 Birmingham People's Marathon I recorded a time of 2:58:50 which, I noted, had been the winning time for the first Olympic marathon in 1896 and proved that I was already 84 years behind the times! The race organiser was one John Walker, a man whose passion for the sport would ensure our paths crossed again.

The only other races I entered were one at a Highland gathering at the local rugby ground, where I placed well down the field, and an event called the Seven Hills of Edinburgh, which was a cross between a road race and orienteering. Some of the top competitors' lack of local knowledge and a few legal short-cuts by yours truly won me third place and £5 prize money! In truth, though, these were very low-key events; in fact, anyone who had previously broken three hours for a marathon was not allowed to enter the Birmingham race!

It was on board that flight to sunny South Africa that my shift from rugby to running was instigated, and an English journalist, Bob Holmes, was one of the major factors in that decision. I had picked up a copy of the UK *Jogging* magazine (this became *Running* and is now *Runners' World*). He had written an article on a 55-mile race from Durban to Pietermaritzburg. I didn't know where the latter city was, but I knew that I was going to Durban and Bob's writing certainly motivated me to take up the challenge!

On arrival in South Africa I didn't have the distraction of rugby, since it was the off-season, and that, plus the attraction of the sunny days, soon saw me running every morning. The talk at my new workplace often turned to the Comrades race and I found further encouragement from my colleagues.

By March I had joined Savages Athletic Club and ran my qualifying marathon. It was during this first race that I met a runner who in later years was to become a very good friend and running companion. We had run together for a couple of miles from around the 14-mile mark when we started to talk, and the conversation went something like this:

'You're running well, what are you going for?'

'I'm just trying to break three hours; what time are you after?'

'Auch, I'm trying to qualify for the Comrades Marathon in May.'

'Have you ever run it before?' I enquired.

'Yes, but you'll have no problem if you can run like this,' came the reply.

Here was a chance to talk to someone who had done the race, so I now wanted to know more and asked the gentleman how many times he had run it. The reply was a bit of a conversation-stopper, as he replied '22 times'. I spent the next couple of miles puzzling at how this apparent 30–35-year-old had managed to run Comrades so many times. In awe at this achievement I didn't remember his name as we shook hands on the run, but I did remember that his father was of Scots ancestry. We split up with about one and a half miles to go, and I couldn't find him at the end of the race (I never looked into the pub!), but in 1983 I got to know Kenny Craig much better when we schemed about how we would tackle the Star Mazda 1,000km race.

Ken's opinion that I would have no problem with Comrades motivated me through the next few months and his words often came back during some of the morning runs when I began to doubt my ability. After all, he was an expert – 22 times and so young! It was only later that I learnt that his youthful looks belied his 48 years.

Comrades went well, with a 7:09, a much-coveted silver medal and very sore legs to show for it. Despite this I was on an emotional high and even ran the club's time trial the next night! A couple of senior club members mentioned how relaxed I had looked coming into Jan Smuts Stadium and already I was being guided towards the ultra events. After all, I knew I didn't have any speed.

I started looking for more challenges of distance and in 1982 entered the track 100-miler. All I intended to do was complete the distance, but two weeks before Tony and Yvonne Sumner suggested that I might be able to make a top placing. I was sceptical, since Derek Kay, who had been the first man to break 12 hours for 100 miles, was in the field. However, Derek was going for the 24-hour record and on the day he had a very bad run in the extreme heat, which gave me the opportunity of a surprise win.

This confirmed it in my mind: I would now become an ultra runner, and the longer the distance, the better. Without testing any speed potential, I had been channelled into the longer events. Now my calendar would centre around the 1,000km race and 100-milers. Even the advent of triathlons in 1983 looked tailor-made for the Williamsons of this world. The Leppin Ironman (13 mile canoe, 65 mile cycle and 26 mile run) and the Carling (three mile surf swim, 65 mile cycle and 26 mile run) both presented the necessary 'distance' challenge. I also seemed to recover so fast after these events and started to cram as many as possible into each year, and it was only in 1984 that the full impact of my mistakes was brought home to me.

The year began with the three-day Duzi 100 mile canoe marathon, followed by the Leppin Ironman, then the Carling Triathlon, then the 55 mile Comrades, all of which was training for the London to Paris Triathlon (a relay for teams of four, involving a run from London to Dover, swimming the Channel, and cycling from Calais to Paris). Having won gold in both the Leppin Ironman and the Carling, jogged Comrades for a silver and captained the Leppin team to a win in the London to Paris, the emotional wave that was carrying me onwards was beginning to give me a feeling of invincibility.

It was during the London to Paris Triathlon that I was exposed to the experience and knowledge of two of the world's great sporting gurus, Bruce Fordyce and Professor Tim Noakes. I was gradually introduced to the idea of peaking and the possibility of overtraining!

However, I had already planned an attack on the John O' Groats to Land's End record with Ken Craig, and the full impact of what I had been doing had not yet taken its toll. One of the most exciting aspects of this record attempt was that I would be returning to my home city and looked forward to being able to display my new-found running ability which, in view of my school experience, would startle many friends. In fact, running had also taken its toll on my figure, reducing my 13-stone hooker's frame to a slender 10½ stone; this alone would cause a few raised eyebrows!

After four days I learnt a hard lesson in what I consider one of the biggest disappointments of my life: I had to quit the run as a result of a stress fracture in my left leg. What made it even harder to bear was that it happened after only 250 miles, just before Edinburgh, so my planned smooth run in the home city was not to be. Instead I hobbled through to Peebles, a distance of about 100 miles, before returning to Edinburgh to borrow my brother's heavy five-speed bicycle to complete the journey.

It was a great privilege, however, to accompany Kenny on the rest of his record-breaking run. Kenny, realising how much that meant to me, has agreed to second me if the chance ever comes up to return to complete that unfinished business. Kenny's record stood for many years, defying attempts from numerous better-known runners. Don Ritchie, a world-record-holder at distances from 50 miles to 24 hours, eventually broke it – but only on his second attempt, despite his local knowledge!

The stress fracture meant no running for five weeks, and with only six weeks until the Hawaii Ironman I was cutting it close – and digging myself into a bigger hole. It should not have come as a surprise that I didn't perform as well in Hawaii as I had hoped. My marathon was, of course, the biggest disappointment, as I recorded 3:42 for the 26 miles. My only saving grace was that I managed to become the highest-placed South African finisher, which was pleasing enough to keep me motivated to tackle the 100 mile track race in Durban two weeks later.

Thankfully, I finally learnt my lesson, although it had been a hard and disappointing one. With more advice from Professor Noakes and Bruce I started to plan my calendar much better and developed a far better understanding of my body's capabilities.

This does not mean that there is nothing more to learn – quite the reverse. There are always new ideas and concepts to be considered. Often they arise when someone has a fresh look at the problem or views things from a different angle. An example of this would be the advice of Richard Turnbull, a coach and bio-kinetist, who finally managed to lay to rest my long-established belief that I was the slowest thing on two legs by showing me that I do indeed have speed potential. By accepting this fact I found new inspiration, and enjoyment, in my running.

From the above it should be clear that I have made some monumental mistakes. The greatest frustration is that these were not new mistakes. They were the mistakes that many runners seem to make, despite the available experience of others. The message seldom seems to be passed on.

Since my exposure to the wisdom of the experts I have considered myself lucky that the error of my ways was shown to me early in my running career. Even after 17 years of running I still look forward to the future and new challenges. However, I occasionally wonder what would have been if I had learnt these lessons earlier. Suppose I had tried speed training and lower mileage when I started in 1981 . . .

To say that I always remember those early lessons would be untrue. Often my enthusiasm or relative success in an event sees me planning another full calendar. A glimpse at the photograph of the dejected runner sitting with a plastered, stress-fractured leg on the monument in Peebles, however, helps to detach myself from the enthusiasm and remember the practicalities.

I would stress, however, that running has been very good to me. I have certainly had opportunities that I could never have dreamt of when I boarded that plane from Heathrow in 1981.

There are a multitude of books on the market which give advice to the runner on how to become a top-class athlete. These are often written by the world's best. There are others that address the absolute beginner. The problem is that these seldom concern themselves with the distance events and, even if they do, most are written on the assumption that the runners' first priorities are running and winning. In my experience this is not the case for the majority of runners. The objective of this book is to give some assistance to the average distance and ultra runner, in order that he (or she) may derive as much pleasure from the sport as possible without repeating the mistakes that tend to trip us all up. That is not to say that the book will give a final answer in the quest for a perfect training plan, but it certainly aims to put to rest some of the prevailing myths about distance and ultra running and to provide a good base from which a specialised individual training programme can be developed.

A number of scientific concepts developed by sports medicine professionals and scientists are discussed throughout the book. Unfortunately these concepts are often discussed in the original sources in language that the average runner is unable to understand. This book aims to make these ideas accessible.

South Africa is privileged to have one of the top sports medicine gurus in the world in Professor Tim Noakes, who spent years putting together a book on the subject called *Lore of Running*. Many of his concepts have been explained in a very basic fashion here, and I recommend that readers further their knowledge by referring to Tim's book.

CHAPTER TWO

THERE IS NO FINISH LINE!

Two phrases dominate the world of running: 'There is no finish line' and 'The race is not always to the fleet of foot but to he who goes the distance'. Although there is an air of contradiction between them, both have long-term messages.

To the competitive runner the first may indicate that no matter how well you race there is always more to be done. People thought a four-minute mile was impossible, then Roger Bannister did the impossible. In the few months after that many others followed suit. The mile record has been systematically whittled down over the years. There is no finish line!

An alternative interpretation of it may be connected to Sebastian Coe's comment that 'There is no such thing as a perfect race'. No matter how well one does, as runners we always look back and wonder where we lost that vital second by going round a corner too wide in a road race, or that essential fraction of a second in a 400m by not leaving the blocks slightly faster. Even when all seemed to go according to plan, the first thing we do is 'scheme' how to improve on it. There is no finish line!

However, I would suggest there is a further way of looking at running, one which, I feel, is often overlooked. My future in running will be a combination of ethos from these two phrases.

One of the most common questions asked of any runner is 'Why do you run?'. It is always very hard to answer with anything that makes much of sense to the non-runner, especially when it has been asked on the spur of the moment.

Running has many benefits acknowledged by the medical men, and there can be no doubt that it is one of the easiest sports in which to participate, but neither of these is the reason I now run. Certainly, my family's poor medical history was one motivation for my initial participation in sport, but it has gone much further than that now. Runners seem to transgress various attitudes towards their sport and yet remain committed to some form of participation. It's even being suggested that running causes some form of 'addiction' without which the runner suffers a 'cold turkey' reaction. I am not qualified to comment on the medical aspects of that but I do acknowledge that the thought of not running for any extended period is not a pleasant one.

So am I doomed to a life of competition, in constant search of a 'win', initially in the sub veterans, then the veterans, then masters and so on? I sometimes wonder what I'll be doing in running in ten years' time, but I never wonder whether I will actually *be* running or not. I fully intend to run until I die, and if I die while I run, even better, since the chances are I'll die happy! But I honestly don't see myself continuing to or wanting to be competitive at any distance for ever. That is not to say that I would stop keeping myself in good condition – that is a feeling that has become too precious to me – but I wouldn't want to spend that vital extra time required to reach a peak in the years to come.

The great thing about running which many runners come to realise over the years is that even when there are no prizes, awards or races to be run, there are still the challenges to be faced and accomplished. Indeed, there is no finish line!

In the begining, the challenge is to be able to run a distance in training so that we can go on to race. Then we challenge ourselves to race faster and beat more people, and then we train to win prizes or be the best in an age group. This tends to be the progression of the runner's career. Some runners accept that they will never win any prizes, and for them the challenge is to improve their times, or to complete a race distance and take home a badge or a medal to 'certify' the fact.

No matter what level of runner you are there is always something that you can take on as a challenge. The lure of a sub-three-hour marathon, completing Comrades, covering 100 miles in 24 hours, eating up a 10km in 30 minutes . . . it's all personal. It's your challenge. There can be few other sports where so many different people all with different objectives get together to meet their challenges at one time.

But not all challenges have to be met in races, and this is what I would encourage runners to realise. Most of my training as an ultradistance runner is done alone, and this is not only because it fits in best with my time schedule, but also because I enjoy it.

When training for a journey event, or even just for the hell of it, I will have planned a 65km run before work in the middle of the week. I write it into my schedule in advance, but as it gets closer I start to get excited about it. It's not going to be a fast run, but it has an excitement and anticipation about it.

In order to do the run and be in work on time, I need to be on the road for just after 3.00 a.m. I have to plan ahead and leave a change of clothes and my car at work the night before. I mentally search out a route. This is flexible to allow me to make the 'challenge' harder or easier, depending on how I am going, but it must take me somewhere in particular. When living in South Africa, the warm overnight temperatures meant that shorts and a vest were still adaquate clothing. The runs would tend to be out and back to the town of Umhlanga and Toti; the location did not matter, but the challenge did.

I head off in the dark of the night, only to meet late-night revellers, security guards, policemen and shift workers. It doesn't matter who it is at that time of the day – we are all defenceless, irrespective of our backgrounds or purpose – and greetings are exchanged. The world seems quiet and perfect and in this pleasant atmosphere I enjoy my run even more.

Four hours later the sun is up as my goal is nearly complete. Despite the distance I still feel a spring in the stride from the success of meeting my challenge and from the thought that I have cheated a few extra hours out of the day! It is a great feeling, and yet there is no measure of time, no position to log, no others to compare my effort against, no exact distance to put down . . . just a sense of achievement, of personal satisfaction.

The euphoria of these long early-morning runs wears off towards the end of the day as the early rise takes its toll. I am aware that there is a need to recover for a couple of days and to take an early night to restore my rest quota, but, that aside, it is a session that has much attraction for me, and I always look forward to it. I see this as something I will do much more of in the non-competitive years.

Running and exploring the high-altitude contour paths in Kwazulu Natal's Drakensberg mountains is a another run that takes some beating. If you are armed with a walkman, some relaxing classical music, a source of water and an easily folded rain suit, the world becomes an idyllic place. The initial climb up to the contour is taxing as you battle the thinner air, and this also limits the speed at which you can run along the path. But none of that matters as you head off towards the horizon, seeing the birds float stationary in the updraught. The mountains seemingly go on for ever, and a point that seems so close is only reached after kilometres of paths winding in and out of the creases in the hillside. The music can make you feel at one with the floating birds; no other sound can be heard. Pace and distance mean nothing up here. There are no kilometre marks, and no car can be taken over the route afterwards. The terrain forbids an even or steady progression; it becomes an enforced fartlek session of run, walk and climb. The direction of the run is unimportant as well, providing some landmark is taken as the point of return! There is no quantifying this run at all and yet it can be extremely satisfying.

Some would argue that it is the effect of the South African climate that makes these ventures enjoyable, but that's not the case. Edinburgh is undoubtedly one of the most beautiful cities in the world. A combination of rural and urban splendour and sufficient paths, parks and trails means that even the fittest distance runner can train off the roads for over three hours without going outside the city boundary.

My first winter back in 1996 saw temperatures reportedly dropping to minus 20°C. With clothing layered, and hidden under the bulk of a gortex suit and balaclava, I commenced my scheduled long run. The snow layered the paths, and crunched under each footstep. From where I live on the hill, I can survey the Forth Bridges, the Pentland Hills and the whole west side of the city. This particular run would take me out to the south-western side and onto paths on the side of the Pentlands. As I commenced my descent from the house, I could see my target turnround point in the distance. The frost had resulted from a clear, cloudless sky and, combined with the early sun, provided picture-postcard views.

Time was not going to be an issue, and distance would be impossible to measure; it was only about enjoyment and an exploration of the challenge of the conditions. I soon warmed to the conditions, as a micro-climate built up under the gortex suit. My stride length varied to meet the needs of different depths of snow or grips on ice. There was a peacefulness, as the city wrapped itself up indoors, giving runners greater freedom and dominance of the paths and tracks. Three and a half hours later, I commenced the climb back through the roads to our house. As it was now almost midday, a few kids were out walking down the road towards me. 'Hey, mister, your balaclava's got ice on it!' With only my eyes, mouth and nose visible, I had not been aware of my external appearance. The layers of clothing and the effort of running had kept me as warm as if I had been indoors. I ran my gloved hand up to my head and brushed off a thin smattering of frost – the heat and perspiration from my head had been frozen on the balaclava. My inquisitiveness had been stimulated. Now back at home, a look into the mirror revealed other winter additions, including ice on my eyebrows. This merely added to the pleasure and satisfaction of the run. In some ways it was another part of conquering the challenge.

Three different runs, three different challenges, and three different experiences. These were not about time, speed, winning or losing; these were about taking and living the challenge of the moment. Failure had no threat; they were merely self-imposed, not self-desired challenges.

My only desire when I think of my running years ahead is that I will keep myself fit enough to enjoy these types of runs. These are the challenges and targets that I hope to be training for, and the point that I hope has come through is that running has something to offer everyone. There is always the challenge, and there is always the need to be fit for the challenge, within the priorities that you set yourself. Even when you become less competitive you can find more and more new challenges. Satisfaction comes from a challenge taken and conquered, no matter what level, and this is irrespective of speed or distance. In running there really is no finish line.

CHAPTER THREE

THE APPEAL OF DISTANCE RUNNING

'The race is not always to the fleet of foot . . . but to he who goes the distance.'

I am often perceived as someone who is only interested in ultramarathon running. There are, however, a number of athletics administrators who have been surprised to hear me campaign for and promote the virtues of short-distance races. I believe and hope that this is underlined by articles I have written over the years and by the content of this book. This said, it is true that my personal preference when racing is for ultradistance events, and not the extended marathons of 30 and 40 miles, but true ultradistance events of 100km and beyond. I hope this chapter will cast a new light on this aspect of the sport and perhaps encourage others to gain similar reward.

Ultramarathons became the focal point of the South African road-running calendar during the years of sporting isolation. They were responsible for the initial growth of road running and its boom over the past 20 years. Much of this is as a result of the TV and media coverage that surrounds the most popular South African races such as Comrades, City to City and Two Oceans. Many runners have been brought into the sport by the 'availability' of the challenge. In the same way as 80,000 people apply to run the London marathon, each year armchair athletes, who see people they know competing in one of these events, realise that they too can take up running and then find themselves motivated to take on the challenge not of speed, but of distance. For most people it tends to be the marathon distance that has this effect, and in each case it is the media support in New York, Boston, Hawaii, Berlin and Rotterdam that promotes this move.

In South Africa, the linchpin of the race calendar is the 90km Comrades challenge. This has had an unfortunate effect on road running there in as much as it annually tempts runners to move up a distance rather than down to shorter events, which is the trend in Britain and the northern hemisphere.

Ironically, however, it is the 90km distance at which most South African runners stop, yet in the true sense of the word this is only the 'baby' of ultramarathons. Indeed, many international runners consider this to be a mere stroll into the magical land of distance challenge, and as for 56km – that is something to be left to the marathoners! Certainly this view is vindicated by the performances of élite marathoners Thompson Magawana (2:11 marathon best) and Frith van der Merwe (2:27), whose low-flying flight over the 35 mile Two Oceans course set world bests at 30 miles and 50km that have stood since the mid-eighties.

Such performances result in many people – runners, administrators and spectators alike – being unable to understand the motivation, athletic endeavour and performances of runners at longer distances. The apparent lack of consistently high performances at longer distances adds fuel to these observers' fires and it is only when the facts are considered that the magnitude of the problem facing the true ultra runner can be established.

Internationally, ultras *begin* with 100km. Nowadays there is an Intercontinental Cup spread over a number of events in five continents. Athletes' best performances can then be compared. There is also the International Association of Ultrarunners (IAU) World Cup 100km, which is recognised by the International Amateur Athletic Federation (IAAF) and became a full-blown World Championship in Belgium in 1993.

Many South Africans initially thought that this distance is comparable with Comrades, and to some extent this is true, but just as there is a 'wall' to be encountered at 20 miles in a marathon and at 40 miles in Comrades, there's another at 53 miles (just when Comrades is finishing) in a 100km event. If you doubt that, just look back at the early performances of top South African Comrades runners' times over the last ten miles of a 100km race. The final 15km in the sanction-bursting International 100km in Stellenbosch in 1989 saw Bruce Fordyce's pace drop from a rhythmical six-minute mile to a hard-fought slog barely under eight minutes per mile. In 1994 Comrades winner Shaun Meiklejohn led the World 100km in Japan, only to grind to a halt, surrender the lead and finish fourth in 6:26:58.

Moving up, there is the challenge of the 100 miles, and many more walls to be climbed along the way. World records here stand for many years. South Africa's Wally Hayward's record of 12:20:08 is still seventh best ever on the road, and that was set on the Bath road to

London in 1953! Don Ritchie's 11:30:51, still the world track record, was set at Crystal Palace on 15 October 1977, and his 6:10:20 record for 100km on the track, set in 1978, still heads the lists.

It was only in June 1990 that he ran his next fastest 100km track time for the distance, 6:46:10, to take the world's best 45–49 age group for 100km. It took even Ritchie, whom many consider the world's best ultra runner, until 1991 to finally match the World and Veteran 24-hour record set by 45-year-old Wally Hayward at Motspur in 1953! Hayward, who won Comrades five times and ran in the 1952 Olympic marathon, returned to Comrades in 1988 to run 90km in under nine and a half hours and in 1989, at the age of 80, became the oldest finisher.

Typically, races over 100km in Europe are won in times between 6:30 and 6:50, with only a few runners getting under 7:00. Even with a top-class international field in Stellenbosch, South Africa, in 1989, attracted by the incentive of vast money to break the sports sanction, only 11 runners broke the seven-hour barrier. In the whole year only 40 runners dipped under 6:58 on measured courses. Most 100 mile races are won in times well over 13 hours.

As we move up again to 24 hours we encounter more 'walls' and the battle against fatigue. By now the Greek wonder, Yiannos Kouros, has come into his own, and he holds both the road and the track record for 12 and 24 hours. He first set a road 24-hour best of 284.853km in 1984 and improved it to the current 286.463 the following year. In between these he secured the 24-hour track record with 283.6km, and subsequently moved it up to a mind-boggling 303km in 1997. This is the equivalent of running seven non-stop marathons, each in 3:20! Kouros holds the top eight 24-hour track performances, with Russian Anatoliy Kruglikov the nearest contender with his 1995 run of 275.982km. In 45 years, only 20 people have bettered Hayward's 1953 mark.

The Europa Cup has been introduced for 24-hour races. Athletes are able to compete in a choice of six races between May and November, their best two performances determining rankings. In 1990 the IAU held an International 24-hour Indoor Championship, with the first international vests being awarded to competitors. In 1989 one runner surpassed 260km, four achieved more than 250km and two surpassed 240km, with the next six achieving just over 235km on the track. There was a similar situation on the road. Top place went to 256.5km, followed by 251.02; only four surpassed 240km and three 235km. Since then teams from European countries annually compete in a Championship race, and there seems the possibility of a World 24-Hour Championship by the year 2000. Notwithstanding the increase in prestige and interest, only Kourus and Russian Ivan Bogdanov were able to get above the 250km mark on the track, and only seven runners topped 250km on the road.

Ultras don't stop there: there's 48 hours, six days, 1,000km, 1,000 miles . . . and so it goes on in the search to find the ultimate ultra challenge. Events are held in every conceivable condition – trail, road, mountain, snow, you name it – and every time someone takes the challenge. Why, then, such apparently poor performances? Maybe not enough people are trying the longer races? Not so. In 1997 teams from over 30 countries competed in the men's world 100km race and 14 competed for the women's team title. In considering only events longer than 70km, there are well over 1,000 events in over 50 countries.

In truth, ultras, by their very nature, require a very delicate balance of conditions. The longer the event, the less likely it is that a new record will be set or an existing one matched. Put another way, the longer the event, the more that can go wrong!

For success, firstly the athlete has to be at his or her peak, then the course has to be suitable for a record, and this also means that it has to be accurately measured, with acceptable amounts of fall (the drop in altitude between the start and finish). Then bring in the major variable, the weather. Ideal ultra conditions are cool and windless. In a 24-hour race this has to be maintained for a full day! Can you remember when that last happened in a normal day, let alone on a specific race day?

It is interesting to note that all three of Don Ritchie's records mentioned above were run in light rain, which doubtlessly cooled the runners. Similar conditions were present when Wally Hayward competed in his record-breaking races in the UK in 1953.

Heavy rain, on the other hand, is a disadvantage. Heat is the ultra runner's greatest enemy. It has been estimated that a marathoner will slow down by 7 per cent in hot conditions, which turns a 2:30 into a 2:35 in hot weather. 'Hot' may only mean raising the mercury to 20°C and a 68 per cent humidity.

Using this same percentage, which is likely to be conservative, would turn a 12-hour 100-miler into a 13.5-hour. Perhaps this explains why in the past 25 years, the 11:56:56 set by South Africa's Derrick Kay has only been beaten twice!

Too cold, too windy or too wet and the times will also drop off. So if, as you run your 10km, 21km, marathon or 56km event, your legs feel weary, or your muscles ache under the jarring downhill, think of the ultra runners who take on the longer challenge and who have yet another 44km, 105km, 20 hours, five days or even longer to go to reach their finish line. Theirs is not the pain of intense speed of marathons or shorter races, rather the slow, numbing pain of distance. It is something that takes as much in guts, courage, skill and ability as their speedier counterparts, but the emphasis on each aspect is different.

It is extremely hard to pin down the exact attraction of the challenge of these longer events, but the fight to conquer the pain and the mind are two aspects. This is made even harder where the incentive is limited to personal challenge. Without close competition it is extremely hard to maintain a record-breaking pace when faced with a further 50 or 100km or more. This too explains the long life of records. There are few ways to describe the 'pain' of the long run, but one incident during the 1,000km race in 1983 will give non-ultra runners some idea. Kenny Craig and I had been running 100km for six days and had just finished a 16-hour session, hampered by injuries. Back at the overnight stop as we undressed for a warm bath, our second George Thompson enquired about Kenny's groans.

'Where does it hurt, Kenny?' he asked.

'Listen, laddy,' came the reply. 'I'm so sore that even my blood aches!'

Ultra running gets like that, but when you have finished, when you have beaten the pain, the distance and the challenge, the feeling is exhilarating – and all you can think of is the next one.

If your running ever seems to be losing its attraction as you finish down the field, or if you feel the need for another type of challenge, then consider a move up in distance. Don't be too concerned about the difference in training; as you will see later in the book, most ultra runners train like a marathoner, with some additional long runs. Ultras have a lot to offer, and are available to everyone. Why do I compete in ultras? Maybe those old words are right – because they are there!

CHAPTER FOUR

UNDERSTANDING THE LIFE OF A DISTANCE RUNNER

In Boston, Rotterdam and London, it's April. In Berlin and Oslo it's September. In Amsterdam and New York it's November, and in South Africa it's 16 June. All are cities and countries engulfed with marathon fever. All share the same rituals. For South Africans it doesn't matter where you live, 16 June is the day that you become involved somewhere, somehow in the Comrades marathon, even if it's only being stuck in the traffic jam between Pietermaritzburg and Durban!

Around the world runners are inspired to enter their local mass-participation event. In the vast majority of cases the greatest distance is 26 miles. Sporting isolation in South Africa brought focus to an event over twice the length of a marathon, and it is for this reason that it became the central feature on a national sporting calendar. Over 15,000 people run each year. Had it not existed, perhaps the focus would have been towards a marathon – but exist it did, and a nation deprived of outside sport took the 1970s running boom to 55 miles. It is interesting to consider whether a similar restriction would have taken Britain's runners to the London to Brighton 55-miler.

What is clear is that it is the same level of 'average' runners in New York, Boston, Rotterdam, Berlin or London who find they are capable of the Comrades. For this reason, let's consider the role of the runner and the impact his or her challenge has on the other aspects and people in his or her life.

In the weeks and months before the event, those 15,000 runners will have been pounding pavements in their quest for a Comrades medal, and the objectives and motivation of each runner vary. For the public at large it is a tremendous spectacle on the day, but few who are not related to one of those 'mad runners' can identify with or understand what it takes to make the Comrades.

There are the stories of runners who were challenged in the local bar and then, seemingly with no training, end up completing the Comrades in order to receive a couple of cases of their favourite tipple. There are the odd occasions when runners claim not to have trained for the event at all, other than the mandatory qualifying marathon between October and April. These few exceptions are generally involved in other sports and draw on that fitness to take them through.

Such anomalies aside, a runner aiming only for a finish needs to complete between 500 and 650 miles during the five-month build-up and will average 30–40 miles per week in April and May. These figures don't seem all that frightening in comparison to the immense distances covered by the top athletes, but it has to be rememberd that the back runners also train at a slower pace and thus will have to put in about five or six hours of running to cover this distance. Add on travelling and changing times and you have a total of ten hours a week that the runner has to find.

In order to complete the Comrades the runner must have the speed to finish a standard 26 mile event in 4:30. Such an effort can be compared over many distances. For example, this would equate to 57 minutes over 10km, or a 45-minute five mile time trial. In fact, most runners' finishing times can be determined long before they line up on 16 June. Calculations based on their best times over shorter distances and the distance they have trained between January and May show that to achieve an eight-hour finish a runner needs a marathon of 3:20 and around 800 miles in training. This means a weekly distance of just under 55 miles. Silver medallists need to be capable of a 3:07 marathon and would cover about 60 miles per week, amounting to 1,000 miles in the five-month build-up.

When it comes to gold, there are many more things to take into account. On the day there are probably 50 people capable of making the top ten positions, but the outcome depends on who is having a good day and who is having a bad day. Then there is the planning. The really top runners have set up the race like a military operation. They know exactly where their seconds (helpers who are able to provide momentary assistance along the route) will be, what they are going to need to drink and when, and who the opposition is likely to be. It is such planning and mental preparation that put nine-times winner Bruce Fordyce head and shoulders above the rest of the field. It is, of course, also true that he had inherited the right genes from his parents to make him a world-class runner, but then so have a few others. Fordyce, however, knew how to make the most of them. To be in with a chance of gold, a runner needs to be able to run a 2:28 marathon and train an average of 72 miles per week, his total for five months being about 1,250 miles. To win, that can be increased to a 2:16 marathon and 1,400 miles.

Running such distances alone will not give the runner a better time – the speed must also be there. Ironically, runners who overdo the distance required in their build-up are more likely to finish with a slower time, since they have not allowed themselves enough recovery for their standard of training. With the correct training, runners' times are virtually a foregone conclusion if they pace themselves well through the race. This just leaves the positions to be sorted out and, apart from the top 50, most runners aren't too bothered about this.

This type of statistics can be applied to any marathon or distance race. A balance can be found between the distance to be trained, the current speed of the runner and the desired finish time. If the balance is right, the finish is predictable.

So, on 'marathon day', be that the local 10km, the London Marathon or Comrades, when you see the coverage of the race on television, don't feel any anguish for the runners; don't sympathise with their pain. If they have done the training, the race is just a formality and, indeed, can be one of the most enjoyable runs of the year. It is this enjoyment that will motivate them to train for the following year's event.

CHAPTER FIVE

YOUR LONG-TERM PROSPECTS AS A DISTANCE RUNNER

'In order to maintain, continue to train!'

One of South Africa's most popular and most remarkable athletes is Willie Mavuma. At the age of 67 Willie still leaves over 95 per cent of the field in his wake, whether he competes at a 10km race or a marathon. In the 15 years I was in South Africa, Willie, who runs for my old club Savages, did not seem to age, and indeed he seems to have slowed down only marginally.

Willie seems to be typical of a growing trend amongst some older runners. Athletes like John Walker of New Zealand, who was aiming to be the first 40-year-old athlete to run a sub-four-minute mile, and John Campbell, who at 41 ran a 2:11:04 marathon in Boston, seem to indicate that some runners have been able to 'cheat' the ravages of time.

Recent research that has been done on the effects of age on running will give runners of all ages some hope, and perhaps some guidance in this regard. One thing is for sure: this is a subject that affects everyone, be it now or a few years down the line. We will all grow old, but this does not necessarily mean that we will get substantially slower.

It has long been held that as we grow older, our ability to maintain our previous level of performance drops off. All those long training hours cannot combat the inevitable slump in times. This seems to be substantiated by the fact that most top-level sportsmen and women retire in their late 20s or early 30s. By 40 it is time to have more respect for our 'fragile' body and take a more gentle approach to exercise. At best this tends towards a sedate training pace, at worst it's regression towards the status of 'professional advisor', a role undertaken by the mass of 'television experts' on sofas throughout the world! Research has confirmed this belief, and shown that even with the adoption of a 'long, slow distance' approach to training, we can still expect a drop-off of around 9 per cent in aerobic capacity for each passing decade.

In South Africa's modern biathlon, comprising a 1km run and 100m swim, 12 bonus points are awarded to those over 27 years of age on the basis of a one-second slow-down in both the swim and the run per additional year of age. Personally I think this is a bit excessive, but it does acknowledge the problem.

A study that included 14 Olympic competitors ratified that even at the highest level, a 10 to 15 per cent reduction of aerobic capacity should be the expectation for a decade of no training. Reduction in VO_2 max and maximum heart rate are two symptoms which are accompanied by an increase in mass. (VO_2 max refers to the maximum rate of oxygen delivery to the muscles, and is discussed further later in the book.) As they say, it would appear that 'the writing is on the wall'. So why continue your training regime? After all, a mere 1 per cent benefit in aerobic capacity is hardly reasonable return for a continuous ten years of training. Couldn't all these hours be put to a better use?

In real terms, the effects of age can be quite devastating, and a drop in VO_2 max of, say, 1ml/kg/min per year would result in a 2:40 marathoner running the same distance ten years later in 3:25. Add to this the fact that we tend to add a few pounds to our bodies as we get older, which tends to show in the form of a constant on-board 'energy belt' around our waists. Such mass increase is in fact of no use and a mere 4lb increase in weight can provide an immediate five-minute penalty to a 2:40 marathoner, along with a further 3 per cent drop in VO_2 max.

Thankfully, the research that confirmed our worst fears also provided an insight into how many of these seemingly amazing veteran athletes maintain their level of performances into their autumn years. What sort of genes, miracle mixture or elixir have these 'demi-gods' discovered that allows them to run times that many people 20 or 30 years their junior are still striving to achieve? The phenomenon is most obvious in track and field athletes, and this may be a clue.

Consider 68-year-old Canadian Earl Fee, who entered the 1997 World Veteran Championships in South Africa with 13 world age-group records on his CV. His specialities are 300m and 400m high hurdles, 400m, 800m, 1500m and the mile. He puts his success down to exercise of some form every day. Even more amazing is that Fee stopped running for 33 years due to injury, but successfully returned to the track in 1982. A daily press-up regime, combined with tennis and skiing on water or snow provided his base during his 33-year racing sabbatical.

Fee is by no means a freak of nature. A trio of octogenarians from Japan competed in the same games, with Kizo Kimura, the oldest at 87, entering 13 events, mixing pole vault, javelin and hammer with runs ranging from 400m to 80m hurdles. His span of events required speed, strength and flexibility. One of his disappointments was leaving his 91-year-old training partner, Kumazo Kashiwada, at home in Japan.

Athletics aficionados will remember the exploits of New Zealand's Derek Turnbull. Now in his 70s, he can still turn out competitive times, with a 2:28.37 at 800m and 18:34.61 for the 5,000m gaining him world age-group bests.

It's not only the men who produce outstanding performances. Which 50-year-old wouldn't be pleased to cover 100m in 12.65 seconds, 200m in 25.72 and 80m hurdles in 12.86, and catapult 5.27m in the long jump? These are the four new world age-group records American Phil Raschker added to her haul in her 50–54 category. The youthful-looking dynamo bagged seven golds, including the heptathlon. These examples are just a few of the thousands of veteran sportspeople who have seemingly found and drunk from the fountain of youth. So where is this Holy Grail?

The benefits of moderate exercise which include an increase in HDL cholesterol and a reduced risk of coronary heart disease were highlighted in a Harvard alumni study of 17,000 men over a 20–26-year period. This landmark research found that each hour of moderate exercise can add roughly two hours to your life! There are limits, however, which prevent us from buying back to 'eternity'. The two-year addition comes in with around 15 miles of weekly jogging, and the upper limit would appear to be around 30 miles per week. In calorie terms this converts to about 2,000 and 4,000 per week. This need not be 'vigorous' exercise, as the research relates to an intensity of about 75 per cent maximum heart rate (about 65 per cent VO_2 max – 10 to 11 minutes per mile jogging).

Given the added known benefits of reduced blood pressure, reduced risk of insulin-dependant diabetes and reduced risk of osteoporosis (particularly in women), it would appear that we have the essence of our goal in basic exercise. However, there is the question of quality in addition to quantity.

Finnish research takes us a bit further down the road. A comparison between endurance sports (running, cycling, swimming), team sports (football, rugby, hockey) and power sports (weightlifting, sprinting) determined that endurance athletes could add six years to their life in comparison to a couch potato, whereas team-sport players could add only four years, and power sportspeople people a relatively miserly two years. As a rider to the outcome, the researchers noted that the power- and team-players enjoyed a higher social status, which probably accounted for their particular increase in life expectancy (better nutrition, health care and so on).

All of the above will probably ensure that those who undergo a relatively minimal amount of aerobic exercise will live through to be septuagenarians. However, to most runners this extension of years is a mere formality, as their life-long commitment to such miserly amounts of low-intensity work is already grafted in stone! The quest is to maintain a level of excellence.

The Harvard research did indicate a link between the low-intensity jogging and swimming with longer life, but found that working in the garden, housework and walking (all often promoted by fitness gurus) did not provide the same results. So the initial link to intensity is evident.

More recently, research on distance runners was undertaken at Ball State University in the USA and included such notable athletes as Frank Shorter, Jeff Galloway and Derek Clayton amongst the 37 élite athletes first tested in 1970. Repeat tests were taken in 1992. In the intervening years eight had taken to the couch, 18 had continued casual training at a low intensity and 11 had kept to a routine of regular vigorous training.

As expected, the eight had experienced a drop-off of 12 beats per minute in maximum heart rate and a 10 to 15 per cent aerobic capacity fall-off. The 18 casual trainers had a marginal advantage, with a 9 per cent drop. However, the 11 who had maintained an aggressive approach to their training with higher-intensity work had managed to maintain their VO_2 max and their maximum heart rate. Furthermore, the fall-off in aerobic capacity was a mere 2 per cent per decade! For one miler, his time of 4:05 at the tender age of 25 had dropped by merely eight seconds to 4:13 at the age of 45.

The basic premise of intense exercise being the prerequisite for maintaining performance is confirmed by the testing of 26 élite athletes (including 14 Olympians) by American coach Jack Daniels. Using less élite but motivated 'average' runners, researchers in Milwaukee, USA, were able to show that regular intense exercise allowed 52-year-olds to maintain their VO_2 max for a ten-year period (i.e. until they were 62).

So, in practical terms, where is the fountain of youthful performance?

The secret appears to lie not with regular endurance exercise, as many have hinted, but rather with regular intense exercise. The endurance work will certainly provide an extension to life and reduction in health risks, but performance will be guided by the rule of 'use it or lose it'!

Considering your heart as a 'rev counter', your youthful range may be from a resting rate of below 50 to a maximum of above 200. The theoreticians tell us our maximum can be calculated from 220 less our age. Thus a 50-year-old has a theoretical maximum of 170, and many use this to guide all their training. This is merely a rule of thumb, however, as many training athletes find that they are capable of going well beyond this. In our early years of training we grind out high-intensity work with little care for how high our heart rates go. Our intensity is limited more by pride and an 'eyeballs-out' creed than by a heart-rate monitor. As we age, we tend towards the conservatism of a watchful eye on the upper limit, and give more credibility to those promoting restrictions on intensity. The problem is that we then fail to use part of the heart-rate capacity that we have developed. If we were weightlifters and only ever lifted 100lbs in training, how would we ever lift 140lbs in competition?

This is not to say that we have to make use of maximum revs at every outing, but rather that the limiting factor to our performance may to some extent be self-imposed. This should not be too surprising.

A study to determine the most beneficial way of training for a 10km was undertaken at the University of Texas by Peter Snell (a sub-four-minute-miler in his own right) with ten club-level runners. After an initial base training of six weeks, they were split into two groups. One group had two 29-minute sessions of lactate threshold training, whereas the other group used two weekly interval sessions over 200m and 400m. Each of these interval sessions was run at a pace between 10km and 5km race pace or slightly faster, and the total distance per session was around three miles. By comparison, the threshold group covered around five miles of continuous running at 12 to 15 seconds per mile slower than 10km race pace. The remaining training sessions for both groups were identical.

After the completion of the study, the interval group improved not only their 800m race time (by over 11 seconds on average!), but also reduced their 10km times by an average of over two minutes. In comparison, the threshold runners, who were effectively only training below their race pace (and heart rate), improved their 800m times by only 6.6 seconds and their 10km by a minute.

There are many reasons for this, but most can be encapsulated in the concept of 'using it or losing it'. This is not only restricted to heart rate, but also running efficiency, co-ordination and the ability of the nerves to 'fire' the muscles at the required rate for leg speed.

It has been shown that simply undertaking one session of 5 x 400m (or 5 x 1–1.5 minutes' effort in other endurance sports) per week, even during injury, is sufficient to maintain basic fitness for around ten weeks. This is primarily related to the fall-off in total body blood volume that occurs when exercise is suddenly stopped.

To maintain your performance, then, it seems you need only incorporate one or two sessions per week which will tax you to the higher end of your capacity. These should be slightly faster, but significantly shorter than the event you are training for. This ties in with the prime training of those World Veterans Championship athletes we identified at the beginning of the chapter.

These same principles can be adapted for any endurance sport. Given the intensity required, the interval work would need to last in excess of a minute and probably no longer than six to ten minutes. Recovery between efforts will obviously vary depending on the speed of the effort, but as a general guide start with the following:

Length of effort	Recovery
30 seconds	40–60 seconds
60 seconds	2 minutes reducing to 60 seconds
3 minutes	3 minutes reducing to 90 seconds
6 minutes	5 minutes reducing to 3 minutes
10 minutes	Around 3 minutes

Going back to those power- and team-players of the Finnish study, it could be that in order to maintain their peak performance they need to do some 'over-distance work'. By their very nature, football, rugby and other team games tend to involve only short high-intensity runs down the wing or through midfield, with fairly long periods of low-intensity 'recovery'. This is probably of insufficient duration to elicit the benefits of interval training (a 30-second run would take the player over the full length of a rugby pitch). A bi-weekly 'quality' session could provide the added boost the older player needs to keep ahead of his younger rivals.

An aspect common to all ageing sportspeople is the natural decline in muscle strength. Muscle density and elasticity both drop off with age, and minimising this requires the move towards a cross-training programme. The older runner or cyclist will spend more time on upper-body strength and a regime of basic plyometric jumps (hops, skips down a stair, and so on), whereas an older swimmer needs to give more focus to the lower body.

The final ingredient to continued performance relates to motivation. For the élite athlete, this is perhaps the most difficult. Having spent eight to twelve years focusing on an Olympic or World Championships medal, how do you maintain the drive? Where do you go from the top? You can only move sideways in the same sport by defending your title. Given the dedication and sacrifices required by top sportspeople, and the lack of reward for those who just fail to make the grade, it is no surprise that they retire early. Thus their decision may be more to do with lack of desire, or burn-out, than with a fall-off in performance (although the two are linked). Perhaps the future will see more élite sportspeople adopt Andy Ripley's approach. The England and British Lions back-row rugby player of the 1970s made the final squad for selection to the Oxford and Cambridge boat race – at the age of 50!

Motivation is where the average sportsperson has an advantage. Unfamiliar with the role of winning, their move into veteran categories will often promote them closer to the victory platform. In some sports there are points added for each year of age, or other method of handicapping, to equate performances. Understandably, there is limited incentive for a previous Olympic athlete to win an age-group veteran title, but for the less talented, or the late starter, the desire for a world or national ranking in veteran competitions can provide the drive necessary to put in those vigorous training sessions.

With athletes such as Merlene Ottey and Linford Christie having competed at Olympic level in their mid-30s, Steve Redgrave winning his fourth Olympic gold rowing medal, 40-year-olds breaking the four-minute-mile barrier and Carlos Lopes not only running a 10km in 27 plus minutes but also winning the Olympic marathon a year later, at the age of 38, it is time to stop thinking of such career extensions as those of freaks. Although we may not reach the same level of performance, adopting the same passion for high-intensity work will help us to maintain our own peak levels for longer.

So our way forward seems to have prompted a new saying: 'Train to maintain; use speed to succeed.'

2

PLANNING YOUR TRAINING

CHAPTER SIX

UNDERSTANDING THE BASIC PRINCIPLES OF TRAINING

STRESS AND ADAPTATION

The whole purpose of training is to bring the body to the state of readiness which will allow you to achieve a specific challenge.

Training is achieved through a process of stress and adaptation. In other words, the body is subjected to a *stress* – that is, more exercise than it is used to. It *adapts* by becoming fitter, and the stress is then increased at regular intervals. This should be carried out over a long period of time. As long as the stress is not too great, benefits will continue to be felt up to a certain limit. Unfortunately most athletes, at some time in their career, adopt more of a 'do or die' approach to training, expecting miracles overnight, or believing they have some sort of superhuman quality that allows them to defy the basic principles.

The concept of stress and adaptation is not restricted to running, nor to training for any sport. The same principle applies to many aspects of life. In fact, the scientific belief in evolution of man is based on the principle that species survive by adapting to the stresses of their environment.

If we look at the different climatic conditions under which man survives, we can clearly see how the process of stress and adaptation has taken place. How is it that some people can follow a normal life at altitudes of 12,000 to 15,000 feet yet others have problems doing the most basic tasks when they visit these places? If the visitors remain there for sufficient time they become more proficient at these tasks, as their bodies adapt to the stress of the lower availability of oxygen.

This is a very simple example, but it illustrates the fact that adaption is not instantaneous; it takes time. It is true that it is necessary to have enthusiasm in order to train, but enthusiasm cannot replace the natural timescale of adaptation and recovery.

The exciting thing about this, however, is that because training and adaptation are long-term processes, so too can be the improvement in your performances. This leads directly to the notion of short- and long-term goals.

We tend to be more motivated by short-term goals than by long-term goals. This is particularly true of novices in a sport, who tend to see dramatic improvements in performance for very little effort. For this reason we often try to bite off more than we can chew and thus fail to achieve our potential. With restraint, planning and a more realistic approach there is a much greater likelihood that we will fare better.

The other benefit of setting short- and long-term goals is that it can supply ongoing motivation and direction over the years. It is surprising how quickly long-term goals become short-term, only to be replaced by more long-term goals.

The only drawback lies in the scientific belief that our maximum potential is largely governed by our inherited genes. Nevertheless, one of the great assets of the sport of running is that our goals can so easily be set in relation to our own previous achievements. Thus there is always room for ambition and improvement.

It is also true that variations in physiology make particular runners more suited to particular events or distances. Nor can it be denied that there has to be a limit to the normal physical ability of an athlete. However, I cannot help believing that this somewhat depressing concept omits to take into account a couple of points:

First, if we accept that adaption is a long and ongoing process, then why should it 'peak out' at a particular point? I can accept that the rewards and improvements may become smaller as time goes by, and that there is a point of diminishing returns, but I have difficulty in accepting that there is some point beyond which each individual athlete cannot go. Recent studies and results in veteran athletes also suggest that there is opportunity for greater improvement than previously thought.

Second, this concept of absolute limits makes no allowance for the psychological aspects of the sport. Without doubt, the longer the distance, the bigger the role the mind plays in keeping the runner fixed on his goal. There can be little doubt that it is the area of mental control and training that offers the greatest opportunity for future sporting improvement. Whilst I have nothing but admiration for the mental strength that Olympic sprinters exhibit as they cope with the suffocating and intense pain of running a 200m race, one must compare this with the mental anguish that multi-day racers go through, trying to combat the constant lower-intensity pain of muscle, bone and joint in their striving to cover several hundred miles.

There is no doubt that the mind can play a great part in a

performance, and this is discussed in more detail later. For now it is enough to remember that what we do in our everyday training is not only physiological, but also determines to a large extent our mental attitude towards the forthcoming race.

My own feeling is that although everyone has a different potential, and the physical side of that has to a large extent been predetermined, our ability to reach goals is a product of our own mental drive, determination and enthusiasm, and these are factors that we have more control over. Thus, to quote the Nike slogan again, 'There is no finish line!'.

I honestly believe that I can improve my running by combining sensible training, motivation and a willingness to learn, both from personal experience and from others. This very basic, but important, concept is addressed later when we discuss the role of coaches and coaching.

THE LIMITATIONS OF LIFESTYLE

If training and hence performance is related to a series of stress and adaptation sessions, then it would appear to follow that the people who can concentrate most on alternating these two phases of training will make the biggest improvement in performance.

This certainly seems to be the case, and most of the world's top runners alter their lifestyles so that they can concentrate on their running and on recovering from it. Other aspects of their lives seem to take a lesser place.

Although Sebastian Coe was undoubtedly one of the world's greatest middle-distance runners of his time, and despite the fact that Bruce Fordyce was the world's greatest runner over the 50 mile distance, one can only speculate as to how well they would have fared if they had been forced to cope with the added responsibility of full-time careers, married life, night school, children or many of the other things that the average runner often faces as a matter of course on a day-to-day basis. This is in no way to detract from what Seb or Bruce achieved; on the contrary, I respect their determination and motivation to be the best there is, and to reach their full potential. However, it does highlight quite nicely the fact that different people have different priorities in life which determine their approach to running.

The point is that people who direct their ambitions in other fields have less energy, mental drive and time to give to running. They therefore have to accept that they will not reach their full potential as runners. They can, however, make maximum use of the time they spend in this field so that they achieve their full potential *within the limits they have determined.*

It has been said that the only time we are free of stress is when we are dead. The next least stressful time in our lives is when we are asleep, which is the 'recovery' period from the stress of day-to-day living. If we miss a few nights' sleep we quickly adopt a 'Jekyll and Hyde' personality, becoming irritable and unable to cope with mundane situations. Everyone has their own capacity for stress, which varies from individual to individual. But once that capacity has been exhausted, we start on a downward trend, both physically and mentally.

The majority of people never come close to using their full stress capacity on a day-to-day basis. An American psychologist has estimated that only 10 per cent of the population actually make the most of this capacity to achieve their goals.

MAKING THE MOST OF YOUR STRESS CAPACITY

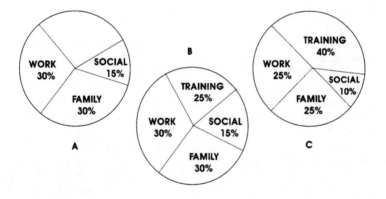

One of the best ways of explaining this concept is to consider your capacity to cope with stress as a fruit pie or a pie graph. No matter what you do, you cannot cram so much apple filling into the pie that you burst open the pastry topping. What you can do is to fill the pie completely without bursting it.

This means that as athletes wanting to achieve our best, we can use whatever space is left after we have coped with the other stresses of our lives to cope with the stress of our training. The contents of the pie – and the proportion of our training stress – will therefore be decided by the priority we give our running. (See charts A, B and C on page 45.)

Obviously, the amount of stress available for training changes from day to day, since the stress from items of higher priority, such as career and personal commitments, changes from day to day. When children are ill, or where there are changes at work, the stress associated with these events will fill more of the pie; hence the training stress needs to be reduced if the pie is not to burst.

Having said this, it would obviously be wrong to try to live at maximum stress capacity at all times. This would be like driving a car at top speed all the time. Although it would cope with this better than with over-revving, it would eventually break down. In the same way, we must also accept that there are periods when we must cut back on the total stress in our lives so that we can recover from this condition. In fact, such a recovery may also benefit us again through adaptation to the stress by improving our overall stress capacity. Perhaps this is one reason we tend to require less sleep as we get older.

GRADUAL ADAPTATION

Following the argument so far, the obvious thing to do is to start by making full use of the stress capacity that other commitments leave over for running training. However, this clashes with another important principle – that of gradual adaptation.

Gradual adaptation fits well with having both long- and short-term goals, but often causes conflict with our enthusiasm and motivational drive.

When starting any training, the traditional wisdom has always been to take it gently and gradually build up. This advice is easy to follow when we first start running, because of the breathlessness and hard work that are part and parcel of the first two to three months of regular running. After that, however, we tend to become enthusiastic at our new-found fitness and the tendency is to chase our goals by becoming over-ambitious in our training.

Such an approach frequently results in injury, and this takes us back to a point where we are even less fit than before.

As with most training concepts, the process of gradual adaptation can be illustrated by a simple physical example. Let's compare the increase in training load to the example of a brick attached to the end of an elastic band. If one end of the elastic band is held and the brick is dropped, the brick plummets towards the ground, building up speed and momentum. By the time it reaches the full extension of the elastic band there is enough momentum to break right through the resistance of the band, which snaps, with the result that the brick hits the floor. The elastic band must then be repaired before the experiment can be repeated.

If, on the other hand, the brick is gently lowered in such a manner that the elastic band is given time to adapt to its gradual stretching, the brick can be lowered until it hangs in delicate balance at the bottom of the elastic band, which is at full stretch.

This latter method maximises the strength in the elastic band instead of destroying it, and this is the objective we must strive for in setting our training programme.

From this analogy it can easily be seen that it takes longer to get the elastic band to full stretch in the second case, but that the rewards are correspondingly greater.

As we shall see in a later chapter, this is also the basis for stretching. In fact, when stretching is applied in this slow way – stretch, reduce force, stretch more – the muscle adapts and stretches further than it would otherwise have been able to. This again indicates the role of correctly controlled stress, rest and adaptation.

REST

So far we have discussed only stress and adaptation, but the key to the training process is rest.

Training is based on the principle of stressing a system to a point just beyond what it has previously been used to, and then backing off so that it can recover and rebuild. In this rebuilding it becomes stronger than it was in the first instance and is therefore able to cope with a slightly greater load.

We are all used to this type of progression. In fact, when we first started running we experienced it in the most obvious form. The first day we went out on to the road, we battled to make the end of the street, or a lap around the block, and we returned home flushed, sweaty and breathless. Several months later we wouldn't bother to change into our running gear if we were going to run only that distance. In the beginning we were forced into this system of stress and rest, but now we seem to forget these early lessons because we have become better able to cope with the stress.

The key process in adaptation is the rebuilding and strengthening which happens during periods of rest. As we shall see later when we discuss track and speed training, even during this higher-intensity work the benefit is achieved not during the run but in the recovery periods between the runs.

Often you will hear runners talk about how they would like to be able to be full-time athletes and have all day to train, but in truth these runners are misguided. The key to the success of full-time athletes is not in having all day to train, but in having all day to rest so that they can put maximum effort into each workout and still recover before their next session.

This was best explained by Wally Hayward, perhaps the best ultra runner the world has seen, who said: 'Being a full-time athlete doesn't mean having more time to train, but means having more time to rest.'

CHAPTER SEVEN

PLANNING AND GOAL-SETTING

This chapter, which deals with the planning required for eventual success, is in many ways the hardest to write. Runners who are looking for a 'magic formula' are going to be disappointed. It is impossible to write a schedule here that will suit your specific needs. After all, it depends not only on what distance race you intend peaking for, but also on your current level of training, how you react to, say, a hard track session, when the race is, what 'season' of training you are in and a host of other things. The objective is to give some basic principles that will allow you to plan your 'ladder to success'.

SETTING THE GOAL

Before you can start a journey you need to know where you intend going to, and thus you must have a goal, or rather a series of goals, which you want to achieve. You set a target and aim to make steady progress towards it.

On completing any goal there is an immediate sense of achievement, followed by an empty feeling as you wonder what to aim for next. Similarly, after any race performance it is necessary to take a break to allow recovery before subjecting yourself to the rigours of even more training. It is during this time that you should be doing the initial planning for the next challenge, which can be anything from a 10km to a marathon, from a local race to an international championship.

One such race could, for instance, be the London Marathon, which is typically held in April. This is an attractive 'goal' for many for a number of reasons:

- It covers a relatively flat course, even although parts of the city-centre section are slightly twisty.

- It is at a time of year when good running conditions can be expected.
- It attracts a very high-class field which will challenge those looking for a top time, and it attracts a large field for those who would rather run in the company of others.
- The preceding winter period provides most club runners with an ideal opportunity to do base endurance work with a scattering of cross-country races to provide quality sessions.
- The London Marathon has an atmosphere about it which provides a psychological stimulus.

This is by no means an exhaustive list of reasons for selecting London, but it will provide us with a good example of how to plan your year towards your chosen major event.

The one other thing to bear in mind before we start is that each year is not an end in itself. The goal of training should be the continued progression week on week, month on month, year on year. This is why top sportsmen often work in four-year cycles, aiming for the Olympics. Their planning in autumn 1996 was geared towards a performance in Sydney in 2000, then in 2000 the goal moves to Athens in 2004. At first, it may be just to make the team, then the focus is towards the final and possibly a medal. Along the way, in each four-year period, there are the national championships and trials, European Championships, Commonwealth Games and World Championships, each of which provides the focus and measure of an intermediate goal. You may not be looking towards such high-profile events or success, but the principles you need to adopt are the same.

Returning to the London Marathon, let's consider a single year commencing from the day after London, and let's assume your objective is to reduce your personal best for the distance over the following two to three years.

If you are a club member you will probably have some commitments to cross-country leagues, road relays and possibly track leagues. These may need to be fitted within your planning, but equally there may be key times, if you are truly going to reach your potential, when you will need to explain to the club that their involvement in a particular event does not fit in with the requirements of your training. In such cases both parties have to remember what it is that they are wanting out of the sport, and in the end it is the goals of the individual athlete that must be allowed to dominate. Remember, life is not a dress rehearsal; you only have one chance of taking on a challenge that is important to you – the key is to know what it is that is important!

The year's planning could look like this:

1. Train to and race the London marathon in April
2. Active rest for two to three weeks (to mid May)
3. Two to three weeks building back to about 50–70 per cent of the pre-marathon endurance training (to end of May)
4. Two to three weeks with 10–15 per cent reduction in mileage, but increasing fartlek and other quality sessions (June). During this period a few shorter but low-key events can act as quality runs.
5. Focus on 'quality' work towards the shortest distances you compete at. (This will vary from runner to runner, and depends on the club activities, league level, etc., but typically 3,000m to 10 miles.) This will take you through to August.
6. Active recovery from 'quality' for two weeks
7. Train and build to focus on an autumn 21km race (8–10 weeks)
8. Active recovery two to three weeks (November)
9. A six-to-eight-week cross-country season, using endurance base from half marathon and improved quality sessions
10. Two to three weeks festive period 'active rest'
11. Commence eight-to-twelve-week build-up towards the London Marathon
12. Taper over two to three weeks
13. Race the London Marathon
14. Return to 2 and set new goals.

It needs to be stressed that the above has been suggested to allow the club runner to participate in the seasonal team activities of the club, and yet focus on his or her own desire to improve in the London Marathon.

A benefit worth more than a second thought is that an improvement in your times over the shorter distances results in an improvement in your potential marathon time. Thus your concentration on improving your speed during the 'summer' season and your 'strength' in the cross-country season will improve your potential in the following marathon. This is more fully explained elsewhere, but the principle is that your performance at all distances from 5,000m to around 100km can be predicted based on relatively simple formula. If the training is done, and all else is equal, the fastest 5,000m runner will also be the fastest marathoner, and the fastest marathoner will probably run the fastest London to Brighton (55 miles) and the fastest 100km race.

The quality sessions of the summer can improve your physiological indicators, such as VO_2 max (see later), lactate threshold and efficiency. This can allow you to 'cruise' at a higher speed in your longer endurance training and hence provide the necessary improvements in the qualities you require for your marathon training.

From this you will hopefully see how each year is built around a few 'peaks', each of which is followed by a short period of recovery. Each 'peak' provides a measure to evaluate the effectiveness of the training in the preceding period. However, for this runner the intermediate 'peaks' may not have the same significance as the major focal point, which is an improvement in the following year's London Marathon.

Top runners, and those more focused towards the marathon distance, will probably want to include a second marathon in the year. Typically the first would be in spring and the second in autumn. Indeed, the autumn marathon is more likely to be the one carrying the higher priority, as it allows the training to be undertaken over the more favourable weather conditions of summer. In such cases, lower emphasis would be placed on the 'quality' work of early summer and the cross-country season, and a longer recovery (perhaps even a two-to-three-week total rest) would be included after the autumn event.

Another alternative that many of the average runners in the London Marathon field should consider is a move up to the challenge of increased distance. If an improvement in your marathon time is of lower importance, why not try to see how far you can run? Having recovered from London, commence a build-up to one of the 30–35-mile races (one of the most popular and scenic is the Two Bridges 35-mile race over the Forth Bridge in Edinburgh in August), and then continue through to the 55-mile London to Brighton classic. Anyone who can run 26 miles in four hours can certainly finish the London to Brighton before the cut-off.

A longer recovery period in October would bring you back to the shorter quality of cross country. The London Marathon would then become a training event for the longer races, and once again a better marathon time will improve your time in both the 35-miler and the London to Brighton. Day-by-day schedules for training for the London to Brighton is included in the book, and makes use of a 35 mile 'training race' (such as Two Bridges) along the way.

The basic outline for the year could look like this:

1. Train to a marathon peak for London Marathon (April)
2. Active rest two to three weeks
3. Train base mileage, then speed to aim for a peak in a 10km (mid June)
4. Active rest for two weeks
5. Train base mileage; run shorter races up until end of July (21km races max)
6. Increase mileage (July–August); add one quality session per week to run Two Bridges or other 30-miler in August as 'training' run
7. Reduced training one week

8. Specific London to Brighton training with strength, endurance and speed
9. Taper for two to three weeks
10. London to Brighton 55 miles race (October)
11. Total rest two weeks
12. Active rest four weeks

Such a schedule does not mean that you do not run other races, but that they become purely incidental in your 'goals'.

Again it will be noticed that there are only two major long races in the year, the marathon and London to Brighton. This is something many runners disregard, yet one only has to look at the very top international runners to see that they will only compete in two or three marathons a year, let alone try a 55 mile race! This has been highlighted even further by Professor Tim Noakes, who advises restricting the total racing distance per year to 100km. Thus a runner could run two marathons and two 10km events, or ten 10km races, or three half-marathons and four 10km events.

In the last edition of this book, I used the example of South African David Tsebe. In the early 1990s people used to point to the likes of him to try to show that it was possible to crowd a race calendar. He would put in a world-class 61:03 one week for the half-marathon and a 2:12 marathon the next, but that was in the restricted racing of isolation in South Africa. There he knew exactly who he would be up against, their strengths and weaknessess and what the race tactics would be.

However, you have to ask yourself what happened to him in 1991. How many races did he win then? Why was he picking up so many injuries? Even compared to his 1989 marathon time, when he was a relative newcomer, he was two minutes slower in 1990! I stated that I was sure he is capable of around 2:08 or better. Shortly afterwards South Africa returned to full international competition, and many top South Africans soon learnt that whilst they could dominate the smaller local pool with weekly racing, to be a big fish in the worldwide pool they needed to be more selective. This has paid off handsomely for them. Tsebe went on to win a number of international marathons including Berlin, and South Africa won the 1996 Olympic marathon gold through Josiah Thugwane, who a year later reduced the 1984 South African record to below 2:08. You no longer see the top South African runners racing each week!

If you want to achieve your top potential then you have to select your races, and your long races in particular, very carefully. In addition you will see that it is important to plan your year ahead so that you can focus on these major points.

As a final 'convincer' on this, consider how top businesses are run. They set goals for one year and five years and then adopt policies and strategies that enable them to achieve these goals. They are forced into this in order to make a profit for the shareholders, and it works. They use a professional approach to get professional results. Try the same with your running and you will get your 'share' of the benefit.

MAKING A REALISTIC ASSESSMENT OF YOUR POTENTIAL

We have discussed the advantages of setting your sights on goals throughout the year, as well as the fact that an improvement in your time in short events will improve your performance in the following year's longer event or marathon.

In order to construct your ladder of progress, however, it is important to have some guidelines regarding what your potential is and what sort of improvements you can expect to make. The goal-setting system will only work when you are setting realistic goals.

There are a number of ways to select realistic targets The easiest method to determine what is realistic for you is to use the following rules of thumb:

For the marathon distance, *either* take your best half-marathon time, double it, and add seven to ten minutes; *or* multiply your 10km time by 4.65 to get your potential marathon time. Thus a sub-39 10km relates to a 3:00 marathon, a 45-minute 10km gives around a 3:30, and to get a 4:15 marathon you need to be able to run 10km in 54 minutes. In terms of the five-mile distance, times of 30 minutes, 35 minutes and 43 minutes would result in 3:00, 3:30 and 4:15 respectively for the marathon.

Obviously from this you can get some feel of the interplay between 8km, 10km and 42.2km performances. The London to Brighton event (55 miles) relates to your marathon time by a factor of 2.42. Thus a 4:00 marathon will give you a 9:45 finish from London to Brighton and a 5:35 finish in the Two Bridges (a factor of 1.40).

This prediction can also be done using a computer programme, which is covered in a separate chapter. It is also useful for determining efforts of runs, potential performances and race predictions (also see the chapter on race prediction). This programme has proved to be very successful and has predicted performances such as Frith van der Merwe's South African marathon record in 1990 of 2:27:36 (predicted as 2:27:35), New York marathon winner Willie Mtolo's half-marathon sub-65-minutes to within ten seconds and Elana Meyer's South African 10km record to within two seconds. It will also help you answer the questions such as what an 80 per cent effort is, or how fast you should run a recovery run, or a fast continuous run, and so on.

A final point in this regard is that your potential can change. If initially the above calculations lead you to train for a personal best of a 3:00 marathon, then once you have achieved this you will find that your potential at other distances also increases. Thus you may then go for a 38-minute target at 10km, which, when reached, may lead you to a 2:55 marathon, and so on. However, as you get closer to the limits of your 'physiological potential', improvements become smaller and smaller. The final limitation may in fact be the ravages of time as each year you get older!

AVAILABLE TRAINING TIME

The next stage in developing your programme is to determine how much time you will have in a week to train. The object of the programme will be to make the most efficient use of this time.

Alberto Salazar once said that in working out a schedule one should calculate how much time one has and then reduce it by 20 per cent. I believe that this is an excellent proposal which re-emphasises the importance of rest.

Instead of 'training time' we should perhaps more correctly speak of 'training time and recovery time'. Each is as important as the other. It's no use planning for 4.00 a.m. rises and 11.00 p.m. bedtimes if you need a full seven or eight hours' sleep to recover. Of all the points in training, a realistic assessment of your capabilities is essential, and this starts with being realistic over the training load you can manage. Just because a top runner does 100 miles per week, don't be fooled into thinking that that is what you require. Such a philosophy does not take account of variation in genetic talent – and that's just for starters.

UNDERSTAND THE LAWS OF TRAINING

In developing a training programme it is important to take cognisance of the 'laws of training' that have been formulated over the years. Strangely enough, many were 'discovered' as early as the turn of the century, and although subject to minor modification, they remain valid today.

At various stages runners have become slaves to one or more of these principles, for example, in the obsession with long, slow distance in the 1970s. The key, however, is to get the combination right and to be fully aware of all the laws.

Once more I have no better reference for those seeking more information than Professor Tim Noakes's *Lore of Running*. Tim has searched old bookshops around the world and found training references for numerous sports. His subsequent analysis and summary has provided a list of 15 laws, which I can do no better than repeat. The name of the author of each concept appears in brackets.

THE 15 LAWS OF TRAINING

1. Train frequently all year round (Arthur Newton)
2. Start gradually and train gently (Newton)
3. Train first for distance and only later for speed (Newton) (Note: this changes for ultras)
4. Don't set yourself a daily schedule; listen to your body (Newton)
5. Alternate hard and easy days (Bowerman and Dellinger)
6. At first try to achieve as much as you can on a minimum of training (Noakes)
7. Don't race in training and run time trials and races only infrequently (Newton)
8. Train specifically – specialize (Newton)
9. Incorporate base training and peaking (sharpening) (Forbes Carlile/Arthur Lydiard)
10. Don't overtrain – listen to your body again! (Newton)
11. Train under a coach
12. Train the mind (Newton)
13. Rest before a big race (Newton)
14. Keep a detailed log book
15. Understand the holism of training

In 1984 I was captain of a team of four in the London to Paris Triathlon, in which one of the legs involved a relay swim across the English Channel. This was the leg we most feared, and we were lucky that the sponsors, Leppin, had had the foresight to make Tim Noakes our manager.

Two days before the event, whilst exploring London's bookshops, Tim came across a swimming book which detailed Captain Barclay's historic Channel swim. After our meal that night we all retired, except Tim, who greeted us the following morning looking very tired but excited. He declared that we were definitely going to win because he now knew how to tackle the Channel. He had spent the whole night reading the book and devising a plan for our swim. We had complete confidence in him and, needless to say, we won the swimming leg, beating a team of British long-distance Channel and national-class swimmers into the bargain. We also won the event – such is the power of Tim's research and a good race plan!

CHAPTER EIGHT

THE COMPONENTS OF A TRAINING PROGRAMME

When we first started running everything seemed simple; all we had to do was step outside and run around the block or over a predetermined route.

At that stage, just completing the route was enough, although often we found ourselves forced to slow down or indulge in walk breaks in order to go the distance. These were included for two reasons: first, our ability to judge the pace that we could maintain for the full course was not good and we frequently went off too fast, and second, we were not fit enough to cover the planned distance. Eventually, however, both of these factors improved until ultimately we could handle the full run and even greater distances.

At this point, most of us continued to use this 'one pace' running style in all subsequent training. The only variations were in distance, the route or the company. Even at this early stage we had lost sight of one of the most beneficial yet basic ways of improving our running: speed variation.

In South Africa, and in Natal in particular, the main motivator in the sport of running has to be the annual Comrades Marathon. This is a national event which in recent years has even helped to create additional public holidays in order to prevent it from falling on a Sunday! English runner John Tarrant commented that the Comrades was to South Africa what the FA Cup final is to England, and that was back in the 1970s before Comrades attracted fields of 15,000 runners!

This obsession with Comrades has been an exceptionally good thing, as it has brought a vast number of people into the sport who would otherwise have been lost to it. On the other hand, Comrades is also responsible for the tendency of all runners to become long, slow, distance runners, irrespective of their natural potential. It has created a belief that speedwork has no place in training for long-distance events.

Other side-effects of the Comrades hype are the handed-down training schedules and the 'old runners' tales' about this or that hero who ran incredible mileages in training. As with most rumours or stories that are passed on by word of mouth over the years, most of these training accounts are exaggerated. Suddenly the hero of the story is supposed to have been running 40 mile runs twice a week, as well as running to and from work, and his total distance becomes an enormous figure that most runners can never attain.

On hearing such a story most runners decide that they are doing too little and thus 'buckle down' to increase their mileage. As their mileage increases, so their ability to vary their training pace decreases and very soon they are always running at the one speed, just pacing themselves from one session to the next. It is ironic that the best illustration that such training is a mistake comes from the novice.

THE NOVICE'S EXAMPLE

New Year tends to signal a new beginning to our lives. It's the time when we try to stick to the resolutions we made during the final week of the previous year, resolutions to become better in some way. For a number of people this will have included some form of commitment to take a healthier approach to life, and this may also have included a decision to start running.

Although most of the people who contact me about the articles I write are experienced runners, it's worthwhile thinking back to the practices we adopted as beginners. In fact, it is amazing what one can learn from the novice runner.

Take my case, for instance. Although I didn't start running until I emigrated to South Africa in 1981, I had resolved in 1973, as a 30-a-day smoker and 13-stone rugby hooker, to start improving my fitness by jogging. Indeed, it was a desire to keep my place in the first team and make a bid for the District side that motivated me to set out in a pair of none too glamorous shorts, plimsoles, long socks and old rugby jersey, to run the perceived gauntlet of peering neighbours to start my first jog.

The reasoning went something like this: if Ron Hill can run a marathon in under 2:10 then surely I can cover a mile or so in 12–15 minutes? So off I went. Remember, this was a 'fit' rugby player!

Perhaps it was the suspicion that people were staring at me, but after 300m this run was not fun, on top of which I was facing a veritable mountain. In truth, its gradient was similar to that of a motorway off-ramp and it was fully 150m long!

As a beginner, fighting for every ounce of oxygen, this was a major challenge, which true Scottish stubbornness allowed me to conquer. The price, however, was an enforced stop at the top of the hill and a total inability even to walk down the other side! It was then that my resolve to give up smoking became a reality.

After a lengthy recovery I was able to jog down the hill, at an even slower pace, and after many similar rests eventually finished my first two-mile circuit, even though my time was somewhat slower than the predicted 15 minutes!

Looking back, I recall that it didn't take long before I could handle this run non-stop in a reasonable length of time, and this added endurance certainly benefited my rugby. No longer did the other forwards have to use delaying tactics to give me time to reach a loose ruck so that I could apply my large mass to flatten it!

This story will be similar to those many runners can tell of when they first started. As a sport, running is one of the hardest to get into. It is totally frustrating, even painful, for the first three months, but this run-break-run-walk system is the universally successful method of getting us hooked into the sport and bringing fast improvement. I am not suggesting that one should run to exhaustion every day, nor that one should follow the example of those novices who overdo it to the extent that they injure themselves. It is also true that our improvement in fitness when we are novices is usually greater that at any other stage, simply because we begin at such a low level of fitness. Many different training methods can produce this rapid increase in fitness in the novice phase. However, what we can learn from these early experiences is the value of varying the pace and regularly exerting ourselves beyond the level of the comfortable jog! Why, then, do we immediately throw this method out of our training to concentrate on slogging out the miles?

Traditionally the New Year sees British runners commencing preparation for the London Marathon, and their South African counterparts begin their annual slogging at distance training in preparation for Comrades. It seems to be almost instinctive. Through-out the following five months what seems to be almost a kind of uncontrollable guilt drives them to grind out a daily diet of even-paced mile after mile. Each mile is well within the capacity of the runner: no more the overambitious, lung-bursting speed of the novice; no more the enforced 'chest-bursting' recovery stop.

This need to vary running speed can be compared to weight-training techniques in which the weight on the bar is increased to 'overload' the muscle so that it will increase its strength during the rest day. Is this not the same way we learned to run? Is this principle not the basis for the fast improvement that we experienced as beginners and now long for as experienced runners?

Reconsider your first steps. Aren't all the principles of fartlek and track training there? Periods of faster work with periods of recovery? Running anaerobically for short periods followed by aerobic recovery? These are the same principles that have been shown to be most effective and adopted by the top international runners in their training. It's ironic that it is the novice runner who comes in search of advice and yet there are many more-experienced runners who have forgotten, or overlooked, those lessons they learned in their early development.

The above illustrates that the correct way to train, for any distance, is to combine runs of different intensity, difficulty and distance in such a way as to form a well-balanced schedule that exploits the runner's potential to the full. If one considers the single-paced runner as having one gear, the runner who varies his speeds in training develops a gearbox of speeds, and perhaps even an overdrive. This can be complemented with other optional exercises and training in order to fine-tune the runner or eradicate a particular weakness.

Since the options and combinations of intensity, difficulty and distance are myriad, let us first classify runs by intensity and then consider some of the possible permutations within each category.

RUNNING INTENSITY

LONG, SLOW RUNS

There is no doubt that there is a place for the long, slow run in any training schedule, but where that place is and how much is necessary will depend to a large extent on what sort of target you are aiming for.

In the case of track athletes, the long, slow run should be carried out during the off-season as a means of building an endurance base. The distance of this run, even for Olympic athletes, is unlikely to be much greater than 25km. By comparison, however, the track athlete's 'slow speed' is quite probably race speed for many road runners. At the other end of the scale, six-day runners will use the long, slow run as the backbone of their schedules and their pace will be considerably slower.

It has to be repeated that London to Brighton and Comrades are not really true ultradistance running, in as much as they are only around 55 miles. Although the definition of ultradistance is any event longer than the marathon, most countries in the world consider the first rung on the ultra ladder to be the 100km, followed by the 100 mile, 24-hour, 48-hour, 72-hour and six-day races.

This is not to detract from such races in any way – they are great events – but they have to be put into perspective when considering the amount and type of training that is required to complete them. It is generally accepted that a top marathon runner will always win a 50km race, and, indeed, one can extend this principle to the 50-mile race as well.

The same principles that apply to training for marathons can also be applied to ultras, but schedules need to be modified to cater for the specific demands of the ultra race. In general, the greatest of these is an increase in endurance, and this is where the long, slow run comes into its own in building up stamina and endurance. This development of an endurance base involves running for extended periods at a comfortable pace. We already know that training is a series of stress and rest sessions which allow us to become stronger. What a number of runners fail to realise is that the stress of a long, slow run comes more from the length of time that it takes than from the speed at which it is run.

Most runners recognise that they have a pace which they seem capable of maintaining for vast distances without ever getting out of breath. This sort of running is said to be in the *aerobic* range, as the runners are taking in as much oxygen as they are using up. When they increase their speed the runners find that the length of the run is dictated both by breathlessness and by a tiring of the muscles. These are the anaerobic range of speeds, where the runner is unable to take in as much oxygen as the body is using to produce energy.

In truth, of course, life is not that simple, and every run is a combination of both aerobic and anaerobic running, but the objective of the long, slow run is to keep as much of the run as possible in the aerobic range. This type of run not only improves the cardiovascular endurance, but also improves the muscular endurance of the runner to cope with the distance of the target race. (Endurance can also be developed using intervals, which will be discussed with other track-training sessions.)

STEADY OR 'THRESHOLD' RUNS

The next level of running intensity is what can be called steady-state running. This is a pace that can be described as being on the border between anaerobic and aerobic. The objective is to try to keep the pace of the run just on the threshold of becoming anaerobic. Thus this pace is faster than that of the long, slow run and its prime purpose is to improve the upper limit of the aerobic range.

Of course, it is very hard to maintain such a finite pace during a run and even the smallest of hills will put runners into the anaerobic range unless they slow down considerably. Likewise, a dramatic increase in speed is required on the downhills if the threshold intensity is to be maintained.

HARD RUNS

Moving up a gear, the third category of intesity is the hard run. This can be used to classify all sessions that are run in the anaerobic range of a runner's speeds.

Obviously there are different degrees of hardness, and in general it is determined by the distance that is being run. A run over a two-mile course will be slower than a run over a one-mile course, but both can be equally hard or stressful. This is well illustrated in the comparative distance-to-speed charts elsewhere in the book, where it is possible to compare the intensity of a race over 5km with that of a race over 21km. (There is also a computer programme capable of predicting and comparing your results at one particular distance based on your previous results at other distances. Alternatively you can use it to determine just how hard you covered a particular distance. This provides an extremely useful tool for determining your individual training schedule.)

In the same way, it is possible to determine what an 85 per cent effort is at a particular distance if you know what a flat-out effort is for that distance. Although the runs are at different speeds, they can both be considered hard when they are in the anaerobic range.

The other thing to realise is that it is necessary to include both short and long hard runs in a training schedule. The words 'short' and 'long' are, however, relative to the distance of the race being trained for!

RECOVERY RUNS

There is one other intensity that should exist in every training schedule, namely that of recovery runs.

These are runs that are performed at very low intensity over the shorter distances, and these are 100 per cent aerobic. Their purpose is purely to assist in improving the circulation throughout the body after a harder session. This decreases the recovery time as fresh blood, and hence nutrients, are pumped to the previously stressed areas and thus the rebuilding and strengthening can start earlier.

These are often the hardest sessions to carry out correctly, as they should be undertaken at a very conservative speed. Most runners find it easier to test themselves when they train rather than easing back and letting things take time.

The real benefit of the recovery run only becomes obvious when runners return to the next hard session and find that they have fully recovered and are able to put a good effort into that type of training.

In many ways this is the most important part of a training schedule, since the training you do is only as good as the recovery. Thus there are likely to be more recovery runs in a training schedule than any other single type of run.

The importance of recovery cannot be overstressed (no pun intended), and the comment by the great ultradistance runner and Olympic marathoner Wally Hayward hits the nail on the head. In 1952, Wally was given the opportunity to be a full-time athlete and was asked how much more training he would be able to fit in. He replied, 'Being a full-time athlete doesn't mean having more time to train, but having more time to rest.'

The relationship between recovery runs and hard training looks like a sinusoidal graph. The easier the recovery sessions, the harder the hard sessions can be. If you run the recovery sessions too fast, expect poor results in your hard sessions. There is only so much stress and energy to go round.

TYPES OF RUN WITHIN THE DIFFERENT INTENSITIES

LONG, SLOW RUNS

We now know that the long, slow run is purely a method of developing muscle endurance and aerobic improvement. It is a steady-state run which, when training for shorter distance events, will tend to exceed the length of the race. For example, if your choice of race distance is 10km, then a long, slow run may be a 10 mile run. However, as you move up in distance towards a marathon, your long, slow run will tend to be either the same distance as the race or, particularly for ultras, less than the race distance.

Even world-class marathoners will tend to make their long runs only in the 20–22 mile range, although a few have gone to 28 miles. Similarly ultra runners will generally not run mammoth distances in their training for 100km or 100 mile races. However, they do use a number of marathons and shorter ultra events to bring them to a peak for a particular race in the season. To this extent they are 'seen' as running many more races than the commonly held 'one ultra a year' regime that has been promoted in South Africa.

In Europe, however, there are definite seasons, and an 'off-season' between November and February is virtually enforced by the climate. This step down in training promotes greater recovery from a hard racing season. In South Africa, and many other countries, the climate is such that it is possible to run distance races all year round, and there is little incentive for the majority of runners to specialise.

It is generally accepted that cardiovascular endurance has been sufficiently developed by the time the runner is capable of completing long runs of 20 miles, and that any additional distance is unlikely to bring significant further improvement. Thus it is muscular endurance that is being developed thereafter, although Professor Tim Noakes has suggested that this also exists on a scale of diminishing returns.

There is, however, a further benefit of the long run is the psychological confidence the runner gains from completing the distance. This is very hard to measure and the need for it varies dramatically between runners. I personally feel that many runners would be surprised at the distances they could run without having done comparable long training runs, providing they paced themselves correctly.

At the longer distances, I am of the opinion that putting two shorter 'long runs' back to back with a relatively short recovery break is probably as good a method of training as one long 'long run'. In fact, there is an advantage, in as much as there probably isn't the same amount of muscle breakdown in the 'double' as there is in the single. The double also assists runners to learn to 'run tired', since they start the second run in a partially depleted state. The ability to 'run tired' is, I believe, a necessity when dealing with the truly long events.

Another aspect of the long run that is often cited as a benefit is that it may help develop the fat-burning energy system. This system, which will be discussed later, is the secondary energy source which becomes predominant once all the muscle glycogen stores have been used up. It is thought that the long training run improves the efficiency with which this energy can be made available. Even if this is so, I don't believe there is any significant disadvantage with my preference for the 'double' training run technique as opposed to a single long run. Again there may be a benefit, in as much as the break between runs will allow a partial replenishment of liver glycogen, which I suspect is a first priority in the body's energy system. Liver glycogen is responsible for brain operation, and thus this double-run system allows runners to complete both runs in a good frame of mind.

To summarise, long runs are an essential part of any distance training programme and, for short-distance races, will slightly exceed race distance. For longer events they will tend to be less than race distance and consideration should be given to using double runs back to back in preference to a single long run.

The benefits of the long, slow distance run are: an improved cardiovascular system, improved muscular endurance, psychological confidence for completing the race distance, and possible development of the fat-burning energy system.

STEADY OR 'THRESHOLD' RUNS

These are runs at a pace which is on the border between aerobic and anaerobic. When runners runs at a purely aerobic pace, theoretically they could go on forever. That is, their oxygen requirement is matched by oxygen intake. In anaerobic running, the demand exceeds the supply and thus a 'debt' is incurred. Scientific studies have suggested that there is a limit to the total debt that a runner can accumulate, and on this basis a runner would ideally like to build up this debt gradually and evenly between the start and finish of the race. This introduces two other scientific concepts concerning a runner's efficiency and the total amount of oxygen that he or she is able to take in.

Professor Tim Noakes has described these in detail in *Lore of Running*. Anyone wanting a deeper understanding of their scientific basis would be hard-pressed to find a better reference source. Thus what follows is a layperson's overview of the concepts, in the hope that it will assist in the understanding of the training principles.

Each individual is able to take in a certain volume of air per minute while exercising, and this must match the requirements of the body if the runner is to continue the exercise. As running speed increases, oxygen requirements increase and a 'debt' develops if the body's requirements exceed the supply. The supply thus has a maximum value, which depends on the effectiveness of the runner's cardiovascular system. Since we have already said that this system can be improved through training, it is also true that the maximum oxygen uptake can be increased to some extent, although it is thought that this may be in the region of only 15–20 per cent.

This maximum oxygen uptake at maximum effort is commonly expressed in the form of millilitres of oxygen per kilogram of body weight per minute. It is known as the VO_2 max and is often touted as the be-all and end-all of an athlete's potential. However, this is not true since there is still the concept of aerobic/anaerobic threshold to consider, which can be regarded as a measure of running efficiency.

Obviously, if one runner can run at, say, 85 per cent of his or her VO_2 max without developing an oxygen debt, then that runner would be able to run faster and hence further than another athlete with the same

VO_2 max who could only run at, say, 70 per cent of his or her VO_2 max value. Runner B would develop an oxygen debt if he or she were to try and match runner A's pace stride for stride and would eventually reach the limiting value and be forced to slow dramatically or stop. Runner A would, however, theoretically be able to carry on, since oxygen demand would be matched by oxygen intake.

Thus the runner with the higher anaerobic threshold will be able to compete at a better level. This is why it is important to try to push up the anaerobic/aerobic threshold point, which is the main objective of these steady runs.

One final point, which is often overlooked in this regard, is that this means that a runner with a lower VO_2 max but a high anaerobic threshold can perform at a higher level than a runner with a higher VO_2 max value whose anaerobic threshold is at a lower percentage. Consider this example:

Runner A:
VO_2 max = 80 ml O_2/kg/minute
Threshold = 60%
Therefore oxygen uptake at threshold = 48 ml O_2/kg/minute

Runner B:
VO_2 max = 72 ml O_2/kg/minute
Threshold = 75%
Therefore oxygen uptake at threshold = 54 ml O_2/kg/minute

The benefit of the higher threshold becomes obvious.

Steady runs are sometimes known as threshold runs and can be done either by running continuously for, say, 5–8km at this pace or by doing a number of intervals at this pace with periods of recovery in between. Generally the distance of the intervals should not be less than 1km, nor more than 3km. The total distance run at this pace in any session should also be kept at a maximum of about 10km, since these are relatively hard sessions and thus require recovery time afterwards.

It is easy to work out what pace is threshold pace if you have a fully equipped lab at your disposal. However, a rule of thumb which will be of more general use is that the pace should be about 30 seconds per mile (20 seconds per km) slower than your flat-out 10km pace.

RECOVERY RUNS

The recovery run is in many ways the backbone of the training schedule. Arguably, it is also the most unstructured training session of all in as much as it revolves around minimal perceived effort. The purpose of a recovery run has been discussed, but since the objective is purely one of improved circulation and ease of movement, speed, time and distance are not of importance. The pressure is off in all respects. Enjoyment can become the prime concern.

I have found the recovery run to be an ideal way to fit a number of errands into an otherwise tight schedule and frequently use this five- to seven-mile jaunt to do things like drop off letters, bank cheques, buy stamps or post letters. Although it requires some understanding from the shopkeeper and other customers, who are faced with a sweaty runner, it's a good way of controlling the workout effort. If I find my pace a bit too fast I am immediately faced with a stop at the first port of call, and hence a recovery. These planned interruptions split the run into sections, which makes it even easier.

Of course, you may prefer just to go out and run non-stop and this is fine, but just let yourself float along in an easy fashion so that you don't feel that any effort is required. You should not feel tired after these runs and in many ways you may feel stronger and more lively at the end of them.

Work hard at making these easy runs, as this will allow you to put greater effort into the hard training sessions!

HARD RUNS

This classification of intensity covers a wide variety and type of training, from fast, continuous runs to intervals, fartlek and hills. One of the most important rules is that the faster the run, the shorter it should be in training and the longer the recovery period required. This applies not only to intervals but also on a day-to-day basis.

Fartlek

This is a method of 'playing with speed' during a training session and can be either informal or more disciplined. The variations of fartlek are as unlimited as the imagination, but here are some ideas to serve as seeds from which to grow your own species.

An informal session would involve running easily for a mile or so to loosen off, then varying the pace over distances from 100m to 1km as you feel able and inclined. The pace will vary from almost flat out to a jog or even a walk for recovery. There is no detailed list of what you must do, but look to cover a complete variation across the spectrum of speed and to finish the session pleasantly fatigued.

Slightly less informal is doing this with one or two friends who take it in turn to dictate the pace. However care has to be taken here to ensure that it doesn't become too competitive. Runners of the same ability are the best companions for these sessions.

These informal sessions do require some discipline, however, since I've yet to meet the runner who really looks forward to a speed effort immediately before starting. This makes the sessions slightly less taxing than the more formal sessions.

In formal sessions the routine is determined prior to starting, using, for example, an easy 2–3km, then repeating four times a series of a minute's hard run followed by a three-minute walk/jog/easy run. After the completion of the full four hard sessions, an easy 2–3km completes the workout.

Terrain variation will also have a part to play. The first hard section may be on flat road, the next up a hill, the next downhill, the next back to flat, or even on grass, and so on. The beauty of fartlek is that it can be done no matter where you are.

Exercises can also be introduced into fartlek as a means of including strength and endurance training. Running around a trim track, with stops at the stations to do pull-ups or press-ups, combined with pace variation between stations is another form of fartlek, which can offer a welcome change to the runner who is feeling a bit bored with just running.

Even the old rugby training technique of having teams run round the outside of the pitch with the back runner sprinting to the front is a form of fartlek. So, too, is the pyramid run, where runners run to the 22-metre line, jog back, then run twice to the halfway line, jog back, then run three times to the opposition 22-metre line, jog back, then run four times to the opposition goal line, and so on.

Fartlek is an excellent introduction to the harder, and more stressful, track training, as well as a good way to develop 'kicks and surges' for use in tactical races. Progression in fartlek can be achieved through increasing the intensity of runs and/or the number of hard sections, or reducing the recovery jogs, or using a combination of these. The method of progression will change, depending on what training aspect is being emphasised.

Hills

Hills are another good introduction to track work, and also develop leg strength and hill technique.

Unfortunately, some runners seem to overdo this training, particularly those who live in a very hilly area and hence find themselves running hills every day. This can actually be detrimental, as it tends to result in their becoming slow hill runners, since even on recovery days they have to fight their way up the hills. Don't forget, one of the keys to good training is variation, not only of pace, but also of terrain.

To my mind there are three types of hill run, although further variations exist within these sections.

The easiest in many respects is just to go out on a run of, say, 10km and push the uphills, recovering on the flats and downs. This is not a run that I am particularly fond of since it doesn't really make allowance for your state of fitness at that particular time. Some hills may be 100m long, others 1km and thus a bit too long to concentrate on for the full length, and then what happens when two long hills such as that are separated by a flat section of only 150m?

This type of run is more in keeping with a fartlek session than a good hill workout. Unfortunately, this seems to be the type of hill session that many runners end up doing, and I don't believe that they are achieving as much as they would if they tried the next type.

In this second type of hill run, the runner finds a hill of the desired steepness and length and, after a warm-up and stretching, runs repeats up the hill to the top *and over*. This may be done only five or six times but the runner now has some measure of effort, since each repeat can be timed and is of equal difficulty. In addition, the recovery is also a measured variable over which the runner has control.

Some books suggest that recovery is achieved by simply turning around and jogging down, then turning around immediately and running back up for the next repeat. This doesn't seem practical to me, although I suppose it depends on what one is trying to achieve in the training session. My own preference is to use the session to develop strength and hill technique but to place less emphasis on the endurance aspect, which I feel can come from other sessions. So I tend to walk at the end of each repeat as I turn and then jog down the hill. I try to get about twice the recovery time as the time it takes me to do the hard repeat. Thus a minute of uphill effort is rewarded with a full two-minute period to get back down and be ready for the next up-section.

Variation in hill gradient and length will determine the emphasis that I want out of the session: steeper hills, more strength; shallower hills, more speed; long hills, endurance and rhythm; short hills, power; and so on. A further 2–3km jog to cool down finishes the session.

Many runners would be surprised at how shallow a hill need be to provide this sort of workout, and care should be exercised to ensure that a good running form can be developed on the hill (the first thing to be sacrificed if the hill is too steep).

The third type of hill run consists of bounding sessions, where the runner is looking to concentrate on strength. Here the runner again does repeats up the hill with downhill recovery, but the action is more one of extending the ankle as far as possible while trying to 'blast' the whole body as high into the air as possible. The other leg is then lifted with as high a knee action as possible. The stride length is short, and speed up the hill is not the main objective. For this reason a shorter, steeper hill is best for this type of work.

Fast, continuous runs

These are run over a distance shorter than your race distance but at your race pace. Thus for a marathon, you may enter and run a 15km race and run it at your predicted marathon pace. In addition to pace judgement, such runs teach the runner to concentrate while under pressure. Ideally these should be over flattish or slightly undulating courses where it is easy to keep a constant pace. Hilly courses require the runner to maintain a constant 'perceived marathon pace effort' as opposed to constant speed, and will not give the desired result.

Club time trials are another valuable but often abused training session. It can, for example, provide an ideal fast, continuous training opportunity for someone training to do a 15km race in an hour. The runner would aim to run the 8km time trial in 32 minutes, not go for broke, as most runners seem compelled to do in club runs. Time trials are training sessions – not races.

Tempo runs

I discuss these directly after the fast, continuous run as I believe the difference between these two sessions has to be highlighted.

The tempo run was developed by the Russians, in a bid to simulate race conditions for their runners without giving them the stress of the full-blown race. These runs are not to be taken lightly, as they are run at a pace probably about 8–16 seconds slower per mile than 10km race pace.

Again, this is an ideal type of session to carry out in a club time trial, but it is very stressful and as such should be prepared for well. This requires the runner to taper down a few days prior to the run, and to allow sufficient recovery afterwards. Each time this session is run it should be run over the same course so that your progress can be measured using a watch and perception of effort or a heart-rate monitor.

Note that this is not a flat-out session; if it were then it would be a race! The tempo run is a training method, and there is no training method that involves a flat-out race, since that would break athletes down rather than build them up.

Tempo runs should only be done once every four to six weeks.

Club time trials

The last two sections lead naturally into a discussion on the place of the club time trial. It appears to me that many runners go down to their time trials each week and run them in the hope of continually improving their time. This will certainly not happen, as improvement is something that occurs in an irregular fashion, with plateaux in between.

The other problem with this approach is that it tends to transform a training session into a race, and that has already been recognised as breaking down rather than building up.

This is not to say that runners should not make an appearance at the weekly time trial – quite the opposite. It can be used in many ways, two of which we have already noted.

In a six-week period of doing time trials (between tempo runs, say), the runner could use the first week as a tempo run and two other weeks as fast, continuous runs. Another two weeks could be used as a formal fartlek session where, for instance, alternate kilometres are run hard and easy. The final week in the group of six could be used for a different type of fast, continuous run where, for instance, the first three kilometres are run at fast, continuous pace, the next two walked and jogged, and the last three run at fast, continuous pace.

The time trial can also be used as a recovery run. At least in such a situation you have an accurate measure of how fast you are running and your objective can be to run *more slowly* than a set time! This could be an opportunity to run with a friend who is substantially slower than yourself.

Use your time trials, don't abuse them.

Track work

Many club road runners only try track work once, before deciding that it isn't for them. This normally results from adopting the wrong approach to the session. Track work is frequently seen as something that has to be run at the fastest possible pace, which is certainly *not* the case.

Let's consider the different types of track session. In order to emphasise the importance of varying speed and recovery we'll look at the entire spectrum of track work, even although the first few types are probably closer to long, slow distance, since the primary development is endurance.

Endurance intervals

It is possible to use the track to develop endurance by running a large number of intervals, say of 400m, with a very short break in between. These, however, are run at an easy pace compared with your best 400m time. Of course, because they are short and there are recovery periods, the intervals are faster than you would run the same total distance if you were running it non-stop. Typically, these intervals are run at 85 per cent or less of your best effort. The recovery is in the order of 30 seconds.

Speed and endurance intervals

These intervals are run slightly faster but there is slightly more recovery time between them and the whole session involves a shorter total distance. These intervals are run at up to 90 per cent effort, depending on the type of race you are training for. The shorter the race, the higher the percentage effort, but again note that you are not running flat out. Runners who run intervals flat out might as well have entered a race on their training night.

The distances of these intervals will vary between 200m and 2,000m, again depending on what event you are training for. The shorter the effort distance and the faster the speed, the longer the rest between intervals.

Pure speed sessions

Pure speed is developed by running very short intervals over distances such as 60m or 70m. These are repeated only a few times and the rest between them is long, maybe as much as four or five minutes. In general, this sort of session has limited benefit to the long-distance road runner.

Power speed repeats/tempo running

The objective of running power speed intervals is to develop power, speed and the anaerobic system. Thus these sessions will cause an oxygen debt and fatigue which must be closely monitored to ensure that the runner doesn't overdo the session. As opposed to the interval sessions, where the benefit of the training is achieved during the recovery phases, the benefit of the repeats comes from the effort of each run.

Power speed repeats are run somewhat faster than race pace. There should be full recovery between intervals, that is, your heart rate will return to 100 or below, depending on your level of fitness. The distance of the repeats will vary with the distance of the event you are training for. This type of session should only be attempted by runners who have already gained some track-training experience.

Some comments on track work

All types of track work are a product of a number of variables: the speed of each effort, the distance of each effort, the total number of efforts, the amount of recovery and the way in which recovery is achieved, that is to say running or walking or jogging.

It is all very well saying that these sessions need to be run at set percentage efforts, but deciding what this means in real terms, in terms of seconds, is what most runners find difficult to do. In fact, this is probably the most common reason why many road runners only ever do one track session.

The main difference between endurance intervals, speed and endurance intervals, pure speed sessions and power speed repetitions is the effort with which they are run and the recovery that is provided between the efforts and the sessions. This is easily stated, but the trick for the athlete is to be able to identify what this means in terms of time.

Obviously, no hard and fast rules can be applied to what time you must run, say, an endurance interval session. It will vary from week to week as a result of many things: how the track is affected by the wind, how you have recovered from the previous workout, whether you had a hard day at work, and so on. The important thing is to have a rough figure in mind when you start. Similarly, it's no use saying that a 42-minute 10km training run is your easy pace, without considering the terrain of the route.

The problem many runners seem to suffer, particularly when first trying track or other speed work, is that they are 'intimidated', both by the other runners and by their own perceptions of how fast they must go.

Consider the average road runner who goes to the track for the first time to try speed work. After a warm-up and stretching, and with much apprehension, he lines up for his first interval. He is unsure of how fast he needs to run to complete the 400m in his target time of, say, 90 seconds, and normally will find he goes off too fast. By the time he gets to 200m he is already feeling the effort but manages to keep it all together to finish the lap in 86 seconds.

He feels happy about this, and although knowing he can slow down now, he commences his second interval after the designated rest. This time he is more fluent, both because he has found his stride and because he knows he can do the task. This results in an even faster lap of 83 seconds, and now the game is on. He resets his target to complete all ten laps in under 86 seconds.

The whole situation becomes aggravated when he finds schoolchildren or other youngsters catching or passing him during his 400m laps when they are doing 800m intervals. Of course, he overlooks the fact that they are training for track races and he is looking to peak for a half-marathon. His pride forces him to faster times. Unfortunately he doesn't then adjust the recovery period as well. Instead he tries to complete the new self-revised schedule.

The result is that the runner *races* his training and, not surprisingly, doesn't enjoy the workout and may even pick up an injury. At best he finds that his recovery from the track is slow and all in all he begins to feel that track and speed work are not for him. He soon reverts to the daily long, slow distance runs. This is just one reason why every runner requires a coach (see later).

This is certainly not the way to do track work. The point of it is to develop a specific aspect of running, and, as we have already seen, this is best achieved by varying speed and recovery between intervals. If done correctly, not only will the results be obtained, but also recovery will be quicker and you may actually enjoy these sessions. If you find yourself going too fast, slow down!

Of course, another reason runners don't like doing track is that it tends to take substantially longer to cover a distance, and most runners perceive training effect to be based purely on the total distance run in any week.

A track session will generally involve hard running over a maximum of two to four miles (more often two than four). Even with, say, three miles' allowance for warm-up and cool-down, plus another mile recovery jogging between intervals, the total is little over six miles, but may take up to one and a half hours! By comparison, the same runner could cover about 20km if he had run constantly for the same length of time, so he sees the track session as being inefficient in his aim to build up distance. This is not the case. In fact, quite the reverse is true; the track session is much more beneficial if built into a balanced programme.

Other runners will argue that a distance runner doesn't need to do 800m repeats, let alone 400s or 200s. These runners are missing the point. These track sessions are designed to develop different energy systems and aspects of training. If runners can be taught to run comfortably at a high speed, even if it is over a shorter distance, they will be even more comfortable at a lower speed, such as that of a marathon. Thus progression in both areas is required. This assists in the development of a gearbox of speeds. Speed work gives one the ability to finish the marathon faster and builds mental toughness, because it is much more mentally challenging to perform a speed work session than it is to go for a long, easy run.

Finally, remember that you can't expect miracles overnight. It will take about six weeks of various track-work sessions before you really see the benefit. In fact, you may even feel slightly leg-heavy in the first few weeks as you adapt to this new form of training, but stick with it. The benefit is well worth the effort.

Table 8.1 compares track speeds and is to be used as a guide for runners as to how the different types of session can be composed.

Table 8.1 Track session speeds

		TIME					TRACK	TRACK	
BEST	BEST	TRIAL	LSD	RECOVERY	LSD	LSD	400 m	1000 m	90
MARATHON	10 km	10 km	10 km	10 km	20 km	32 km	REPEATS	REPEATS	km
3:00:00	39:15	41:00	45:00	50:25	1:33:10	2:34:30	1:28	3:45	7:15
3:30:00	45:15	47:20	52:00	57:50	1:47:25	2:58:43	1:42	4:20	8:28
4:00:00	51:00	53:25	58:40	65:00	2:01:30	3:23:00	1:46	4:55	9:40
4:30:00	56:50	59:20	65:10	72:00	2:15:10	4:36:45	2:09	5:30	10:54

WARM-UP AND COOL-DOWN

There is one more intensity of running which needs to be considered, and I have deliberately left it under the heading of hard runs even though it is the easiest of all. Of prime importance in any training session is a warm-up and a cool-down.

In every book that you ever read about training, be it running, rugby, football or swimming, there is a section on warming up and cooling down. The physiological benefits of this are well documented, and it has been shown that the body will perform better when it has been forewarned of a hard effort as opposed to being dropped in at the deep end.

However, one has to be practical about these things, and many runners find the idea of spending 10 or 15 minutes warming up and another 10 cooling down before a recovery or distance run in the morning something they cannot bring themselves to do. One reason for this is that they judge their training purely by the total distance run in a week, rather than by the quality and quantity of their workouts.

This is something that we can all identify with, but I believe there is a way around this problem for the easier early-morning runs. I really enjoy my sleep, and although I find the very early-morning runs amongst the most enjoyable, I don't enjoy getting out of bed one minute earlier than is necessary. So I set my kit out the night before, and, after a trip to the bathroom, I'm out on the road – total time no longer than 15 minutes from the alarm.

At that stage I don't feel the impulse to warm up and stretch; instead I purposely take the first mile very slowly, and since I inevitably seem to start up a hill, I try to overemphasise my style and take short strides. When I reach the flat the stride is gradually increased over a couple of 50m repeats, after which I seem to get into a rhythm fairly quickly. This seems to work for me, but failure to do this tends to lead to bad runs which I am keen to get finished.

Such an approach would not work for harder sessions, however, and for these I suggest that each runner work out a standard warm-up and cool-down procedure. The reason it should be standard is that when it is used under pre-race situations, the runner knows the 'success' it has brought in training. If it were changed, there would always be the anxiety that the changes might affect the race performance.

My preference is to commence with a jog of about one and a half miles. I must admit that I frequently have to control the speed of my jog carefully, as pre-race nerves tend to speed it up! This is followed by six or eight stretching exercises and, if necessary, a change of shoes into racing shoes or spikes. I am then ready to do three strides over 80–100m, starting from a jog and building to a sprint over about 15m. I walk back to the start each time as recovery. For longer races I will run a single 400m distance at the same pace that I would do ten repetitions on the track. A final short jog, a visit to the toilet and a drink, then I'm ready. I try to time my warm-up so as to finish within ten minutes of the start of the event. A basic rule is to make your warm-ups longer for the shorter, more intense races. This may mean slightly more jogging, strides and stretching. For longer events, just keep to your basic format.

The weather may also require a modification to your warm-up. In cool or cold conditions, do your routine in a rainsuit or windproof jacket. This creates a micro-climate within your clothing and helps to get you warm. Conversely, in hot and humid climates try to find a shaded area, to minimise the dehydration and sunburn effects. The warm-up is equally important in both cases. Even though you may feel warm, the exercise of the warm-up gives your body's systems a boost and preparation for the task ahead.

The cool-down at the end is somewhat similar, with the exception that there are no strides.

This seems to suit me, but each runner should find a routine that suits him or her. Runners who suffer badly from pre-race nerves may find that they require shorter warm-ups to get themselves ready, or that they need to do them on their own. Other runners who find it hard to get motivated may need to do more in the company of others so as to benefit from the atmosphere of the event. Any method is acceptable as long as it both prepares you physically for the race or hard session ahead and brings you to a suitable mental state of readiness. In this latter regard, the use of a walkman with music or a relaxation tape can help you to visualise the task ahead or dispel those over-anxious thoughts.

One thing is certain: not to warm up is to run the danger of injury, and will more than likely result in a below-par performance. In training, a warm-up will ensure that you are making the most efficient use of your training time.

These, then, are the different running components that will help make up a training programme. In many cases the programme will be augmented by additional exercise, where time allows, but one always has to remember that, in general, where time is limited, the rule 'running is the best training for running' will hold true.

The next chapter deals with various additional types of training that can be used to supplement and vary your programme.

CHAPTER NINE

SUPPLEMENTARY ACTIVITIES AND CROSS-TRAINING

Having looked at the various different types of running training, let's turn to the role various other exercises can play in developing a runner's full potential.

The concern with overtraining has been well aired throughout this book and in many ways this is the biggest problem faced by the motivated runner. Often runners see the objective as being to put in as many miles as possible. The higher the weekly mileage, the fitter they are – or so they think. This is certainly not true.

As previously stated, your training can only ever be as good as the rest and recovery available to you. It's no use piling in the mileage if your body never gets a chance to rebuild the microscopic muscle tears that occur in training. It is this recovery that improves the muscles' performance.

Similarly, there's no point in simply grinding out distance, as this only improves one aspect of your performance and, as we have already seen, a really good performance involves combining a number of different factors, including speed, endurance and power. Such variables as weather, psychological preparation and terrain are among the other factors affecting performance.

The benefits of supplementary exercises are manyfold and include giving variety to a training programme. Some long endurance runs could be substituted by a long cycle, for instance; although different leg muscles are being used, the cardiovascular system is unaware of whether you are running or cycling, it just knows that it has to supply air!

Supplementary exercises can also be used as a means of training through an injury. A number of world-class athletes have run in water when they have been injured and unable to take their full body weight on their legs. Exercises such as weight training have been shown to be the most efficient way of developing specific muscle strength.

The permutations when doing supplementary exercises are endless. Athletes who are training to maximum capacity in running can use these additional exercises to take them slightly further up the fitness graph to a slightly higher peak. It has to be accepted, however, that these additional exercises are generally less efficient methods of training for a runner than running is, and should not be considered as a substitution for running if you really want to reach your potential.

INPUT AND OUTPUT

Figure 9.1 is an input/output graph showing the relation between the training effort put in and the improvement one can expect as a result of that effort. This graph is purely indicative of the above concept. Initially it is seen that the graph is a straight line, indicating that up to a certain value the amount of training effort that one puts in is directly proportional to the results that one can expect. However, after a certain point the return that can be expected will diminish, that is to say, a greater amount of time will be required for the same improvement to be forthcoming.

Figure 9.1 Input and Output

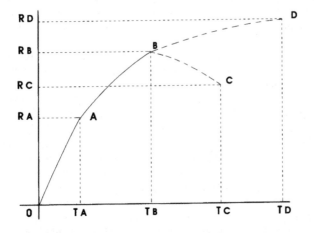

Where this point of diminishing return is located will depend on the individual, the type of training, the available rest and other stress-related factors. Thus the point may in fact vary at different stages in an individual's life. As a rough guide, however, some scientists believe that it is likely to be about 70 miles per week for a serious athlete, and hence I would guess that it occurs at around 45 miles per week for the average runner who has work, family and other obligations to take into account.

If even more time is put into training, the performance actually tends to drop off, and this is the overtraining principle. This shows that the body is not getting enough chance to recover before it is put under stress again. Obviously, the ideal is to get to the crest of the graph for the race you want to peak for.

The line coming off the crest is indicative of the role that supplementary exercise can play. By removing stress from muscles that have already been taken to their limit, and by training other areas, it is possible to improve the performance even further. It is important to note, however, that the return from such exercises is not as great as the return from running at the beginning of the graph.

The above places the role of supplementary exercises into perspective in relation to running training. The next question is what form of exercises to undertake.

THE IMPORTANCE OF BALANCE

Have you noticed the differences in the way runners run? It is possible to identify runners from quite some distance by their stride; each has a distinctive 'footprint'. I believe that this is largely a result of the mechanical imbalances of the runner. In some cases this includes such inherent 'defects' as a shorter left or right leg, excessive pronation or supination, turning in or out of feet, and so on. The list is virtually endless and it is doubtful that there are any runners who are truly perfect in their strides.

It is, however, noticeable that most track runners have a much more fluent style than most road runners. Perhaps this is one of the reasons that they compete on the track. On the other hand, the road runner concentrating on the longer distance uses a much more economic stride that his track colleague, who seems to bound along. The longer the distance run, the lower the kick-back of the leg as it follows though to start the next stride.

During my 1990 visit to Scotland from South Africa, I was lucky enough to get IAAF press accreditation to one of the Grand Prix series and there witnessed the then new sprint star Michael Johnson of America. Apart from the fact that at the Edinburgh meeting he ran a 19.85 200m time, he also ran a 400m in the relay and clocked 44 seconds. What was impressive was the rigidly disciplined stride he used in the final straight. Unlike most 400m runners there was no evidence of 'tying up'. Close inspection of his style will reveal that he tends to use a very low knee-lift action in his running. This is a vast contrast to the average sprinter, and has obviously come with extensive practice. A number of athletes have tried to adopt a similar low leg lift, recognising its energy-saving qualities.

What is the value of all of this to roadrunners?

Well, as discussed previously, there are times when we should reduce our mileage and concentrate on improving speed. Speed is a combination of stride speed (cadence) and stride length. To a limited extent, increasing either will increase your speed. However, you have to be careful of overstriding since, if you do this, your centre of gravity remains behind the point of landing and then you have to work against gravity to keep the forward motion.

Your ability to reach your full potential in stride length is directly related to your flexibility, particularly in the hip and hamstring regions. Obviously, the more mechanically perfect you can get your style, the more efficient you can be in your running. This means that you can either run faster, or run further at the same speed.

Have you ever considered that your 'style imperfections' may actually be a result of muscle-strength imbalances? Perhaps the tendency of your foot to overpronate is as a result of a tight inner set of leg or foot muscles? Suppose, then, you worked on strengthening the antagonistic muscles on the outside: could this not balance you and help to reduce the problem? Have you ever put a mirror down the centre of a photograph of a person? The new reflected image is different from the 'whole' person because no one is perfectly symmetrical. The same applies to most of our muscle groups.

Muscles work in pairs, but unfortunately they don't always gain strength at the same rate. Take running, for example. When we run we strengthen the muscles down the back of our bodies, particularly the hamstrings and the lower back. This causes them to shorten. The muscles in the front are not getting this workout and so they don't shorten as much. This explains the tightness that many runners develop, becoming unable to touch their toes, or even suffering back pain. Part of the answer, then, lies not only in stretching these back muscles, but also in strengthening the front muscles – hence the importance of sit-ups to the runner.

How do you find out just how imbalanced you are? One of the best methods is testing. In most cities there are at least a couple of Akron or Cibex machines and biokinetics clinics which can do this work for you. After the test you will know what areas you need to work on. If you are in a period of training where your mileage can be reduced, you will presumably have a little extra time to undertake a couple of workouts per week to strengthen your weak areas. This in turn will improve your style and hence your efficiency. As a result your speed can improve, and this brings us back to an improved race time.

It is no coincidence that track athletes spend many hours developing their style. Wins on the track are measured in hundredths of a second over short distances. If efficiency is important over short distances, then surely over longer distances it is even more important? It is worthwhile developing a schedule of exercises that you can use in a couple of sessions per week to improve this area.

Let's now consider different types of supplementary exercises that you can use to balance your training programme.

STRETCHING

Stretching is perhaps the most logical exercise to look at first in running training, and, if you have already looked at the track-training section in chapter eight, you will see that stretching has already been emphasised as part of the essential warm-up before training sessions.

The need for stretching becomes obvious as soon as one realises that an exercised muscle will tend to shorten, and in fact running tends to shorten most of the muscles down the back of the body. If this is true then the range of movement of various parts of the body must also be changed and restricted. This could result, for instance, in a shorter stride length. Since the speed at which a runner can run can be considered as a product of both the stride length and the number of strides taken in a minute, it becomes obvious that a full range of movement will be nescessary for achieving maximum speed.

(As with most things there is a point of diminishing returns, and overstriding will result in a slowing-down due to basic mechanics of running. If a runner overstrides he then has to fight against gravity to 'roll' over into the next stride. For this reason runners should not assume that simply lengthening their stride will result in faster times.)

Similarly, a shortening of the back muscles will result in a bowing of the back and hence a stretching of the stomach muscles. Thus it is obvious that if an erect posture is to be maintained, the stomach muscles must be worked on to bring the body back into line. (This also leads into weight training.)

There are many stretches that can be done and, strangely enough, many runners find themselves doing stretches without anyone even suggesting it; this even happens to novices. The usual stretches seem to be hanging forward over their feet (this would stretch the back to some extent), putting one foot up on a wall or other higher object (this tends to stretch the hamstring area), and the ever-popular 'push over a tree or wall' exercise (stretching the ankle and calf areas).

The point being made is that it appears that these stretches are prompted by the body itself. It has become apparent to me over the years that the cravings and prompts given by my body tend to be the very things that I need to do. Stretching, then, is an excellent, if not essential, part of training for running, and should take the form of a regular, well-rounded variation of exercises undertaken as often as possible.

Stretches are easily included in a schedule by doing them when watching TV or when relaxing outdoors. The important thing is to make the stretching a regular habit. The complete session may only involve six or eight stretches and take about 15 minutes, but, done regularly, it will provide substantial benefit.

A possible session could be as follows:

1. *Forward-hanging stretch*
Place your feet apart and bend forward at the stomach to let your upper torso hang over your feet. Keep your legs straight and knees locked. Gradually move your hands to one side, then towards the other foot. Feel the stretch but do not try to take it past the point of initial pain. This is a good way of warming up for later stretches. If you do this again at the end of the session you will see that you are able to go lower before reaching the initial pain point.

2. *Standing cross-leg stretch*
Cross one leg over the other and keep the heel of the crossed leg off the ground, with only the forefoot on the ground. Now bend forward and hang down towards your toes and hold the stretch for a few seconds. Raise the torso and stretch backwards, then repeat the forward stretch. Repeat the procedure with the other leg crossed. The knee of the back leg should remain locked and straight at all times.

3. *Hamstring stretch*
Lying on your back, pull one knee to your chest, with a fully bent leg, and raise your head towards your knee. Repeat with the other leg.

4. *Abdominal and upper body stretch*
Lie flat on your stomach with your hands shoulder-width apart at chest level. Push up with your arms, bending up from your lower back. Do not pull with your back. Try to keep your pelvis on the ground.

5. *Quad lunge*

Stand facing forward and take one stride forward so that your front leg is parallel to the ground. Now move forward to enable you to drop the other knee towards the ground. Keep the upper body vertical. The stretch is on the back leg. Repeat and then repeat with the other leg forward.

6. *Sitting quad*

Kneel down on both knees and sit back on to your heels. The stretch will be felt in the quads above the knee. Some runners may find it possible to sit right down between their heels; if this is so, care must be taken to ensure that the knee joint is not damaged.

7. *Back stretch*

Lie on your back and gradually and slowly bring your legs over your head to touch the ground behind. Care must be taken with this stretch to ensure that you do not damage your back by jerking it over. Use your hands to guide you and support you.

8. *Calf stretch*

Adopt a pushing position with your hands against a wall or other fixed object. Keeping one foot firmly on the ground, slowly bend the supporting knee until you get the feeling of the stretch. This can be modified with the use of a wedge of wood or similar object to assist in improving the flexion of the ankle. Slight variation in movement will move the location of the stretch.

There are a couple of basic rules that should be adhered to in stretching. First, under no circumstances should you bounce during the stretch. Bouncing actually causes the muscles to shorten and thus a further stretch can cause injury. Just take the stretch to the point of feeling it, hold it there for a few seconds, then ease back and apply it again. The second and third stretches will take you further.

Ease into stretching and don't measure yourself against others; work within your limitations.

Don't stretch when totally cold; rather, do at least some minor form of warm-up. Ideally do your stretching at the end of another training session.

It should be borne in mind that muscles operate in pairs: one pulls whilst the other relaxes. Muscles cannot 'push'. Strengthening exercises and stretches are required in combination to 'balance' the runner.

The dangers of cold stretching were highlighted in a survey of the

Honalulu Marathon. Researchers eliminated from the survey any runner who had previously had an injury, and compared those who stretched before the race with those stretching after. It was found that whilst Asian runners were able to stretch before or after without injury, white runners were 33 per cent more prone to muscle tears or similar injury if they stretched before the race. It was speculated that this was partly as a result of insufficient warm-up and their lesser affinity to regular stretching.

AEROBICS

This is a logical extension of the stretching exercises and will improve not only your suppleness but also your aerobic capacity.

Most gyms have aerobic classes and the benefits are fairly obvious and don't really need further discussion, other than to note that such sessions are also a good method of recovery after a race.

Don't be disappointed or embarrassed if you find yourself lacking in co-ordination in some of the movements. Despite appearances, even the best instructors had that problem when they first started!

TREADMILL RUNNING

I have included this here as it is something that can offer an alternative when either the weather prohibits training or you are looking for a different session. With treadmill running you have the opportunity to do any or all of the normal running sessions expressed in the book. However, you will not make any friends if you use the local fitness-club treadmill for your two-hour-long run! Normally sessions on a club treadmill will need to be limited to about 30 minutes in order to let others get through their training.

Treadmills offer some benefits. They force you into a leg speed – it's either keep up, or be forced off the back. They often have a more cushioned tread-board, which reduces the leg pounding you get from tar or the track. This is particularly useful when making a return after injury, or just for a change. Most treadmills also provide an instantaneous read-out of speed, distance and time, and thus can be useful for short speed sessions.

On the negative side, it has to be said that treadmill running uses a different stride technique. You can, however, do two things to compensate for this: set the treadmill gradient at 1 per cent, or alternatively raise the speed by about 1km/hr above your target pace.

This will provide about the same perceived effort as your target pace. The use of the incline is preferable.

Although you will not have to push aside any headwind or move air when running on a treadmill, you will also not benefit from the air's cooling effect. Make sure you take a cloth or towel with you when treadmill training, as your sweat will not be a welcome present for the next user – and you can be sure that you will sweat more in the warm indoor climate.

A greater mental tenacity is required to do your training session on the treadmill, since you are going nowhere and see the same scenery all the time. The treadmill can, however, offer a good transition session from road to track training, as it builds the confidence of handling speed and distance. Doing short, very fast repeats on the treadmill is a good way of improving leg speed.

As with most of these supplementary exercises, the treadmill is a useful tool, but not one to overplay.

WEIGHT TRAINING

There is a distinct difference between weight training, weight lifting and body building. Body building aims to develop muscle bulk, something that a runner doesn't want. This, of course, becomes obvious if you remember that the VO_2 max discussed in chapter three is measured in units per kilogram of body weight. Hence the lower the body weight, the higher the VO_2 max.

Weight lifting is concerned with the maximum 'one-off' effort to lift a weight in a prescribed fashion. By contrast, the sport of running is concerned with a series of movements that are repeated many, many times per kilometre, and thus weight lifting is of no real interest to runners.

Our interest in weight *training*, on the other hand, is concerned with the development of strength in an endurance mode. The strength requirement, like all aspects of training, varies with the distance over which you want to compete. There is a high strength requirement in sprinting, as opposed to marathon running, where the requirement is much lower.

Looking at the physical differences between, for instance, Linford Christie and any of the Kenyan distance runners highlights the different requirements. In Christie we see a highly developed, muscular frame, a power-packed explosive frame that is 'designed' to catapult its way off the blocks and over 100m. In the Kenyans the muscle definition is still there, but there is much less bulk. The muscles have been trained to do the same exercise many, many times over. In other words, the key is strength endurance.

There are extremes in strength training. Obviously, the closer one gets to the sprinter, the more 'explosive' strength is required; the longer the competitive distance, the more strength endurance becomes important.

There are many ways of developing strength. Essentially, anything that causes the muscles to be 'overloaded' will result in a strengthening when they rebuild and recover. Overloading can be achieved through the use of hills, running in water, running through sand or rough grass, bounding or, more commonly, through the use of weights or other training machines such as elastic cords or springs. Many track runners have dragged tyres or training partners behind them in order to produce the resistance they require to improve their strength!

The key is that in each case the runner performs against a resistance to cause the muscles to 'break down'. During the recovery period between training sessions the muscles repair and get stronger; they adapt to this resistance and are then able to tackle a greater resistance.

At first sight it would appear that the only muscles that a runner would be interested in strengthening would be those of the leg, but in fact a stronger upper body can also be beneficial to the long-distance runner. In the case of the sprinter or 400m runner, the arms and shoulders are very important for developing the high arm drive required. In addition, a good all-round tone to the upper body will assist with correct running style.

The objective for the distance runner is not to increase body bulk but rather to develop strength for endurance, thus a schedule will concentrate on a high number of repetitions with relatively light resistance.

In the case of weight training, this means doing, say, 12 to 20 repetitions of an exercise, and performing these groups of repetitions three times. Each group of repetitions is called a set, and a short rest of about 30 seconds is allowed between sets.

A basic all-round schedule for a distance runner could be:

1. Warm-up (a 2–3km easy jog, or skipping, or cycling on a stationary bike)
2. Stretching
3. Bent-leg sit-ups x 20 x 3
4. Leg extensions x 15 x 3
5. Leg curls x 15 x 3
6. Lunges x 15 x 3

7. Calf raises x 15 x 3
8. Bent-arm dumb-bell pull-overs x 15 x 3
9. Bench presses x 15 x 3
10. Upright rowing x 15 x 3
11. Bicep curls x 15 x 3
12. Incline leg raises x 20 x 3
13. Stretching
14. Cool-down (easy jog, skipping or cycle)

You may wonder why I haven't described in detail exactly how to do each exercise, but this is not an oversight. Since you are dealing with weight additional to your body weight, weight training does carry a certain risk of injury. It is very important that these exercises are done properly and I therefore recommend that the first time you attempt weight training you go to a gym instructor and ask to be shown the correct procedures.

Furthermore, you should initially select a slightly lighter weight than you think you can handle, since this will ensure that you concentrate on doing the exercise properly to begin with.

The session I have described will only take about 30 minutes and would therefore fit nicely into a lunch hour. Thus this training can be done without having to compromise other running time.

Another alternative is to buy a home gym, which would allow you to do this training whenever you want. Such a machine should be solidly constructed and stable so that there is no chance of it moving or tilting over during use. It should allow you to do a variety of exercises, without being as complex as the equipment in a professional gym. Buy from a reputable dealer and get advice from other runners first.

Such a weights session would be performed three times a week during the base training period, and would reduce to twice a week during the pre-competition period. During your racing season (or your taper period before a major race), no work is done with weights.

As with track work, don't expect dramatic results overnight, as it will take a few weeks before your body adapts to this training and you see the benefits. In fact, for the first six weeks your legs may even feel a bit heavier than usual – but after that you will find your times improving.

Circuit training can provide a good transitional phase for runners moving from base training towards strength training. This is done over four to six weeks and combines running with basic exercises. Whilst it is fairly easy to improvise at the trackside, it is particularly easy to do in a gym where you have access to a treadmill.

Commence with a warm-up and stretch, as always. Then move on to the treadmill for a 400m at your 5km pace. Immediately run through the following five exercises: burpess (6–10), pull-ups/chins (4–6), abdominal crunch (12–20), push-ups (10–15) and fast bodyweight squats (20–30). Then it's back to the treadmill for another 400m (building to 800m after three weeks). Then it's off again for squats and dumbell presses (6–10), elevated feet press-ups (6–10), low back extensions (12–20), bench or chair dips (10–15) and lunges (10–16 each leg). Once again go back to the treadmill for another 400 or 800m at 5km pace.

One circuit on the first week becomes two on the second, and goes back to one on the third, but with 800m intervals. On the fourth week the intervals become 600m, but the circuit is done twice, and finally, on the fifth week, it's three circuits with 400m intervals between exercises.

Don't be fooled into thinking that these are easy. By the time you have worked your way through the combination of strength and speed, you will know you have worked!

OTHER STRENGTHENING EXERCISES

Although most people consider that the only way to improve strength is by the use of weights, this is not the case. Any session that causes the muscles to be overloaded will develop an improvement in strength in those muscles, providing, of course, a sufficient recovery period is allowed to enable the repair of the muscles.

Since our objective is generally to improve the strength in the muscles used whilst running, it would seem that some form of overloading whilst running would be the most efficient training method. This principle has been tried in many sports, by using, for instance, heavier golf clubs or tennis rackets when practising. The problem is that such methods tend to change the person's swing or grip, since more and different muscles need to be brought into play in order to handle the heavier equipment.

Similarly, running with weights also tends to change your style and therefore in general is not a good idea. A possible exception to this would be to use a container that distributes the weight evenly through the centre of the body. In this regard the liquid-filled Tripper discussed in the chapters on running gear and energy replacement could prove to be the answer.

Because of the possible impact on style, we look for other forms of resistance which still allow the development of strength without impairing running style or, indeed, do so whilst actually improving running style. There are many suggested methods such as running in calf-deep water (along the beach, say) or running on sand or on hills (see chapter three).

For many years the British athletics team, as well as many teams from other sports, have gone to the sand dunes in Wales, where they do repeats up and down one of the steep dunes. Other athletes have tried dragging car tyres across grass as a means of developing both strength and a good driving style for their running. The tyre is attached to their body by means of a harness which passes over each shoulder.

These sessions would be preceded by a thorough warm-up and stretching session and would then comprise five efforts over 200m to 400m, with sufficient recovery to allow the session to be completed. Such a session falls more into the category of running training as described in the previous chapter than weight training, however.

In all cases, the actual effort put into the repeats, the distance covered and the amount of recovery will vary depending on the objective of the session. Runners must decide whether they are trying to develop pure strength, or speed endurance, or style improvement, and so on.

Care should be taken when trying any running on sand, since your feet tend to sink into the sand, putting greater than normal strain on the Achilles tendon. There is also the problem of the slope of the sand towards the sea, which can result in knee injuries. When running hard on sand there is a tendency for some people to twist their feet, and this can cause problems as they are not running with their natural stride. An adaptation period is necessary for all of these reasons.

A similar excercise can be undertaken on stairs. Again, as the emphasis of your training changes, so you can change your stair training session. Running up 30 flights of stairs in an office block, stepping on each tread, obviously does more for strength endurance than does sprinting up the short but very steep grandstand stairs of a rugby ground.

Most of the exercises discussed above are designed to develop leg strength, but upper-body strength is also important in the correct carriage of arms and the aiding of breathing. A trim track can be used for this purpose, with the runner stopping at various stations to do pull-ups, dips, sit-ups, press-ups and a host of other exercises against gravity and body weight.

Hand weights can also be used to tone up the upper arms, but again it is important not to use weights that are too heavy, as this will alter running style. Weights in the region of 0.5kg per hand are ideal.

Another form of strength training that has gained a lot of favour recently is 'plyometrics', which consists of exercises involving 'elastic bounding'. A plyometric series could be: two strides, a hop, a hop, and then a double-foot deep jump; or dropping off a step and immediately doing a deep jump. The variety of exercises is unlimited, but a full session of these may take 20–30 minutes. These exercises improve not only strength and power but also co-ordination. One of the most famous users of plyometrics was Sebastian Coe. He regularly undertook a session of plyometrics that would have him bounding over vaulting horses or jumping astride over a low box.

Similar exercises can be developed to improve rhythm, style and co-ordination as well as strength. An example would be to run 50m whilst concentrating on kicking your heels up to your buttocks as many times as possible. Obviously your arms would need to be moved in synch throughout this exercise. Another example would be to repeat the same distance with high knee-lifts and very short strides.

These may all seem very simple exercises, but try this session a couple of times and you will soon notice how it works muscles you never knew you had.

A good introduction to plyometrics is simply to hop down a set of stairs. Pick a flight with around 10 or 12 steps and hop down on one leg, then walk back to the top and hop down using the other leg. The handrail can provide the early safety and confidence you require, and the small eccentric bounding prepares you for some of the more substantial bounding exercises that you can move on to. Starting with a total of around 20 hops, you will soon build up to between 50 and 80 on each leg.

To get the maximum benefit from these sort of exercises you should aim to do the explosive sections at around the same pace as running. (approximately 85 steps per minute). One of the disadvantages of most weight training is that it is only done at a much slower speed. The strength is not 'specific' to running, whereas fast plyometric work is. Aim to keep it fast, rhythmical and explosive – you'll soon see why you don't have to do much to get big gains.

CYCLING

Cycling was a boom sport in the 1960s in Britain and has experienced a 'second wind' both from a recreational standpoint and also as a result of the development of the sports of biathlons and triathlons. More recently this has been further bolstered by the explosion in mountain-biking, either for off-road use or simply to get to and from work.

Cycling, like running, is basically an aerobic sport, although it can be used to develop all the same aspects as running, namely endurance, strength, speed, and so on. Once again it depends what sort of training session you undertake.

Is there any carry-over between cycling and running? This is a hard question to answer, but in my view there must be some cross-over benefit. Certainly there has to be a similar improvement in cardiovascular development in the two sports, provided the cycling is strenuous enough, and surely cycling benefits from the improvement in the leg-muscle strength that results from hill repeats? Similarly, the 'spinning' action (fast, low-gear pedalling) undertaken by cyclists must surely help in improving the leg cadence of runners.

The biggest drawback to any cross-training benefit is that cycling does not use exactly the same muscles as running; hence there is no direct relationship.

In terms of time benefit, one American triathlon source suggests that, since one rides at approximately twice the speed at which one runs, it would take an hour of cycling to equate to half an hour of running. I'm not convinced that this is quite true; I feel the ration is more likely to be 3:1.

One thing I have proved with runners I have coached is that there is a definite benefit to hill running from cycling training on hills. Cycling teaches the need for changing gears and shows how to tackle a long hill with a rythmic approach. It is an excellent way of teaching a runner how to run up long climbs in races.

The spinning involved in cycling, where legs turn over at a speed in excess of 90 revs per minute, has also been of benefit to a number of runners I have helped. In fact, friends and I have run some very fast sessions immediately after a short cycle. (Such sessions are, however, extremely taxing and must be used with care; see triathlon training.)

Cycling has certain drawbacks, however, and in my view the greatest of these is the additional danger. This is not always a rider's own fault, and no matter how safety-conscious you are, the fact that you are sharing the road with high-powered motor vehicles means that there is substantial risk. A very dear friend and team colleague, Dave McCarney, died after being hit from behind by a large truck. I therefore advise cyclists to take all possible precautions in the equipment they use, even to the extent of having mirrors and reflectors fitted to their bikes. It may not be fashionable to wear a hard helmet, gloves and bright cycling top, or to fit a handlebar or helmet mirror, or to have a host of reflective material over the bike, but it's better than becoming a statistic!

Whatever you do, be bright, be seen and stay alive. A useful tip for cycling past road junctions at which cars have stopped is to watch the wheels rather than the bodies of the vehicles. Small movements are much more easily detected.

One training session that is exceptionally hard and yet 100 per cent safe involves using indoor wind trainers. Here the bike is fixed to a rig and a fan is turned by the rear wheel to create resistance. This is a very taxing session and allows the rider to do various high-intensity repeats. Since you are indoors, it tends to get very humid and hot. It is also very tiring mentally, since you are always stationary. On the other hand, it is possible to combine this exercise with various testing and monitoring procedures, which allows a standardised testing procedure to be undertaken.

Regular tests can be used in this manner to assess fitness and it is even possible to determine VO_2 max and threshold levels with the use of a heart monitor. However, this result can only be used as a guide, since your technique in cycling may be slightly better or worse than in running and hence there will be a minor variation in the results.

SWIMMING

Swimming is another excellent sport and one that tones up just about every area of the body. If you go for a swim, notice how firm your muscles feel when you've finished even a relatively short session.

Exercising both the upper and lower body, swimming makes major demands on your cardiovascular system, and the fact that your breathing has to be controlled into the stroke means that swimming is a good way of learning to regulate your breathing.

In swimming your body weight is totally supported by the water and so it is the most useful sport in cases of injury.

RUNNING IN WATER

Many world-class runners have used 'water work' as a means of training thorugh major injuries and then come back to record significant performances shortly after resuming running. Water work involves not only swimming but also running in the water. This is achieved by being supported in the water in a vertical postion whilst driving with the arms and legs. It sounds easy, but a 15-minute session like this is a heavy workout, so water work should be undertaken gradually. In such exercises the resistance is not only on the downward foot drive but also upwards against the water, and your muscles will remind you of this fact for the following two days!

The main problem with swimming is that it is a high-technique sport. Indeed, if you were not taught to swim properly as a child, the chances are that you will take a great deal of time to learn the required techniques. Often you will have to 'kick' certain bad habits that you have developed through casual swimming, and this can prove to be almost impossible.

It is interesting to note that most champion swimmers are relatively young, and even schoolchildren who take up the sport seriously are subjected to 10,000m of swimming per day. Obviously this is far in excess of the swimming that one would use as an alternative or supplement to running training. Here a session might involve swimming a total of between 1km and 3km. This is not done in one continuous length, but rather in intervals of anything from 50m to 200m.

In the same way that track speed and recovery are varied to suit your needs, so must swimming speed be varied. However, rather than specifying a set recovery period, it is common in swimming to specify a 'turn-around time'. In other words, the instruction might be to swim 50m on the minute. This means that you swim a 50m length every time the second hand reaches the 12. Thus if you swim hard, you get a longer break before starting again; if you swim slowly, you have a short break.

Swimming is the least taxing and damaging of the three triathlon sports – running, cycling and swimming – and thus recovery from a hard swimming session is fast. This is one reason that young swimmers are able to cope with such long distances.

Anaerobic capacity is also thought to be improved by swimming distances underwater, hence limiting the oxygen supply. This would tie in with some research done with runners who performed breathing exercises for six weeks. Basically they practised breathing against resistance both on inhaling and exhaling. This was found to improve their VO_2 by a substantial amount. It would seem that just learning how to breathe and how to build and exercise those breathing muscles could be an easy way of making some progress. It certainly would make a relatively easy day of active rest.

Other variations in swimming include using hand paddles to increase the water resistance in the arm pull, kicking only, tying the feet and pulling with arms only, and so on. Long swims of over 600m are unlikely to be of much benefit to non-swimming runners, since the pace is likely to be too slow owing to inadaquate technique.

CANOEING

I have included canoeing in this list since it is a popular sport amongst a number of runners who also participate in the canoe triathlons and other outdoor activities. Canoeing can obviously be used as an alternative sport, but since it is predominantly concerned with upper-body movement, the benefit to running is much more limited.

MASSAGE

Although this can hardly be called a sport or exercise, it certainly has a place in training programmes. Massage can be used as a worthwhile tool in training, race preparation and recovery. The first problem for the novice to such treatment is what type of massage to go for and what to look for in a masseur.

Massage is an excellent way of improving blood circulation to muscles and joints, improving the alignment of the muscle fibres and the flexibility of the muscle, and treating minor and potential injuries. It also has a stress-reducing and psychological benefit to the athlete.

The emphasis on each of these areas can be altered through the use of different types of massage strokes. A trained masseur can use one massage method to mentally atune an athlete who is lacking in motivation for a competition, for example, and use more relaxing strokes to bring down the anxiety level of an athlete tied up with apprehension before a major competition. Massage method should vary according to the stage of training, and can be widely classified into three areas: preparatory massage, pre-competition massage and recuperation massage.

Preparatory massage is used during the training period. It is intended to aid the recovery of the athlete after a heavy session and also to prepare him or her for the next quality sessions.

Pre-competition massage is used to bring the athlete to the right state of physical and mental arousal immediately before competition. Obviously this will vary depending on whether the event is a sprint, which requires many short, fast strokes, or an endurance event, which will tend to need longer, deeper massage techniques.

The recuperation massage is undertaken after the competition to improve the athlete's rate of recovery. Again the techniques will vary with timing of the competition. A deep massage immediately after the marathon is not going to be the most beneficial or most pleasant experience, but a light massage a week later will have little benefit.

The masseur must obviously have a thorough understanding not only of the massage techniques but also of the athlete's objectives at any point in his or her training. A background in physiology and, to a lesser extent, psychology is important. A good masseur will also be capable of work on minor injuries and assistance in prevention of potential injuries. For these reasons it is essential that athlete and masseur work together over an extended period to develop the necessary rapport.

Obviously, such regular attention is viable for many runners only if a friend or family member is suitably trained in such techniques. It may therefore be more beneficial to attend a course on massage than face the relatively high cost of regular attention. This again depends on the priority one gives to reaching peak performance.

I suspect that the general attitude towards massage is one of suspicion, which is probably reinforced by the experiences of some runners at under-qualified establishments. However, the practice of mixing massage and training has been shown to have major benefits to world-class athletes and I have no hesitation in stating that it is a practice that, when applied properly, will benefit runners at all levels.

Remember, your training is only as good as your recovery, and anything that improves recovery will allow you to train more effectively.

CHAPTER TEN

THE DIFFERENT PHASES OF TRAINING

This section helps you to put the 'meat' on to the skeleton of the schedules. Obviously the type of schedule will be different for each training season, since the objective in each season is different. I am a firm believer in knowing exactly what I am trying to achieve every time I cross the threshold to go training. I can go further and say that I know what my session this time next week will be trying to achieve.

You have to know where you are going and how you are going to get there if you want to reach a destination or goal. It is therefore important to plan for that. However, as the great Rabbie Burns put it, 'The best laid schemes o' mice an' men gang aft a-gley' (or often go astray, in more common usage!), and the fourth law of training tells us to be flexible.

If I have a track session planned and a work commitment means that I can only train at four in the morning, then I must have the flexibility to change my sessions around, since to try track work at that time is more likely to cause injury than benefit. Conversely, I mustn't use this flexibility as an excuse to get out of training sessions that don't initially appeal to me. It is not a way of developing excuses!

ACTIVE RECOVERY

The active recovery schedule is probably the most flexible since its objective is to give the body a chance to recover fully from the competition season, whilst at the same time maintaining a basic standard of fitness and movement.

This weekly schedule should incorporate a few rest days of total inactivity. It also provides an ideal opportunity to make use of some or all of the supplementary exercises discussed earlier.

A possible schedule is shown in Table 10.1.

Table 10.1 Active recovery schedule

Day 1:	Rest	Day 5:	5 miles off-road/cross-country
Day 2:	Cycle 1 hour	Day 6:	Swim 1km
Day 3:	Run 5–6 miles	Day 7:	Run 6–7 miles
Day 4:	Rest		

The permutations are endless and will vary with your fitness level, but this is a time of no pressure, and if you feel like missing a session, you may do so.

BASE TRAINING

Once you have recovered you are ready to start tackling your next goal, and one of the first rungs on the ladder you have to climb is re-establishing your endurance base. Thus most of your running during this phase will be of the long, slow nature – but not all of it.

The training schedule for this phase will also introduce weight training after a few weeks, and may use some cycling to provide an alternative way of developing the long run.

I find that one of the easiest ways to start setting up a schedule is to determine which day you want as a rest day. Not many years ago I made the mistake of not having at least one day's full rest a week. When I eventually got wise and included a rest day, my running improved immediately, since I had a renewed zest the following day. Now, although I may actually train on days that I have scheduled as rest days, I still abide by the principle of having regular, complete rest days, and benefit from the physiological and psychological renewal they provide.

Some runners will find that they need two rest days a week, and this is fine. Remember the sixth law of training: try to achieve as much as possible on the minimum of training. Don't let yourself get into the obsessive training routine, or become a slave to weekly distance. These are wheels that have been invented and re-invented many times – and on each occasion they have been proven not to work!

The next step is to divide up your training runs so that your week includes one long run, one medium run, one fartlek-type run and some short recovery runs. This in effect gives you three harder sessions and three easier sessions, plus a rest day.

What constitutes a long run will of course be decided by what you are training for and what level of fitness you are currently at. The fartlek is included in the schedule to prevent a one-pace format developing in this training, and may be as simple as speeding up from training pace to 10-mile race pace three or four times in the session. These faster sections may be only a few hundred metres long but will prove invaluable. They should not be hard efforts, simply a change of gear.

Runners who have never done any speed work tend to train at their marathon pace almost all the time. However, the élite marathon runners train at much slower than marathon pace – but then their marathon pace is slightly under five minutes a mile! Seiko of Japan actually carries out many of his distance training runs at eight minutes a mile, despite being capable of running sub 2:10 marathons. Once average runners have become involved with speed work they too develop a relatively wide range of gears and speeds at which to train. Remember, long, slow trainers become good long, slow runners.

Bearing in mind the fifth law of training, you must apply the alternating principle to your weekly long runs. Thus, if your maximum weekly long run is currently 10 miles and you are building to 18 miles, try scheduling your build-up as in Table 10.2.

Table 10.2 Long run schedule

Week 1: 10 miles	Week 6: 12 miles
Week 2: 8 miles	Week 7: 15 miles
Week 3: 14 miles	Week 8: 12 miles
Week 4: 9 miles	Week 9: 18 miles
Week 5: 13 miles	

This may seem slow, but remember the second law of training! In any case, this approach will allow you to recover well and will establish a good base.

So, in general terms, a weekly base schedule will look like Table 10.3.

Table 10.3 Weekly base schedule

Day 1:	Rest
Day 2:	Medium run (*about 20% of weekly total*)
Day 3:	Short run
Day 4:	Fartlek (*about 12% of weekly total*)
Day 5:	Short run
Day 6:	Long run (*not more than 35% of weekly total*)
Day 7:	Short run

The short runs would then each be one-third of the distance left in the weekly total after your other runs have been accounted for. Thus if your total is 50 miles then a long run would be 15–18 miles, the medium run 10 miles, fartlek about 6 miles and the short runs about 5–6 miles each.

This, then, gives a nice rounded schedule, and after a few weeks a couple of weight-training sessions could be introduced. Depending on availability of weights, these could be on days two and seven or three and one. Do not mix them with the hard sessions such as those on days six and four. Day seven's run could be replaced by a cycle of an hour, which would again assist in recovery and prevent mental staleness by providing variation.

RACE-SPECIFIC TRAINING

After a base has been established it is possible to include training sessions in your schedule that deal with the specific needs of your chosen event. Generally these will be speed-orientated, but training for some of the trail races that are run, particularly in America, may emphasise running on trails, for example, while training for a race over a hilly course may emphasise hill technique. The point is that this period of training specifically adapts the runner to the needs of the competition that he or she is aiming for.

Again, the objective is not to become obsessed with these requirements but rather to develop a balanced programme around them. You cannot do everything at once, so during this period, which may last between 6 and 12 weeks, the emphasis may change to cover all the requirements in gradually increasing difficulty.

For example, if your chosen event requires speed, this period of training may introduce a couple of sessions of fartlek per week, then change to one fartlek and one hill session, then to one hill and one relatively easy track session, then finally to two or even three track sessions per week. In general, of course, there will not be more than three hard sessions per week, as this would not allow for recovery.

Initial fartlek sessions will have been included in a very easy format in the base training and so to a certain extent there is a carry-over effect between these two training phases. Hills may be introduced towards the end of the base training phase. The progression is generally from endurance, to strength, to speed, to taper (sharpening and recovery), to competition.

With this in mind, the average runner training for a half-marathon may have a schedule something like Table 10.4.

Table 10.4 Half-marathon schedule

Day 1:	Rest
Day 2:	Track (3 or 4 x 800m for speed endurance)
Day 3:	Recovery run (7 miles)
Day 4:	Track (5 x 200m for speed, 5 x 400m at 5km pace)
Day 5:	Recovery run (5–6 miles very easy)
Day 6:	Cross-country race or fartlek
Day 7:	Slow distance (10–12 miles)

This schedule would result in a total distance of about 38–40 miles for the week, and certainly provides variation. If the hard sessions are done hard and the easy sessions taken at an easy pace, results will be felt.

This schedule is just a guide, and the track content will vary as the training season develops. Notice the reference to a cross-country race as an alternative to a fartlek session, but remember that the runner and the coach should agree before the race on the runner's finishing time or place. It should not be a flat-out effort. This approach to races requires supreme restraint and will power, and perhaps most runners are incapable of such self-discipline and would do better to avoid such races. What tends to happen is that they see a runner they know they can beat, or a friend whom they always 'dice', and then the game is on. What should be a training race becomes a flat-out effort and instead of developing their fitness with training, they end up drawing deeply on their reserves in a race situation.

On the other hand, as you approach the race you are trying to peak for, it is essential to sharpen up in a couple of races. This allows you to experience the pre-race anxiety, the race tactics, the conditions, and so on, but once again these are not necessarily 100 per cent flat-out efforts. Many of the world's top marathon runners use a 10km race about ten days before their marathon as an indication of how they will perform. It is important to note that the race they use is run over a shorter distance, and, indeed, this is where a club time trial can come in handy. A three-mile time trial would be ideal for a 10km race, and so on.

The Americans have a rule of thumb for determining the recovery period after a flat-out race, and that is to allow one day of recovery for every mile raced, before building up again. Thus after a hard three-mile time trial one should allow about three easy days. This again emphasises the problem of 'racing' the club 5-miler every week – no sooner have you recovered than you have the next week's time trial to run!

ACTIVE REST

In any build-up to a distance race there are periods of heavy training, and each of these should be followed by a shorter period of recovery before moving on to the next period of heavy training. This recovery period allows the body to 'repair' and benefit (adapt) from the overload (stress) effect of efficient training.

One should enter into periods of high distance fresh and eager to train. In the weeks that follow, as you try to squeeze in the distance, there may be times when it seems that there just aren't enough hours in a day. Starting the endurance training block with an easy week of active rest will allow you the opportunity to get things done in the rest of your life that your training may make impossible later.

What makes up a recovery week of active rest? It doesn't mean doing nothing, nor does it mean just going for slow runs. The idea is to keep to the basic training principles but to reduce the workload enough to enable your body to rest and recover fully from previous effort. This also means that it is no use reducing the training just to replace its stress by working all hours of the day and night.

Taking a whole week off is not as beneficial as this balance of reduced stress and activity, but there is nothing wrong with adding an extra day's total rest to your schedule. Where your work allows, shift your early-morning runs to early evening or even lunchtime. This will allow you to enjoy an extra hour or so in bed – something that may have to be sacrificed in the following weeks.

It is important to ensure that you continue to use a variety of speeds during the week's training, and a single high-quality session will ensure that you don't lose any of the fitness you have already built.

Your week, then, could look like Table 10.5.

Table 10.5 Active rest schedule

Monday:	Rest
Tuesday:	5 miles easy (marathon pace or slower)
Wednesday:	5 miles with 5 x 100m pick-ups at 5km pace
Thursday:	3 miles moderate (10 mile to half-marathon race pace)
Friday:	Rest
Saturday:	Track 4 x 400m at 5 seconds faster than best 5km pace with full recovery between each
Sunday:	7–12 miles easy

Such a schedule could be used as a recovery week in a marathon or ultra build-up.

The following week you could start your new training schedule and then begin moving towards your specific goal.

The difference between the recovery week and active recovery is only minimal. The recovery week maintains a higher level of 'quality' work and is a temporary lull in the build-up to an event, whereas active recovery is more orientated to circulation and 'ticking over'.

TAPERING

Every schedule that builds to a peak performance needs a period of tapering. I feel that this is so vitally important that it warrants a chapter in its own right. The influence of this will also be seen in the section on racing and the schedules given at the end of the book. Tapering is an essential part of your race preparation.

A FINAL WORD

In all of the schedules outlined above you can see that there is and must be a balance of effort and recovery. Although it is implied in many of the 15 laws of training, there is a principle that needs to be stated again forcefully: where there is any question or doubt about hard training, take the conservative option. It is better to go into a race slightly undertrained than to go in overtrained. At worst you can always improve for the next race, whereas if you race when overtrained you will only go further down the spiral and may even be sidelined by injury.

CHAPTER ELEVEN

SEASONAL TRAINING

I have always felt that one of the biggest disadvantages facing the average South African runner is that they don't really have seasons. This is, of course, the same for any country situated around the tropics, and in particular in the southern hemisphere. In comparison with their European and American counterparts, there really isn't an off-season for South African runners. Such countries virtually have 'year-round' summers (certainly compared to Scotland!), and hence even their largest races are held in adverse heat conditions.

Let's consider the problems associated with such a climate and how our British seasons, although an irritation in some ways, are beneficial to the planning of our training and racing.

In South Africa, every month of the year there are a substantial number of races around the country which attract runners to compete. To some extent the international isolation made this matter worse, since exceptionally large sponsorships were ploughed into local events, which provided a large number of high-profile races to run in. This leaves the average South African runner with a choice that tends to centre not around the question of what to race but rather around the question of what to leave out. It is rather like having a London Marathon or a Great North Run every month!

Let me state emphatically that I am 100 per cent in favour of and grateful for the sponsorship that goes into our sport, making it a multi-million-pound affair in this or any other country. The point is that a 'clustered' fixture list of high-profile, highly sponsored events in countries such as South Africa presents most runners with a problem of self-discipline in fixing themselves an off-season where they can get back to recovery and then base training. There is an alternative, which is to do base training throughout the year and never to peak for any particular race, and indeed this is what tends to happen to many South African runners as a result of the wide choice of events.

Consider the typical year for a South African runner. October to

February is concerned with running a Comrades 'qualifying marathon', then in March and April they focus on the short 30–35-mile ultras (Two Oceans, Milo Korkie, Bergville, etc.). Each has substantial reward of gold, silver or bronze medal, each attracts over 8,000 runners and each has the atmosphere of a London Marathon! Then in June it has to be Comrades, a 55-mile race which attracts 15,000 runners and full-day television. You aren't considered a runner in South Africa unless you have finished the Comrades.

July sees the start of the provincial championships at the 15km and 21km distances and, of course, the 10km road-race series, all of which are open to all runners and attract major sponsors and great handouts. In August it's the City to City 31-miler, September the increasingly popular Durban Marathon, followed by the Soweto Marathon in October, and the year ends with a mass of festive races, national championships and the track season. In addition there is cross-country between April and September for those who enjoy a bit of off-road, and then the nine or so ultra races for those wanting to do 100-milers. Where does the average South African runner rest? This doesn't even include the weekly races which have also become more and more high-profile, attracting fields of over 1,500 runners.

In 1996 John Disley, the IAAF Measurement Co-ordinator for Africa, on a visit from the UK, noted that a half-marathon in Johannesburg had to have the start delayed to allow one of the other club races to clear a section of the half-marathon route. Two races, one day, one area and over 2,000 runners in each! Whilst this public and sponsor interest may seem utopian to some, they would be overlooking the benefits of our seasons.

In Europe our seasons are well defined. Winter and cross-country lasts between late October and February, March to October is the road season, with most marathons distributed to spring and autumn and ultras tending towards the end of summer. Track season starts in late April and goes through to a championship peak in August, leagues finalising in October.

As a result, runners can build from active rest to base training, to speed and sharpening, to competition, before returning to active rest. The temptation to compete at a high level all year round in search of elusive medals or cash prizes is not there. Even if it were, one would suspect that the weather would help to control the urge! Although the local ultra runners tend to run a number of ultras in one season, they are virtually forced into a period of recovery as the weather turns.

Obviously, then, our UK and northern European situation is more in keeping with the 15 laws of training, and any runner who wants to reach his true potential has to recognise the need for training seasons.

So the next move is to identify your competition season, then work backwards to allow a taper period, your sharpening (peaking) season, your base season, and finally your rest or recovery season.

Incidentally, rest and recovery need not mean doing nothing; in fact, to do so would contradict the first law of training. It does, however, mean cutting way back on distance and effort and having an active rest. Conversely, there is nothing wrong with doing absolutely nothing for a short period of time, particularly after a hard race or competitive season.

This is emphasised again by the fifth law, which instructs us to alternate hard days with easy days. This prinicple should be extended to the wider situation, where hard periods of training are followed by easy periods. Three weeks of heavy training may be followed by an easy week, and so on.

How long should a season be? This again is a difficult question that really requires an individual answer for each athlete. Elite athletes seem to be capable of sustaining ten to twelve weeks of heavy training before the overtraining symptoms start rearing their ugly head. My experience suggests that the average runner, who is under more pressure from work, family and the like, can only handle about six to seven weeks of hard training before something has to give. Inevitably, the priorities in their life dictate that it will always be the running first.

The length of the taper period is somewhat easier to determine, but again it will vary, depending on what distance you intend to race. A short race may require only an easy couple of days beforehand; an ultra or marathon taper can be as long as two to three weeks. Another variable determining the length of the taper period is just how hard you have been training in your build-up.

Base training to a limited extent can be handled for substantial periods of time, since it is not necessarily that taxing if distance is kept under control.

WHERE SHOULD THE SEASON START?

As the IAAF take greater cognisance of cross-country, road running and ultramarathons, this question is going to become more and more confused. The answer will relate to the aspect of the sport that you wish to make the greatest improvement in. If that is, for example, cross-country, then obviously your 'peak' season is winter; if your interest is in track, then the major events are in July and August. Marathon runners typically have their major championships in August and city events in spring and autumn. World championships in all aspects of athletics have now forced élite athletes to become more specialised in their training, and the opportunity to get to the top in both middle-distance track and cross-country will soon disappear as the calendar become more crowded.

Since many of the runners reading this book will have been involved in marathons, let's consider how they could view December and June.

THE SPRING MARATHONER IN DECEMBER

This is truly one of the few occasions when road runners are virtually forced into taking a rest, at least from races. The reason is simple: there just aren't that many races on the calendar. The pre-Christmas festivities and the risk of bad weather keep organisers at home!

So, apart from the odd 'turkey trot' run, runners not wishing to do cross-country are left to their own devices. Unfortunately, many see this as an ideal opportunity to start their build-up to the marathon and set about tackling some long runs. This has to be one of the biggest mistakes that can be made.

It is easy to appreciate that runners don't want to lose the fitness that they have developed over the last few months by running shorter distances at a faster pace. However, most of the world's top runners, those who reach their objectives, recognise the need for an off-season. A classic case of this was Sebastian Coe, who, in the years that he dominated the middle-distance events, ran a total of only about 12 cross-country races. His reasoning was that he first needed to recover from the competitive track season before concentrating on working on his 'weaknesses' to improve for the following season.

Surely we have the ideal incentives to give running and training a break . . . they're called snow and ice!

One of the major problems with taking a break is the guilt complex that we develop when we stop training. Another factor, as previously mentioned, is the concern that we will lose our hard-earned fitness. However, research from America has come to the rescue. It suggests that with only two sessions per week for, say, a three- to four-week period, we can retain that fitness. What will come as a surprise to many is the type and amount of training that is required to achieve this result.

A simple example would be to go to the track and, after a warm-up, run four to five repeats of 1,000m at your best 5km pace. The rest period between repeats can be fairly lengthy, say three to five minutes. Follow this with a cool-down and then you can go back to the roaring log fire or join the rest of the family at the festive celebrations.

As you read through this book you will see that this type of session has been found to be effective in many areas, including rest, injury and even ageing!

This session would be repeated twice a week only, and can even be a once-a-week outing if you are willing to live with a small drop-off in fitness over the full three-week period. This apparent 'high-quality' training without base work will surprise many, but it does have a logical background. It has been found that the major reason for loss of fitness is a drop in blood volume. When we are fit we have a higher blood volume than the 'average' person, and this partly explains why, for instance, we seem to have a low iron level. Of course, with this greater blood volume comes a greater oxygen-carrying capacity and hence a higher VO_2 max. When the blood volume drops, so too does the VO_2 max and hence performance. Thus, if we can keep the blood volume up, we can maintain most of our fitness.

Although other areas of our fitness, such as muscle endurance, enzyme action and so on, do deteriorate, the drop-off has been shown to be very much slower and to have a relatively insignificant effect over the break period.

Thus, if you are planning to run the London Marathon, December is the time for you to take that break, refresh the mind and the body and enjoy the spare time that holidays offer, in the full knowledge that you will be able to start back in mid January only slightly below your current fitness level but fully refreshed and eager to go. Hopefully this will only add to the Christmas and New Year celebrations!

THE POST-MARATHON MONTHS

Having got the marathon over for another year, it is time to capitalise on all the endurance work that has been put in over the past months. Obviously the first requirement after the 26-mile race is rest and recovery, and the wise runner will have used at least the first two weeks as active rest. The muscle damage that many will have suffered over the final ten miles will require up to a month for a full recovery, but the post-race period is the time to select a few shorter race goals for the second half of the season.

Depending on whether the marathon was in spring or autumn, there will be a choice between the start of the track season and the start of the cross-country season. The strength and speed developed in cross-country is an ideal base for road races, and these races are over manageable distances, typically four miles for women, five to six miles for veterans and six to seven miles for seniors.

No one can give another runner goals to aim for, but, with summer providing many shorter races and road relays on the local calendars and even the opportunity of track racing in open graded or low-key events, there should be no shortage of incentive.

One of the hardest things for marathon runners to come to terms with is the need to change their philosophy totally for training for these shorter events. The total weekly distance is likely to be about three-quarters of that used in the marathon build-up, but each week should now include two to three 'quality' sessions. The other good news, particularly for your family life, is that long runs will not require to be more than 10 to 12 miles unless you are looking towards a half-marathon, and even then they may only stretch to 15 miles.

The real work, however, comes in the form of the faster sessions. For those who have no track experience, this can start with a formal fartlek session on the road. Start with a one or two-mile jog and then break for some stretching. Follow this by a hard run for 60 to 90 seconds, with between three and five minutes of easy running as recovery. Repeat five to eight times, followed by another easy jog to cool down. The 'hard' pace should initially be somewhere around your 5km to 10km pace, and there is no set recovery pace – just run it as you feel. This can be repeated twice a week but should have at least one or two days' easy running between session.

Add to that a time trial or a cross-country event and you will have a good basic schedule for this period. It is very important to note, however, that the time trial or cross-country events must be run below your best pace. The objective is to use them as training for the race for which you want to peak.

After a few weeks of this training, you can introduce the more formal speed work of track sessions. When these sessions are performed correctly, they can not only be of great assistance to your running but can also be very motivating.

Track training in winter can be problematic, unless you have access to a fully lit all-weather venue. However, making use of a treadmill can overcome this. Just remember that you need to set the incline of the treadmill to 1 per cent to get the same effect as running outdoors. If there is no incline option on the treadmill, add an extra 1km/hr to the speed. In other words, if your target speed is six minutes per mile (this is equal to 3:45 per km, 90 seconds per 400m, 16km per hour, or 10 miles per hour), then set the treadmill to 17km per hour or 3:31 per km (5:38 per mile, 84 seconds per 400m). This roughly equates to the running effort.

Another alternative is to mark out a 1,000m section on a local path or cycleway. Put marks down every 100m and use this area for your training, but beware, running speed sessions on tar can be very tough and you need to be sure you get ample recovery between sessions.

The above plan would make more effective use of the large volume of endurance work that was done in the first part of the season in the build-up to the marathon. Obviously you would expect better results in the short events after a spring marathon than after an autumn marathon. The top marathon runners would have to delay such an active participation in short, high-quality racing for an even longer period after the marathon or ultra race, since their recovery time will be longer. But the same principles are used by them.

CHAPTER TWELVE

TRIATHLON TRAINING

Although triathlons have existed in the world of sport since 1978, my introduction to them came in 1983 when they were first held in South Africa. Even the early events attracted relatively large numbers, which augered well for what has become the boom sport of the '80s and '90s.

Whereas running and cycling races took years to progress from the small fields of competitors to today's large and sometimes restricted entries, triathlons have in a brief period grown to a point where fields consistently number a few hundred competitors.

The problem with such rapid growth in a sport is that a tried and tested recipe for training for a triathlon has not had time to develop. This, combined with the fact that triathlons are a combination of three established endurance sports, each with their own requirements for dedication and skill, makes the mere training for such an event a challenge on its own.

I do not consider that I can necessarily provide the solution to the problem. Instead I wish only that you consider the merit of the approach that I have adopted, and which has brought relative reward both to myself and to friends who have reworked their training to fall more in line with the following thoughts.

There is perhaps a basic rule which, like many of the other comments I shall make, applies to all sports. We can never run the perfect race – we always feel that there is room for improvement. After each event we should analyse the good and the bad and learn from the answers we come up with. It is without doubt better to discuss this with a training partner or colleague, for they can see the merits and the flaws easier than we can. During my short running career it has surprised me how often a novice has come up with an idea that has been overlooked by seasoned runners, and this reminds me that we are never too smart to learn.

In deciding whether or not an idea has merit, I ask whether it sounds logical; if it does, then it is probably right. However, this approach will only work if we are able to look at ideas objectively and without emotional involvement.

Much of what follows is echoed elsewhere in this book, but I felt it important to provide a complete strategy for people wanting to set themselves a target in the triathlon.

SETTING GOALS

The first step in any programme of training is to know what you are trying to achieve. It would be futile to decide to train for triathlons without any idea of the events, distances or disciplines you want to aim for. The training for the Hawaii Ironman, for example, differs from that for the '1.5 swim, 40 cycle, 10 run' format, in the same way that marathon training differs from that required for success at 10km. Then there is the question of whether you are aiming for canoeing or swimming triathlons. Training must be specific.

For this reason, we set a long-term target and a number of intermediate goals, each of which will bring us closer to our long-term target. Choosing the long-term goal is normally easy; the difficult part is not only to determine our intermediate goals but also to keep them relevant. These intermediate goals can be as simple as learning to balance in a canoe or as seemingly formidable as completing a half-distance event. The object is purely to build yourself a ladder with which you will reach the final target and to keep that ladder as straight as possible.

After two years of running in ignorance I found myself performing reasonably well in endurance events and therefore concluded that I could tackle anything that required competitors to test their ability to stay upright for long periods of time. There were numerous challenges – 100-milers, ultratriathlons, canoe races – all of which I wanted to combine with the usual weekly shorter social events.

This jack-of-all-trades approach ensured that I was training at base-level intensity all the time, and no sooner had I completed one event than the next one was three weeks away! There were times when I did not know whether to pack my swimming goggles or my canoe splash-cover, or both.

One other problem reared its head: the possibility of breaking down or injuring myself in the events that really did matter to me. All the incidentals resulted in accumulated fatigue that could knock me back just when I really wanted to do well.

My mistakes were brought to my attention by the seconding team for the 1984 London to Paris event, but it took a further three months, much persuasion from that team of Bruce Fordyce and Tim Noakes and another ruined hope to see them clearly. This story is told in chapter one.

The reason I refer to this story again is that it illustrates not only that we must be specific and the outcome of failing to be specific, but also how set in our ways and blind we can be when we are emotionally involved. What concerns me is that I could see the same thing happening to another triathlete in 1986 and, despite similar warnings from three people, my colleague made the same mistake. It appears that many of us learn only from our own mistakes, but those who are truly clever will take heed.

So, remember to set your long-term goal and then plan your intermediate short-term targets so that you stay on the straightest road. Don't get involved in training for the sake of it, since this rarely leads to progression and usually becomes boring.

TIME MANAGEMENT

There are few better examples of good time management than successfully fitting a well-rounded triathlon training programme into an ordinary life. Triathlons are truly time-management events.

To achieve the necessary skill in time management we need to identify all the aspects of our lifestyles and determine the priority of each in relation to our desire to reach our long-term target. (These priorities are often short-term and change after we have attained our goal.) Normally we need to apportion our daily and weekly time among family, career, socialising, sleep and sport. Although sleep and sport are listed separately, we shall see that the two are very closely linked.

Having allocated an amount of time to each aspect of your life, you must make the most efficient use of the time you have dedicated to each. I tend to picture my day as a pie chart and try to fill it so that there are no gaps between the sections. For example, you might leave your car at work and cycle in the next day. It might normally take 20 minutes to drive to work, whereas it now takes 40 minutes to cycle. Even if you allow 10 minutes for changing (good transition practice!), you've still only used 30 minutes of training time. We need to ask ourselves questions: What do we do during lunch? What is the minimum time it takes to get out of the house in the morning? Is this the most efficient use of our time?

It is obvious that the professional triathlete or the student has more time and more flexibility than the rest of us within the confines of the 24-hour limit, but good planning can go a long way towards closing the gap.

The next step is to consider which of the three disciplines will give you the most reward for the time spent on it. Again this is a time-efficiency problem. It may be more pleasant to spend two hours swimming intervals or distance in the pool, surrounded by those scantily clad bodies, but more return may be gained in the next event by spinning over the hills and valleys on country roads.

So, you have determined the proper place for triathlons in your life, identified the amount of time that you can commit to it and determined the priority of each of the three disciplines (running, cycling and canoeing or swimming). Only now are you in a position to try to determine what you are going to do.

CONSISTENCY

The hardest part of any endurance event is the correct training that precedes it. Unfortunately for those of us who enjoy the ultras, the longer the event, the truer this becomes.

Because triathlons are made up of three events, they are always billed with each of the individual distances, for example, 1.5km swim, 40km cycle, 10km run. At first glance we may sneer at such distances. We may know what it is like to do each of these events separately, but the combination can be a totally different proposition.

If we consider that the élite triathletes take in the region of 1:50 for such an event over an ideal course and in ideal conditions, then perhaps we can compare it to a road race of 35km, a cycle of 75km or a 8km swim. Suddenly it becomes more apparent that the triathlon is an endurance event.

The reason for highlighting this fact is to ensure that everyone realises that success at this sport cannot be had by the three-day-a-week training that some people manage to use to prepare themselves for the rigours of rugby or football. If we are to achieve our goals in triathlons, to do more than just battle our way to the finish post and exhaustion, then a more dedicated approach is reqired.

This more consistent approach to training has physiological reasoning as well. It is obviously better to increase one's training load gradually than to subject one's body to the shock treatment of irregular heavy sessions. For every action there is a reaction, and the reaction to shock treatment can easily be injury and enforced rest.

If we look at the two running schedules in Table 12.1, we can see that it is possible to reach the same overall mileage in each case. Schedule A, however, demands that three large quantities of time are set aside each week for three relatively large volumes of running. Such an approach is very likely to result in substantial periods of recovery both after each bout of exercise and after the probable injury. Schedule B, on the other hand, requires only a small amount of time each day and will result in quicker recovery. In addition, this schedule allows more flexibility and opportunity to vary the pace, time or location of the exercise, and therefore keeps it interesting.

Undertaking smaller periods of regular training not only makes it seem easier to handle, but also develops a routine which in turn makes the training easier and more pleasant.

Table 12.1 Running schedules

	A (km)	B (km)
Monday		6
Tuesday	21	9 km time trial and warm-up
Wednesday		18
Thursday	22	10
Friday		Rest
Saturday		10
Sunday	42	32
TOTAL	**85**	**85**

ADAPTION AND PROGRESSION

Two words are very closely linked to consistency, and these are progression and adaptation.

As previously discussed, the system of adaptation and progression can be understood by imagining a weight attached to an elastic band. If the weight is heavy enough and dropped from a resting position, it will plummet earthwards, breaking the band instantly. However, if the same weight were lowered in a gentle, controlled way, it could be suspended at the full extension of the band. This latter case is what we are trying to obtain in triathlon training. We want to reach our physical limit without snapping the band.

In finalising our programme we also need to consider the effects of the input/output theory we discussed in the chapter on supplementary activities and cross-training (see graph on page 80). Whilst initially there tends to be a direct relationship between the amount of time we put into an exercise and the improvement we see as a result of that time (0 to point A), after a certain point the rate of the improvement peaks (point B) and begins to diminish. Additional time spent in similar exercise after this point may well result in reduced benefit and is indicative of overtraining.

In a single sport, the object would be to train at time B during our heavy training period, possibly extending our returns by a supplementary exercise as shown by line B to D. However, in triathlons it is doubtful whether it is possible to train at that intensity for each sport. In fact, I can think of no surer route to competitive suicide than to undertake all three training loads that the single-sport specialist does for his or her discipline in one week.

Luckily, triathlons, particularly the longer events, require us only to be *capable* in each discipline, not expert. Obviously, however, the more capable we are in each leg of the event, the more successfull we will be. As a result of this, it is probably better to try to train each discipline at time A, but we must realise that A and B are only relative to our state of fitness at any one time and that our programme must be formatted so that these points will move further and further from the origin.

At the very top end of the scale, the professional triathlete who has all day to train will be looking to become expert in each of the sports. But then he or she will have the time for recovery that will allow that amount of training.

An advantage of triathlon training is the cross-training effect. This refers to the enhancement of our running and swimming fitness, for example, as a result of our cycling. At first this appears to be a contradiction of the earlier decision to be specific. On closer examination, however, you realise that your cardiovascular system is being trained by all three disciplines and this will show better results than a training schedule which required only a comparable amount of running.

Whilst it would be inefficient for runners, who are committing only enough time to their sport to get to level A, to spend time cycling, a triathlete, who is compelled by the nature of the sport to train at each of these disciplines, can use the effects of cross-training to advantage.

It is essential that a recovery period is allowed after the period of stress, in order that development and growth can occur. In the case of the elastic band, the weight is lowered in increments to allow the band time to adapt to the stress of the weight. So, too, in training it is necessary to plan recovery both by the use of alternate periods of hard and easy work and by the occasional rest period.

In 1986 a new triathlete entered Durban's triathlon scene. She came from a swimming background and quickly came to terms with the basic hard/easy, train/recovery principles. She soon won a trip to the Hawaii Ironman as the women's winner of the Durban 2.5 mile swim, 90 mile cycle and 20 mile run triathlon. These basic principles stood her in good stead and within a few years Paula Newby-Frazer not only had a string of Ironman wins, but also dominated the professional triathlon scene in America. Throughout her career she stuck to the basic principles and proved that a limited amount of quality training far outweighs the benefits of large quantities of low-intensity distance work.

A couple of years later there was a similar story with another young athlete from Durban. Again from a swimming background, he concentrated on the shorter events, maintained quality not quantity in all his training and soon departed Durban for London. Simon Lessig now dominates the UK and European circuits. Both Paula and Simon followed well-defined training programmes that were goal-orientated.

It is not only the daily progress of our training that should be based on the principle of hard work followed by easy work – so should our weekly progress. Determining what constitutes a hard and what an easy session can best be done by monitoring the body's reaction to the previous day's load. Parameters such as an increase in morning pulse, loss of weight and increase in thirst are the tell-tale signs of too much, too soon, too often. (See chapter 15 on heart-rate monitoring.)

With the limited time available and the amount of effort that needs to be crammed into a week of triathlon training, it would appear at first sight that overtraining is inevitable. The only alternative seems to be arriving at the start under-prepared.

It is, however, possible through careful planning to combine the less stressful items in one discipline with the more stressful items in another. A hard session in cycling one day is followed by an easy run the next. Within each discipline it is important to mix both the distance and the pace of the training and, although running cannot be described as a highly skilled sport, time can be well spent in technique sessions in the other two disciplines.

In order to improve, it is necessary to increase the stress as you continue to train. In the same way that you first undertake base training and later add speed training when you train for running, so too must you adopt this principle for the triathlon.

Finally you get to the stage where you have written down your programme for each session of the day and each day of the week. It encompasses the principles of training for each individual sport and yet offers a balance of the three sports, a balance which has been determined by the requirements of the event in which you wish to compete. Your programme is not one of rigid finality but allows enough flexibility to substitute, for example, the less taxing effect of a cycle for that of a joint-pounding run when your body is telling you to beware.

Flexibility must not be mistaken for laziness. Often I have been tempted to substitute a cycle for a series of hard swimming intervals when I have been listening to my preference for cycling rather than my training need. Great determination is often required for me to complete swimming sessions, but the greatest will power is required to stop me from overdoing the running. An honest appraisal of your own programme will always reveal preferential faults, and when this is changed, better time management results.

A SUGGESTED SCHEDULE

The object of this chapter is to assist with the formulation of a suitable training schedule and thus would not be complete without an example. The problem with such an exercise is that, like all training, a training programme for a triathlon has to be personally tailored and specific for the event at which it is aimed.

This being the case, I have used the skeleton programme that as team manager and coach I gave to ten of South Africa's top triathletes when they were selected to make up the Leppin London to Paris squad in 1985. These triathletes were selected in May and asked to prepare themselves for a trial in early July. They were told that the trial would be of similar format to the event, and were given the above guidelines and a possible peak week training schedule in the hope that it would assist them to prepare themselves for the rigours of the event.

Those of us who are familiar with the event know that, despite the fact that it is of a relay nature and spread over a three-day period, the 100 mile run, 20 mile swim and 190 mile cycle requires each of the four team members to be in peak fitness and to work together like a machine. I can report that there were those amongst our squad who questioned the difficulty of such an event but, during stolen moments of recovery in Cape Town during the trials, confided to Tim Noakes and myself that this had been one of the most taxing weekends of their sporting lives.

Table 12.3 gives the details of a typical week's training before the trial. Distances have been omitted from this table deliberately. It is important to see that the programme has been biased towards the swim in the same way that the event is biased towards the swim. The other important feature is, of course, the combination of sessions of different difficulty during one day and throughout a week.

As I have mentioned earlier, it is important to have intermediate goals, and at least some of these can be progress in training. It is important for us to attain each of these smaller steps as this creates confidence about our chances of succeeding in our long-term target. Once we have set up our plan of attack, we must have confidence in it and give it the chance to work for us.

Table 12.2 Training components

RUN	CYCLE	SWIM
6 days	1 x fast distance	1 x surf
1 x track	1 x long cycle	1 x distance
1 x long	1 x technique	2–3 interval
1 x fartlek	1 x slipstream	technique
		time-trial
		(bi-weekly)

Table 12.3 A typical peak week

DAY	RUN	CYCLE	SWIM
Monday	recovery	fast distance	intervals
Tuesday	track		technique
Wednesday	recovery	slipstream	time trial/ intervals
Thursday	fartlek		distance
Friday		technique	intervals
Saturday	recovery	long cycle	technique (optional)
Sunday	long run		surf swim

THE RECOVERY OR TAPERING PHASE

After the gradual increase in overall stress, and after our period of peak training, we require a period of gradual recovery. Unfortunately, during this stage we are often feeling so strong that we want to go and test our strength, feel that we can still benefit from 'just one last hard session', or ignore the warnings of the last ten days because we will have a recovery period soon. To succumb to any of the above temptations is a sure way of waving goodbye to our long-term goal. The trouble is, it is so easy to do.

The importance of monitoring your body and using self-control during the latter weeks of preparation for an event cannot be overemphasised. Bruce Fordyce's suggestion that it is better to arrive at the start slightly undertrained than overtrained must be kept in mind constantly during this time.

It is during the final recovery or taper period that we gain the strength, physical and mental, that will allow us to dig deep into our reserves in the final section of the event. This is what makes the difference between just finishing and truly succeeding.

The training procedures for triathlons are similar to those for most other endurance sports. The problem for most of us is that we find it hard to know where to begin and how to proportion our training. We seem to be running when all our peers are cycling, or swimming when they are going for a run. We continually question whether we are doing enough in any particular sport, and even if we are doing the right thing.

The object of this chapter has been to suggest a structured approach to developing a suitable training programme within the limits that each and every one of us sets, and to making the most efficient use of our time within those limits. Doing this, with the help of the basic training principles outlined here, should give you the confidence of knowing that you have established the best possible basis for attempting your long-term goal.

3

GETTING THE MOST OUT OF YOUR TRAINING

CHAPTER THIRTEEN

WHY EVERYONE NEEDS A COACH

It is not easy to prepare runners to get the most out of their running. Too little preparation, the wrong mix or too much training and they will fail to reach their peak. The fine line between optimum training, too little and too much puts the runner on a razor's edge. As if this were not enough, there are also questions relating to race preparation, planning and the building of confidence to deal with.

Some will point to the fact that most of these things are personal and individual in nature and therefore therefore runners are themselves best-qualified to know how their bodies are reacting to the preparation. Certainly, there is a need for runners to become totally aware of their bodies and their reaction to situations and conditions. But the problem is that runners are not in a position to be objective about themselves.

What, then, of those very successful runners who, it is claimed, coach themselves?

According to the commonly held view of what a coach is, perhaps it is true that they coach themselves, but I am sure that each runner will also be using at least one other person as a sounding-board to get an objective assessment of his or her performance.

How many times do we hear people at the club talking about another runner and saying, 'Joe can't expect to do well this week, he's been doing so much distance and run so many races, that he's overtrained,' or something similar? Runners can easily spot the early signs of overtraining in other runners, but have great difficulty in seeing it in themselves.

Runners tend to feel invincible, particularly after doing well in a race. Floating along on an emotional high the week after their success, they become motivated to train harder and may even enter another race. Even as I write this, I know it happens to me, and yet in the cool calmness of my office I can't put my finger on the reason behind this temptation.

The fact that we had a good race means that we will have put substantial effort into achieving the result. Thus the more logical thing to do would be to rest and recover before building up for another challenge.

What would a coach do in this situation?

Most people think of a coach as someone who, in conjunction with the runner, sets the training schedule, evaluates the results and progress, assists with the planning and gives the runner mental and physical support. The coach may be down at the track timing the intervals, or acting as the second on a long run; the coach may even be the person the runner confides in, the runner's closest friend.

The popular image of a coach is embodied in Sam in the film in *Chariots of Fire*, who becomes the mentor of Harold Abrahams. The duo become inseparable in their quest for Olympic gold. Such coaches do exist, and the British Athletics coaching structures have long been the official 'production line' for the development of coaches. Whilst generally admired for their high standards, it is unfortunate that there has been a tendency for coaching progression to require candidates to recruit top-level athletes to their squad, rather than developing a system that encourages assistance to runners of all abilities, be that the novice jogger or the élite national athlete.

I make this special mention of 'runners of all abilities' because I think there is a great need for administrators in particular to realise that coaching should not be restricted to the élite, although this is a commonly held belief, even amongst runners.

This belief is so deeply rooted that awards, coaching qualifications and appointments tend to be based on the number of district and national athletes a coach can lay claim to. This seems to me to be the wrong way round. Sure, the élite runners need to be coached, but many of them have enough talent to get to that level without a coach. They also have the motivation to do it for themselves. The role of the coach is then to take them to their absolute peak, but the chances are that even if the coach fails, the athlete will still have enough talent to perform at a high enough standard to assure the coach of the award or qualification. This award system also promotes the 'poaching' of athletes by coaches.

Consider the alternative, where emphasis is placed on improving the ability of the *average* runner. An improvement here will result in the élite runner now being challenged by runners previously considered to be of lesser ability. In order to stay at the top, the élite runner will work harder. In addition, many of the so-called average runners will find that they have a talent for the sport that was not previously exposed because of poor training methods. This will again result in an improvement at the top levels of the sport.

I have yet to hear of a successful business whose major effort went into developing its upper echelons and who left the base of the pyramid to develop itself. Yet this is an inherent part of the previous BAF structure. The Eastern Bloc countries thrived on a system of early assessment of an athlete's potential. They were then channelled to maximise this potential. The point is that the initial emphasis was at grass-roots level; they developed the champions. They didn't wait for élite runners to find themselves.

I expect one argument against this to be financial, but the cost of even mass education or coaching material in the form of videos, training charts, newsletters and so on would be small in comparison to the numbers of athletes it could reach. Coaching incentives don't have to be based on élite athletes. Surely those coaches who work to bring runners into the sport and develop them are serving the sport and the athlete just as much?

It's amazing how many women runners an event like the Imperial Cancer Race for Life series has brought into the sport. Many have been coached or encouraged on a one-to-one basis by people at club level or existing athletes, others by coaches writing in athletics magazines. I doubt whether many of those runners have yet made district or national status, but surely these 'coaches' have a place within the sport? Taking novices through to the point where they have reached their maximum potential is surely just as much 'coaching' as taking naturally talented athletes through to their maximum potential, especially when we think that many coaches only have contact by phone with their 'élite' charges? The difference is purely in the starting and finishing points of the journey.

Once again we must ask: what is a coach?

The major point to be made is that each runner's requirements of a coach will be different from anyone else's. One athlete may only require distant contact as a sounding-board, whereas another may demand virtually full-time attention from the coach. The extent of the coach's attention may also change as you develop in the sport. There should be no stigma attached to coaching. It should not be reserved for the élite runners, but is something that we should, and quite frankly *must*, all have access to.

It's all very well reading books, listening to lectures, gathering information on training techniques and even knowing how to put a training schedule together, but when it comes down to it there is no tried and tested formula that applies to everyone, and it is here that objectivity comes into play.

Human beings are not good at being objective and therefore, at the least, it is worthwhile having someone who can assess what you plan to do or have done, and who can give you some informed comment. This kind of feedback is often enough to bring to light a glaring omission or even a subtle point overlooked in your schedule.

I repeat, it's remarkable how even the runner with the least experience can spot overtraining in another runner. Conversely, it is even more amazing how a runner with a vast amount of experience can overlook the same symptoms and make the same mistake many times.

A sad story that illustrates this point well is that of Tony Venniker, better known to many South Africans as 'the radio doctor'. Tony had a regular radio slot and helped many people. He was always willing to listen to problems and give assistance to others. A very knowledgeable man, he was gifted enough to be able to spot troubles in others early enough to ensure fast and efficient medical treatment. However, by his own admission, it was his failure to diagnose his own illness early on, and to do something about it, that led to the illness becoming terminal. Tony was one of the oldest novices ever to compete in Comrades and his real-life story is symptomatic of most runners' inability to coach themselves.

What does a runner require from a coach? Perhaps the most important factor is that you must have confidence and trust in him or her. It is no use asking people for advice or looking to them for encouragement if you have any doubts about their integrity. For this reason, the world's best coach, if there is such a thing, may not be suited to the world's best athlete. The relationship between coach and athlete, whether the sport is running, golf, tennis or whatever, is based on a sound understanding between two people.

The remaining requirements will vary in terms of what you expect your coach to do. If it is total control of everything to do with your sport, then look for someone who has done the studying and has plenty of practical experience. If it is purely a sounding-board for ideas that you are after, then a fellow runner may be able to help you, since all you're really looking for is some objectivity and someone to play devil's advocate. Perhaps you could coach each other.

If you already have the knowledge and know how your body reacts to various conditions, it may be possible to ask your boyfriend, girlfriend, husband, wife or other good friend to act as coach. He or she could pick up enough knowledge from a few books to be able to assist you in questioning what you have done, what you are going to do, where you are going, and whether your planning is correct. For some runners, such questioning will be enough.

The coach-runner relationship is based on interaction, not demands. A coach works *with* a runner to develop a training programme. Not every runner responds to the same training in the same way. The athlete must always be given a schedule and surroundings that he or she is comfortable in. There is only one thing more tiring and destructive to an athlete than heavy racing, and that is emotional stress. Thus the successful programme and regime is one that suits the athlete, not the coach. I was amazed to hear that a coach had instructed a national-class athlete to leave her family and move nearer to him! Often the administrators and officials seem to forget that without the athlete there is no need for officials. Without officials, I can still run. There wouldn't be the same standardisation or organisation, but I would still run.

An issue that has reared its head recently is that of payment of coaches. The argument goes that if athletes are winning big money and the coaches are helping them to do so, then the coaches should be paid. Certainly there is a logic to this argument.

Another point a local coach put to me was that if coaches charged a regular, small monthly fee, athletes would tend to be more committed to turning up at coaching sessions. This is a very valid point, since many runners seem to think that it is acceptable to make contact with a coach, let him or her spend time writing out a training schedule, and then disappear into the distance with what they consider to be a magic formula. It certainly doesn't work like that, since a suitable training schedule can only be written by a coach who has come to know the runner's abilities.

Second, and perhaps more importantly, runners should realise that they have no right to demand time from a coach unless they are going to show the coach some respect. This would mean at least letting the coach know how they were finding the training schedule. Some athletes seem to lack this common decency.

On the other hand, I don't believe there is a coach in the country who would turn away a runner who wanted assistance but was unable to pay for it. Indeed, I and many others have never asked for or accepted payment for coaching any individual. However, there are coaches who rely on funding to enable them to be available throughout the day to take after-school classes.

It all boils down to a personal choice in individual situations, and I don't believe that coaches who charge for their services should be considered inferior to those who don't charge. After all, it is their time that they are giving up, and they must put whatever price on their time they feel it deserves.

Perhaps the best way to end this chapter is to refer you to the regional and district athletics bodies, who should be able to put you in touch with coaches in your area. These addresses appear at the end of the book.

CHAPTER FOURTEEN

KEEPING A TRAINING DIARY

Dr George Sheehan called training 'an experiment of one', which highlights the need to learn from experience and the fact that what is good for one person may not be good for another. We must keep note of what we do, how we feel and how our bodies and running performance react to the training. This will allow us to look back and tailor our training to the specific requirements of our racing.

Unfortunately, human nature is such that we tend to forget things after a time, frequently recalling the highlights but forgetting the critical detail that is the key to analysis. When training sessions are written down at the time they are completed, the exact distance, time and feeling is recorded for posterity and becomes an unarguable record when we later want to refer to it.

I remember asking Dave Box, the 1970 world record holder for the 100 miles, what training he had done before setting one of his 100-mile track records. He said he thought he had done a weekly 60–80km run over weekends and several fairly long runs during the weeks. However, he added that he had it all written down and would find it for me. When he did so he was surprised to see just how little he had done in the build-up to the race. Memories play strange tricks!

KEEPING A RECORD

Why look back at your training? Frequently we aim for a specific target in the beginning and find ourselves full of enthusiasm for what seems almost a mission. Fired with this enthusiasm, we find ourselves plotting our training for the target, building in weights, track, hills, fartlek and endurance runs.

Nine times out of ten, this initial schedule will be too ambitious. A better approach is to look back to the last time we ran a race that we felt was our best performance and base our plans on the training we did prior to that success. This training obviously suited us and thus should only be modified slightly for the new target. Similarly, there is benefit from looking back at the bad races to see what training we did leading up to them. This should teach us what we need to avoid doing!

This, then, is the theory behind the training diary, but it is only of as much practical use as the information it contains. Simply recording the distance run and the time taken is not really of any benefit; other information is necessary. In general, the more information the better. Everything that seems important at the time will be of importance when looking back.

HEART RATE

Your body's response to the previous day's training can be judged by your pulse immediately after waking. This information should be logged each day. After just a few days a 'baseline' or average pulse can be determined; a variation from it will give you an indication of the intensity you should train at on that day. If your pulse is high, you have not recovered fully from the previous day's effort and should take it a little easier in training. As you get fitter the baseline reading will decrease, but on any specific day it may still rise if you have not recovered fully.

For example, I know that at my fittest I have a waking pulse of 38 beats per minute, but in 'tick-over training' it tends to be about 41 or 42, and if I have done a hard session the night before it may rise to 44 or 45. This indicates the need for an easier day. If it is above 46, a recovery day is required.

I have actually got to the stage of knowing when I am ill or even about to become ill, because my pulse will be up despite two easy days of training. This helps a lot when I go to the doctor, who tells me that my pulse is 'normal' and I have to point out that it is in fact up ten beats a minute or 25 per cent! After all, the doctor's judgement is based on the fact that the average pulse is around 60 at rest.

To sum up, then, morning pulse is one of the measures that can be very useful in determining your reaction to training.

Similarly, heart-rate monitoring during exercise has the advantage of providing a measure of the intensity of the training session. The specifics of this are covered elsewhere, but having taken this information it is important to keep a record of it. A particular benefit of this record is that the intensity of the session can be compared to the current level of fitness. In this way, if you are commencing training at a lower or higher base fitness, it is possible to modify the required heart rate to match the intensity of the proposed session. The times might differ but the intensity will be the same.

WEIGHT

Early-morning weight, measured before eating anything and after having been to the bathroom, can also be used as an indicator of training response. Tim Noakes regards a sudden drop in weight as a possible sign of overtraining. Whilst not disagreeing with that, I also believe that runners, in very humid climates in particular, may also experience a gain in weight as a sign of overtraining.

Tim also notes that an increase in the amount of fluid taken at night is another indication of over-stressing, as is water retention by the body to assist with repair. Runners who train in very humid climates tend to lose large amounts of water during training. I could 'lose' 4lbs during a 10km run on a summer morning in Durban before work. This was only water, however, and not a true weight loss. If I was not careful to replace this water each day on finishing the run, I would soon become stressed. My weight would 'see-saw' over 6–8lbs in a day and in fact my early-morning weight tended to be up! This has always happened when I have been overdoing things, so I watch out for it.

Another experience which substantiates this belief is that my joints and limbs have swollen in the long-journey runs I have done, and this too is a direct result of water retention. This occurs, of course, under extreme conditions where one can be running over 75 miles each day for a week or more.

Weight is, therefore, another useful factor to log.

SLEEP

Throughout this book there is much emphasis on the need for recovery. It therefore makes sense to log the amount of sleep you have each night. This allows you to spot any tiredness resulting from the lack of proper sleeping recovery.

In this regard one should remember that in general it is not the night before the day of tiredness that causes the problem; rather, it tends to be the night before the night before. That is to say, if you feel tired and washed out on Wednesday, it is probably as a result of poor sleep on the Monday night. Similarly, in race preparation, an anxious, restless night immediately before the race is not as detrimental as a poor night's sleep two nights before. That is the really important night's rest.

TRAINING INFORMATION

Then there's your actual training, and here you should log the route, the distance and the time, as well as your feelings about the run. Was it a good run? Record what your objective was. Was it recovery, or fast, continuous effort, or long, slow distance? Alternatively, you may have set out to do a track or fartlek session, in which case you should record the details of the session. The more you record, the more helpful the data you will have later when you look back.

Some runners record data such as what shoes they wore, the weather, and who they ran with. All of this can be of assistance and thus you should develop your own personal diary format.

PROBLEMS WITH DIARIES

Just as a diary can be of assistance, so it can also be the downfall of a runner, particularly for those who believe quantity is everything. Runners can become obsessed with achieving weekly distance targets as opposed to having a balanced, quality training week. Similarly, logging exact routes and times can tempt runners to try to test themselves continually and improve their times over routes on each outing. Such approaches are doomed to failure.

There are going to be times when your runs are slower than before, when the pressure of a hard day's work has tired you and takes its toll in an extra few minutes on the road. There are times when you must go more slowly, such as on recovery runs. There are times when your weekly mileage drops, while the amount of your quality running increases. All these factors will depend on the period of training you are in and what you are trying to achieve.

The point is that it is tempting, and dangerous, to become a slave to filling in your diary. There is nothing as satisfying when recording training than a full page showing good training, but there are times when an empty couple of days may look bad but result in a much better performance when it counts – in the race.

A serious warning: don't make the mistake so many runners make. It is not the distance covered that makes an athlete, but *how* the distance was covered. I repeat: Don't become a slave to weekly distance.

HIGH-TECH LOGS

With the advent of personal computers it was just a matter of time before a running diary was developed for the PC. It started in the United States and has now found its way around the world. I have reviewed a number of them, and whilst they do provide a method of recording one's training, most have substantial drawbacks.

In most cases the amount of space allowed for recording your training is limited and thus the detail has to be omitted. Ironically, the detail is the very thing you tend to want when you look back in later months or years. The other problem is that the computer diaries don't allow you to format them to include the information that *you* think is important, such as pulse, weight, time and so on. If you want to substitute a cycle or swim for the run, you can't log it properly. The flexibility just isn't there, in comparison to a handwritten log.

However, these computer records are very useful for producing graphs which show weekly or daily distances, personal bests and so on. It's much easier to see trends in this way than by flicking through a book. Bearing this in mind, I believe that a combination of computer diary and personal log-book is probably the best. What I am sure of is that there is a place on the market for a well-written, flexible programme that allows runners to log their training in their chosen format.

A PERSONAL PREFERENCE

My personal preference for a running log is at present a day-to-a-page diary. This allows me to record exactly what I want in a way that suits me. I rarely run out of space, even if I train three times a day. I can record my cycling, running, swimming, weights or anything else, as well as how I feel, my pulse, my weight, hours of sleep, eating habits, and so on, without having to draw up new sections or squeeze my writing into a set space. In my profession I have been lucky to receive calendars and diaries at the end of the year. Each December I eagerly await an A5-size page-to-a-day diary, which I will then use for the following 12 months as my training log.

CHAPTER FIFTEEN

HEART-RATE MONITORS

THE PRINCIPLES

The 1992 drug controversy in rugby in South Africa prompted Tim Noakes to say that most rugby players could improve their performance through bettering their basic fitness instead of abusing drugs. He was responding to the fact that chemical manipulation is often seen as a shortcut to peak performance.

Far better and safer is the efficient use of training time. Until recently, however, the capacity to monitor the body to ensure that training was being done efficiently was restricted to a privileged few top sportsmen and women under the guidance of sports scientists.

The advent of accurate personal heart-rate monitors has changed that. They provide an accessible, efficient and effective way to monitor training. Although detailed information is spread throughout the book, a summary of the benefits are given below.

Performance in any sport relies on energy, and there are four basic energy systems. Depending on the speed and duration of the exercise, energy will come from a different system or combination of systems. Athletes try to train the energy systems they require in competition to make them more efficient. For each individual, performance within these systems can be related to a particular level of heart rate. Hence, by accurate and constant monitoring of your heart rate during training, you can ensure that you train effectively on each occasion.

The energy systems, and therefore training, of sprinters differ from those of distance runners. Those of rugby players and footballers vary not only from those of cyclists and other sportsmen, but also with the positions they play. The use of heart-rate monitoring means that training can be tailored to the specific requirements of each athlete.

The heart rate is also a good measure of recovery. The faster it returns to normal at the end of exercise, the fitter you are. It is the need to stop during exercise, and this fast drop-off in heart rate, that make the ordinary practice of measuring a pulse over a ten-second period and multiplying by six inaccurate. Therefore manual methods prove inadequate for exercise monitoring. Likewise, a rise in an athlete's waking pulse is an indication of poor recovery from the previous day's training or the onset of an infection. Thus, keeping a record of early-morning pulse can help ensure that training is not overdone.

But the benefits are not restricted to the competitive sportsperson. Recreational runners, cyclists, walkers and even those just wanting to commence an exercise programme can gain substantial benefit by using some form of heart-rate or pulse monitoring.

What is the difference between pulse and heart-rate monitoring? Your pulse is taken at the wrist or neck, and is a 'reflection' of the pulse of blood being pumped from the heart. Heart rate is measured at the contraction of the heart muscle, and is recorded by a electronic heart-rate monitor. Hence we use the term pulse when measuring at the neck or wrist and heart rate when using a cardiograph or heart-rate monitor.

In order to improve cardiovascular condition it is necessary to exercise within a set range of your maximum heart rate. As we age, our maximum heart rate tends to drop by around one beat per year, and the rule of thumb used for determining maximum pulse is to subtract your age from 220. By determining your waking pulse it is possible to calculate a heart-rate range through which you can exercise. This is done by subtracting your waking pulse from your maximum heart rate. Hence various levels of exertion can be calculated as percentages of your heart-rate range.

For example, a 30-year-old with a waking pulse of 60 would have a maximum heart rate of 220 - 30 = 190 and therefore a heart-rate range lying between his waking pulse of 60 and his maximum of 190, i.e. a heart-rate range of 130. Thus 65 per cent effort would be 130 x 0.65 + 60 = 144.5

It has recently been suggested that a more accurate formula for maximum heart rate might be 214 - 0.8 x age for men and 207 - 0.7 x age for women. These formulae are thought to be more appropriate for people who have exercised.

The best way to get a true maximum heart rate is to run an 800m flat out, take 30 seconds' recovery and repeat another 800m. You will get your maximum heart rate during the second 800m. If you don't fancy running 800m, use two 300m sprints up a steep hill with about 20 seconds' recovery. You will need a 600-metre-long hill, so that the recovery is kept to a minimum. In both cases a heart-rate monitor that either memorises maximum heart rate or records heart rates at five-second intervals will give the best results.

An improvement in fitness will see a decrease in waking pulse over the months.

You can also measure your fitness improvement by performing a set exercise procedure on different dates and comparing your pulse rates. As fitness improves, the heart rate needed to perform the same exercise will decrease. Thus, if one month you run for ten minutes on a flat course with a heart rate of 140 beats and cover 2km, the next month, using the same time and heart rate, you may cover 2.3km. It is easier and less destructive to use this sort of measure than to try the flat-out exertion of seeing how fast you can cover 2km on each occasion, as that is basically a race condition and thus requires recovery before any training can be resumed.

COMMERCIAL HEART-RATE MONITORS

Over the years there have been many attempts to produce commercial pulse monitors, but few have ever proved accurate unless they have had detectors attached to the athlete's chest. These, however, have tended to be bulky, expensive and inappropriate for use during exercise. Earlobe and finger monitoring pick-ups have failed for most people during exercise as a result of inconvenience and sweat disturbance of the reading.

Recognising the advantages of such monitoring, I have tried nearly everything on the market over the years, but failed to find anything that was remotely accurate during exercise until I bought my first wireless heart-rate monitor in 1989. Technological advances and micro-computing now allow a simple elasticated chest band to hold electrodes against the chest whilst a transmitter sends pulse readings to a receiver in a watch strap, so that the monitoring of your pulse is literally at the flick of a wrist.

This technology has resulted in a whole range of functions, from a simple digital pulse recorder, to sophisticated range alarms (alarms which can be set to indicate when you have reached the top and bottom of your pulse range) and memories that can be used in all sports, including swimming. Models at the top end of the range can keep a record of the pulse at five-second intervals throughout exercise and then download this data into a computer for graphing and analysis.

After18 months of using them, I was so convinced of the benefits of these monitors that I moved up to a model which would allow direct downloading. This allows close monitoring of my own training, as well as providing an excellent way to gauge the condition of a number of the athletes I assist in training.

The point of all the above is to emphasise that if you are going to consider investing in a heart-rate monitor, you should go in as high up the range as you can afford, instead of buying the cheapest and finding later that you want a device with more functions.

Although something of a contradiction of the above, and an apparent backwards step in technology, coaches and runners would be well advised not to overlook the features of the Cardiosport Heartspeak 20, which was launched in 1997. Whilst it took years for manufacturers to get rid of the wires from heart-rate monitors, this is one of the keys to the success of the Heartspeak 20. It consists of the same chest belt. This is connected to the match-box-sized processing box by two wires. A second wire leads to an earphone, with a comfortable behind-the-ear hook to hold it in position. A simple in-line control adjusts volume.

Plugging both wires into the unit starts the monitoring period. A voice reports the heart rate at 20-second intervals, and the elapsed time every ten minutes. The benefits come both from the simplicity and from the audio feedback. The wires ensure that there is no interference when used on a treadmill or other gym equipment. This makes it ideal for testing of runners, with the coach able to wear the earpiece to monitor the heart rate at 20-second intervals. This prevents the athlete from being psychologically affected by an awareness of the heart rate. Since the feedback is audio, the coach has his hands free to take lactate samples or do other work. Connecting the unit to a tape recorder can provide a record of the heart-rate tests.

The benefits don't stop there. Arm movement makes it difficult to read a heart-rate monitor whilst running long intervals or fartlek sessions, whereas with Heartspeak 20, if hard efforts are two minutes long, it's simply a case of listening for seven announcements of heart rate (i.e. six no. 20-second intervals).

Recovery runs can also benefit. Frequently we think we are taking it easy and then gradually turn up the speed, ruining the recovery effect. The Heartspeak 20 almost nags you into an easy run! It can also be used as a tool to assist in relaxation before visualisation and to prepare mentally for competition.

One of the major concerns of the newcomer to heart-rate monitoring has been removed with the recent release of the Cardiosport Autozone model. This is the ideal starting point for those who find calculations of training zones just too mysterious. It is a very elementary watch in terms of the 'running features'. It provides a readout of your heart rate, the training zone you are currently working in and a percentage of maximum heart rate. In addition there is an exceptionally good night-light which remains lit for about three seconds.

Although there is no stopwatch or time of day, this model will do all the calculation work for you. In the 'set' mode you have the option of setting rates on the basis of age, or inputting your maximum heart rate, which is the more accurate method. The watch will then set up four training zones for you, and an alarm can be activated to identify when you either exceed or fail to get into the chosen zone. In addition you can specify a particular training zone of your one. This is ideal, as you can ensure that your threshold training, for example, is tied down to a narrow band.

It is important to note, however, that the percentage of maximum is calculated as a direct proportion and makes no allowance for resting heart rate. The heart rates and zones referred to elsewhere in this book take into account the resting heart rate, as this can differ quite considerably from one person to another. However, it is fairly simple to make a modification to compensate for this.

This is one of a complete new generation of heart-rate monitors and with each year the technology has allowed forward-thinking companies such as Cardiosport to develop products that closer match the requirements of the runner. At the top end the sophistication of the watch allows for countdown timers, training zones, lap memories and the downloading of workouts directly into software for analysis and saving in training logs. All the normal watch features are gradually being included, so that now there are fewer reasons to have both a training watch and a heart-rate monitor.

Advancement is not only being seen in the watch/receiver units, it is also being reflected in the design of the transmitting belts. The latest Cardiosport range of heart-rate monitors uses a shaped and much thinner belt than others on the market. The pick-up terminals are more precisely placed and since the receiver is smaller and thinner it is more flexible and hence is better at taking up the shape of your chest. One of the previous problems with belts has been that people have different shapes of chest and some belts were not flexible enough to keep the terminals in contact with the skin. For this reason readings became erratic. Alternatively the belt had to be set so tight that it almost interfered with normal breathing. As opposed to most of the other belts on the market, Cardiosport have stuck with models that allow the user to replace the battery. This replacement of a small lithium battery is a relatively cheap operation. The sealed units of other manufacturers require to be sent back to the distributor and a replacement belt sent out. This involves not only substantially greater expense, but also the loss of use whilst the belt is in the post.

I can only reiterate that it is important to be very careful in your consideration of which model to purchase.

Such are the benefits of heart-rate monitoring that an American sports body gave consideration to the banning of such monitors in races after a runner set a new American record in a 50-mile race. They felt it could be regarded as 'unfair technological assistance'. This is surely testament to their effectiveness. A meeting of the IAAF in the second half of 1992, however, determined that the use of heart-rate monitors in competition was legal. Either way, athletes dabbling with syringes would be better investing in heart-rate monitors!

USING A HEART-RATE MONITOR

Since the energy systems that you use at different speeds can be related to your heart rate, you can also use your heart rate as a guide to the level of exertion of your training. All that is required is an initial laboratory test to determine your heart-rate and lactate levels at various speeds and hence the energy systems you are using. You can then set various heart rates for each type of training session and be confident subsequently that you are achieving maximum efficiency for the time you spend in training.

Before we go any further, it is worth saying something about lactate, a substance which has caused much confusion among runners. Lactate is a substance which is produced in the muscles during exercise. The amount of lactate in the exercising muscles gives an indication of the intensity of the exercise. When these levels become excessive, they prevent that intensity of exercise being maintained. This is a form of safety system to prevent the muscles from being damaged by being pushed too far. However, lactate is not responsible for sore muscles. When exercise recommences at low intensities, the excess lactate will be used as a source of energy.

The four most commonly used 'training zones' are given below in the sample training schedule and an explanation of the energy systems they relate to is given in chapter 24 on energy replacement.

The amount of time you spend per week at each level of exertion will vary with the distance of the race for which you are training. So a track athlete, for example, will spend much more time in the 'ATP + creatine phospate' energy levels than an ultra runner, who will concentrate training at the 'fat-burning' energy level. Obviously, time spent at the various energy levels will also vary with the different stages of training throughout the build-up period.

One of the first things that many runners will notice when using the sophisticated device is that they have been training too hard during 'easy' days and too easy during 'hard' days. This is an unfortunate side-effect of the marathon boom of the 1970s and '80s, and the desire for fast improvement in fitness.

Here follows a sample training schedule for an athlete using a heart-rate monitor.

SAMPLE TRAINING FOR 10KM USING A HEART-RATE MONITOR

Identify four training heart-rate 'zones' (by testing at a lab on a treadmill).

Session (zone) types

A   Fat-burning/recovery (55 per cent to 65 per cent max heart rate)
B   Endurance (65 per cent to 85 per cent max heart rate)
C   'Threshold' (85 per cent to 90 per cent max heart rate)
D   Anaerobic (90 per cent and above max heart rate)
E   Rest

The percentage of maximum heart rate given in brackets serves as a guide for calculating the various 'zones' in the absence of a lab test, but this should be used only as an interim measure while awaiting professional lactate testing. Days with D-zone sessions could begin with a 3km easy run in the mornings. Distance will change, depending on the standard of the runner.

Some guidelines

- A thorough warm-up and cool-down have been allowed for before and after each C and D session; these will take about 10 to 15 minutes each.
- Generally, D sessions can be swapped around within any 10- to 14-day period. Likewise, there is a flexibility among C sessions. However, the overall order of sessions should not be drastically changed.
- Time is less important than keeping your pulse in the correct ranges.

A suggested schedule

	Session type	Example
Week 1		
Day 1	E	rest
2	D	(1 x 200, rest 30 sec, 1 x 400, jog 400 or rest 2.5 mins) x 3 to 4
3	A	5 km easy
4	B	8 km moderate
5		C3 to 4 km steady (10 km pace) (keep constant pulse)
6		12 km moderate
7	D	4 x 800, rest 2.5 to 3 mins
		Total 52 km
Week 2		
Day 1	A	5 km easy
2	C	2 x 2500 (10 km pace), 2 km jog between
3	B	8 to 10 km moderate
4	D	(2 x 400, rest 2.5) x 4
5	A	5 km easy
6		1 x 200, rest 30 sec, 1 x 400, rest 1 min, 1 x 600
7	E	rest
		Total 53 km
Week 3		
Day 1	B	12 km moderate
2	C	4 km (10 km pace; same pulse as week 1)
3	A	5 km easy
4	D	(1 x 200, rest 30 sec, 1 x 400, jog 400 or rest 2.5 mins) x 4
5	B	12 to 14 km moderate
6	D	3 x 800, rest 2.5 mins
7	A	5 km easy
		Total 65 km
Week 4		
Day 1		3 x 2000 at 10 km pace, jog 5 mins (or 5 km race at 90%)
2	B	8 to 10 km moderate
3	D	2 x (1 x 200, rest 30 sec, 1 x 400, rest 1 min, 1 x 600, rest 1.5 mins, 1 x 400, rest 1 min, 1 x 200)
4	A	5 to 6 km easy
5	C	2 x 1500 at 10 km pace, rest 2.5 mins
6	E	rest
7	B	12 to 15 km moderate
		Total 64 km
Week 5		
Day 1	B	8 to 10 km moderate
2	D	6 x 800, rest 2.5 to 3 mins
3	A	5 km easy
4	B	15 to 18 km moderate
5	D	(1 x 400, rest 1 min, 1 x 200) x 4, rest 3 mins
6	A	5 km easy
7	C	8 km time-trial (10 to 15 km race pace), keep to set pulse
		Total 73 km

A suggested schedule (continued)

	Session type	Example
Week 6		
Day 1	E	rest
2	B	8 to 10 km
3	C	3 x 2000 at 10 km pace
4	A	5 km easy
5	D	(2 x 400, rest 45) x 5, rest 2.5 mins
6	B	15 to 18 km moderate
7	D	4 x 800, rest 2.5 to 3 mins
		Total 52 km
Week 7		
Day 1	A	5 km easy
2	C	4 km at 10 km pace (use same pulse as weeks 1 and 3 – compare time)
3	E	rest
4	D	1 x 800, rest 3 mins, 1 x 600, rest 2 mins, 1 x 400, rest 1 min, 1 x 300, 1 x 200
5	B	8 km moderate
6	C	1 x 3000, rest 5 mins, 1 x 2000, rest 2 mins, 1 x 1500 at 10 km pace
7	B	12 to 18 km moderate
		Total 46.8 km
Week 8		
Day 1	T	5 x 400
2	A	4 x 400
3	P	3 x 400
4	E	2 x 400
5	R	rest
6		rest or 1 x 400 at 1500 pace
7		race 10 km race
		Total 16 km
Week 9		*(Recovery week – your next target starts here!)*
Day 1	E	rest
2	A	3 to 5 km easy
3	B/A	6 to 8 km easy/moderate
4	E	rest
5	A	5 km easy
6	B/A	6 to 8 km easy/moderate
7	E	rest
		Total 26 km

Some guidelines

A thorough warm-up and cool-down have been allowed for before and after each C and D session; these will take about 10 to 15 minutes each.

Generally, D sessions can be swapped around with any 10- to 14-day period. Likewise, there is flexibility among C sessions. However, the overall order of the sessions should not be drastically changed.

Time is less important than keeping your pulse in the correct ranges.

CHAPTER SIXTEEN

RUNNING BETTER ON LOWER MILEAGE

Sometimes, less can be more. This is a difficult but important lesson for all runners to learn, particularly those who run marathons and longer races.

It is not unusual for me to make comments about the apparent obsession many runners have for distance. It is a feeling that I have experienced myself, and a trap that I have fallen into, particularly in the first few years of my running. There were times when the driving force behind my training was to maintain a 'set' target mileage per week, in the mistaken belief that this alone would ensure success. In 1983, for instance, my weekly average was over 88 miles for the full 52 weeks, and that included periods of illness or injury. During that year I ran over 1,600 miles in races, in addition to competing in many triathlons, which also required cycling and swimming training.

This regime meant that the vast majority of my training sessions were done at one pace – there was no alternative, because I didn't have any energy left to do quality work! By Thursday each week I would find myself totting up the distance run since Monday and planning how to reach the magical 100 miles by the end of the week. Come hell or high water, I wouldn't be truly satisfied unless I did.

Luckily, by this time I had selected long ultras as the races I wanted to take seriously, and to a limited extent this sort of training suited that choice of event. It certainly made me a good one-pace runner, but did nothing for my speed and left me sadly lacking in shorter-distance races. Most runners don't share my liking for the long races and yet it seems as though the average runners are automatically drawn to making this 'distance obsession' the backbone of their running.

In South Africa I was reminded of this each weekend. The lack of a local race resulted in many runners going on their own training runs. As I drove into town on Saturday and Sunday I would see a number of runners obviously just finishing another long, slow distance session. Although this can to some extent be understood in the build-up to a marathon, the same situation could be seen at all times of the year, even when there were no marathon races in the coming weeks. Many runners just don't seem to consider it worthwhile to run short races unless they are on their doorsteps.

Ironically, these shorter-distance races can provide ideal quality training sessions if you don't want to race them flat out. If you are looking to put in a top-rate performance at such a distance, then the longest training run you would need would be about 10–14 miles; the longer run is of little or no benefit.

This also reminded me of my interview with Sebastian Coe. We were talking about travelling and running and the fact that some top runners even go for a run round the airport grounds whilst they are in transit. He thought this was pointless, since the only time he went for a run was when he could do quality training, be it ten miles or a track session. Those 'airport runs' certainly couldn't be quality workouts, so why waste the valuable energy?

The long run benefits only muscle endurance, mental strength and ability to withstand time on the feet, and this has been recognised by some of the world's top marathoners. Seiko of Japan, for example, will run 30 miles at eight-minute-mile pace in training. However, his quality workouts are hard. He has been known to take a surveyor's wheel and mark out a 1km distance on the paths of a London park and then run ten repeats of 1,000m in about 2:35, with a rest of only a minute between repeats. This is the sort of session he was using before running a prestigious 10km race in the UK in his build-up to the London Marathon. He obviously understands the principle of hard and easy sessions

The difference between longer and shorter races must be mirrored by different approaches to training. Thus, when you are not training for a marathon or longer event, the key to improving performance is dropping mileage. This does not mean that you will necessarily find the total weekly training load any easier; indeed, it may actually seem more stressful, particularly for the first six weeks.

Whereas the marathon is run at a fairly even rate of energy expenditure, races over three to six miles require the runner to keep the pressure on at all times. Thus there is no point in doing speed work on the track with long breaks and recovery periods – you won't be able to stop for breaks during a race! A better training session would be a track session of three or four repeats of 1,000m at best 10km pace, with a minute's rest between repeats. This is closer to the requirements of the 10km race and will improve the average runner quite considerably.

Including a warm-up and cool-down, this session would add only five miles to the training distance, and would take the best part of an hour to do. The benefits, however, would far outweigh those gained from running a long, slow seven or eight miles.

There is, of course, a place in the training week for a continuous run, probably three times a week. These could be over, say, twelve, seven and five miles. However, the pace of these continuous runs would be slightly faster than the normal pace used in the marathon build-up.

There are many theories on how fast these runs should be, but heart-rate monitoring is the best guide. Nearly all the theories boil down to running at a pace around 65 per cent of your working pulse range. For a 40-year-old with a resting pulse of 60 and a maximum of 180 (220 less 40), the working pulse range is about 120 (220 less 40 less 60). Thus this runner would aim for 138 (120 x 0.65 + 60) as a minimum pulse during these runs. He would not, however, want it to go much above 150 for any length of time.

When I first started monitoring my heart rate regularly over a three-month period I found that only after the first ten to twelve minutes of a run did my heart rate reach my required range. If nothing else, this proves the need for a warm-up. If this is the intensity required to benefit from training, it becomes obvious that the benefits of a 20-minute jog or very easy run, even over a long distance, are minimal to those wishing to improve in the shorter races. The role of those short, easy runs is purely one of active recovery.

So it makes sense to reduce mileage, do two or three quality sessions per week, add three shorter continuous runs and see how less can be more! Your total distance may be only 30 or 40 miles a week, but your training will have the same energy demand as 65 to 70 miles of one-pace running.

Another point to remember is that, even if you don't find racing these shorter distances challenging, a period of lower weekly distance with higher quality running every year will assist you in the longer events. It is recognised that the athlete who is faster over the shorter distance has the potential to be faster over the longer races too.

A variety of training and a reduction in distance will also give your body and mind the recovery required to allow you to go into your next marathon build-up fresh and eager to take up the challenge.

SPEED AND DISTANCE DON'T MIX

If you have been following the advice of this book, you will have probably been doing more speed work and quality sessions than before. If you are an experienced runner you will also have seen your weekly distance reduce in comparison to your previous training. For most of your training for the longer events, you will only be covering about 60 to 70 per cent of your total distance capacity.

Whilst marathons require good endurance, the mistake many top runners make in their attempts to 'go for gold' is to undertake frequent speed sessions or races and at the same time try to increase their weekly distance. This is impossible. In the early months the objective is to improve your basic endurance, whereas later in the build-up the emphasis moves towards speed endurance. In training for events longer than 50 miles, the reverse is true. Initially the training is aimed to increase speed capacity, whereas later the emphasis will change to improving your endurance.

Unfortunately we tend to think that if a little of something is good for us, then a lot must be even better. This is not the case. There needs to be a balance and the basic training principles must be observed.

If training for an ultra, as the need to increase distance predominates, then the number of quality sessions will drop from, say, three to two. Even in those two sessions it may be necessary to increase slightly the recovery between intervals, or to reduce the number that are done, but these sessions should not be stopped completely. On the other hand, runners who normally train only once a day may add in an extra session on one or two days during the week. The midweek long run would be gradually increased by 10 to 15 per cent, and the run at the weekend increased on an alternating basis. This should allow your weekly distance to increase by 10 to 15 per cent so that it will peak out at your maximum distance capacity about six weeks before the race. You can then hold that distance for three weeks before commencing a taper down to your chosen ultra.

If, however, you are training for a marathon or a shorter race you will find that the endurance and speed blocks of training are reversed, so that you first build on endurance and then improve speed. The endurance is decreased by 10 to 15 per cent and the number of speed sessions are increased from two to three. The recovery interval is then reduced. However, the same principles regarding the need to recover between these training segments must be maintained. Remember: your training is only as good as your recovery.

CHAPTER SEVENTEEN

COPING WITH THE ENVIRONMENT

There can be little doubt that the climate in South Africa is very conducive to training and vastly different from that of the UK. Different environments affect our ability and motivation to run.

What follows is a short discussion of how I perceive various weather conditions to have affected my running, and some recommendations about how to counteract the effect of the weather. Wherever possible I have made reference to scientific research but, quite honestly, there does not seem to be a lot of information available on this in some cases.

HOT WEATHER

This is the greatest problem encountered in South Africa and the need to keep cool is well documented. This is best done through the use of 'airy' clothes such as mesh vests and fabrics that are light in both weight and colour. The body's major heat-producing areas are the large muscles, since they are the ones that are working hardest, and these are therefore the ones to sponge down.

It always surprises me that Bruce Fordyce does not like his hair to be wet, since he recognises the fact that much heat can be dissipated through the top of the head and to keep this wet seems to me to be logical. Perhaps the irritation of wet hair is more of a problem to him. This is simply a matter of personal preference.

For the same reason, the use of a hat in hot conditions is not wise. In my view one should opt for a peak such as the promotional foam peaks that are regularly handed out at races. The need to keep well hydrated is also important. The importance of drinking enough has been dealt with in another chapter.

Whether to wear suntan lotion or not is an area of controversy. I don't like putting anything on my skin as it may prevent easy sweating and, since this is my prime cooling method, I sacrifice all for it. Rather than use a suntan lotion, I prefer to go into the race having already had some exposure to the sun. Again, I would stress that this is based on personal preference rather than proven fact.

In general, the message for hot-weather running is wear as little as possible and get as much air to the body as you can. This is based on the assumption that the running takes place in a fairly or highly humid environment. When running in a very sunny, hot but dry climate, I have found a pure cotton shirt to be the best protection from the sun, and there is no problem with chafing.

For the British runner who goes overseas to run, the biggest challenge is to adapt to the heat and get used to the humidity. Adaption to heat will generally take a minimum of about ten days. This is a good time to use a heart-rate monitor, as it allows you to put the same effort in for your sessions, but these will not be the same speed. As with all adaption it should be undertaken gradually and gently increased, so start with perhaps 30 minutes and build up to about 90 minutes over the ten days. If you can spend more days in the heat prior to the race, then all the better. The big temptation is to get a suntan as soon as you arrive. This can become a problem, so build it up gradually, particularly if you have fair skin. It is worth while increasing your consumption of vitamin A when you arrive in a sunny country, as this will assist with sun protection.

You will note the wording 'get used to the humidity'. I do not feel that you ever adapt to the humidity and often its effect is confused with that of heat. As humidity increases, the ability to cool through sweating decreases, as the air is too moist to take the sweat away. It is the removal of sweat that aids cooling. High humidity, be it during exercise or simply normal living, places a big drain on the body, and it is absolutely necessary to increase the amount of fluid you drink each day. Furthermore, humidity will tend to reduce the amount of sleep you get and therefore longer recovery may be necessary between sessions. Taking a siesta during the hottest part of the day may help regain some of the lost sleep, but staying indoors in air-conditioned rooms all day will not prepare you for the energy-sapping effects of humidity. The key to dealing with humidity is to get used to the effects and modify both your target time and fluid- and energy-replacement strategies to cope with it the best you can. Cities with high humidity often have high pollution levels, and this can be seen by looking at them from the top of a hill outside the city. Often you will see a yellowy-brown layer of pollution hovering at skyline level. Take that into consideration in your preparation. When the flag has lowered on the 1998 Commonwealth Games in Kuala Lumpar I am sure several UK coaches and managers will have changed their views on the effects of humidity!

COLD WEATHER

The chapter on running gear deals with the type of clothing you can look for to ensure that you do not get cold. One piece of advice is to wear the amount of clothing that allows you to walk outside at the beginning of the run feeling just slightly cold. When you start running, the heat from the energy expenditure will get you back to a comfortable temperature. If you are warm at the start of the run, then you will soon overheat.

The key areas to think about in cold weather are the extremities, i.e. hands and feet. It is worth while to make the first part of your training run a short loop which will allow you to return to base to make additions or reductions in the clothing you are wearing after you have been running for a while.

Because we live in a very temperate climate there is a perception that we do not need to drink, as there is limited evidence of a high sweat rate. This is a fallacy. The cooling effect still takes place but is not as noticeable. Furthermore, if the weather is so cold that you need to wear a windproof jacket, you effectively create a microclimate inside the jacket and this can become very humid – hence the reason the inside of the jacket is so wet. There is a definite need to increase your fluid intake under such conditions. This means taking fluid both on the run and afterwards.

ENVIRONMENT AND PERFORMANCE

There is a dearth of information on how the environment affects performance. Although it is recognised that the ideal running conditions are windless and slightly overcast with a temperature of 11 to 16°C, few references tell you how other conditions may alter your performance.

It may be helpful to look at extremes such as the 100-mile records.

The world records set up by Derek Kay and Dave Box in Durban between 1969 and 1972 were set in what were considered 'bad' conditions: raining, cold and overcast. Likewise, the current world best set by Don Ritchie on the track in 1978 was also set in cool conditions. Although many have tried, Ritchie's record has never been bettered.

Even Wally Hayward's 1953 record still makes the top listing; Derek Kay's is still the fourth-best.

There are many reasons for this. Running a race like this requires the athlete to be at a peak for the full 24 hours, as many things can go wrong in such a long event and, most importantly, the weather must be kind for the full length of the race. A full 12 hours without strong wind (a gentle breeze can be a bonus), a constant temperature between 11 and 16°C and even a light rain will make for ideal ultra conditions. Heavy rain means the need to wear protective clothing and the possibility of a poor foothold on the road. Light rain, on the other hand, is cooling and refreshing.

Now consider the running of 100-mile races in South Africa or any other hot climate. Many runners have been within the same times as Kay or Box for shorter distances, but have never matched them over 100 miles. It is true that they might never have reached the same peak, but one must also look at the conditions. Typically, over the last years, the 100-miler track races have been run in weather where the heat has gone up to and even over 30°C. The slow times are scoffed at even by administrators of the sport because the races have been won in 14 or 15 hours.

How can one compare these times with times set under more favourable conditions? Well, the hot-weather results may not be world-record times, but Dr Stephen Browne has done a limited amount of research into hot-weather running and he classifies a 'hot' race as one where the effective temperature is over 20°C and a 'cool' race as one where the temperature is less than 20°C. Effective temperature is a combination of both humidity and air temperature, and can also be increased or decreased by the effect of wind. A head wind will obviously have a cooling effect.

Racing times in hot conditions, according to Browne, can be expected to be at least 7 per cent slower than times set in cold conditions, and this increases with increases in temperature.

Two other researchers, Foster and Daniels, have estimated that for every degree above 7°C on the dry bulb, the running time in a marathon will be 40 seconds slower. This comes from a *Runner's World* article written in 1975 and I suspect that since then more has been discovered. I know that Tim Noakes is also looking at this problem and will no doubt come out with more detailed research on the subject, but this discussion does give some idea of what to expect.

In other ultras, such as the 1988 Komani 200km race, during which 'bad' conditions prevailed, good times resulted. On the other hand, over that same course when conditions were hot, times were worse.

This principle suggests a beneficial effect for hot-climate runners who run in, say, European conditions. If runners from hot climates can run 2:10 marathons in hot and humid conditions, imagine what they could do in more ideal conditions in the London or Boston Marathon! Obviously, 7 per cent at that level means much less in terms of minutes and seconds than at 100 miles, but the principle is the same.

Having been lucky enough to experience many races in a number of countries, I agree with Browne. I remember being in London a week before the 1985 London to Paris Triathlon. Tim Noakes and I were on the management team and, having been given the weekend off, we decided to take a trip up to visit my family in Scotland. With only 48 hours' notice, and hence no specific training, we took the chance of running the Edinburgh Marathon. If was certainly cool and, in that regard, ideal. Despite a very strong head wind for much of the run, I recorded a 2:36, which was a personal best by three minutes. Similarly, in 1983 I ran the London Marathon in 2:43, again a personal best, and the next day ran the Boston Marathon in 2:45.

In terms of Browne's formula, anyone running a 2:35 in hot climates can expect to do a sub-2:30 in ideal conditions and vice versa. Similarly, anyone running around 3:08 in hot conditions could achieve a sub-3:00 in cool conditions.

WIND

This is perhaps the environmental factor most disruptive to running. Winds are never constant. They gust through built-up areas and are prone to tunnelling and eddy effects, all of which disrupt the rhythm of the runner.

Even a direct head wind on an out-and-back course causes times to be slow. More effort is needed to counter the effect of a head wind than is gained from the effect of a direct tail wind. Don't expect the loss of time when running into the head wind to be gained when you turn. It won't be!

Another problem with winds is that they have a cooling effect, and Table 17.1 shows how wind can reduce the effective temperature considerably and even lead to hypothermia. The table comes from research done for cycling and thus deals with speeds higher than those of running, but the principles for running are the some. A tail wind will cool you off less than a head wind and has a dehydrating effect because you don't notice it as much, although it is causing sweat to evaporate.

Table 17.1 Calculating wind chill

Wind speed[2] (km/h)	Air temperatures (degrees Celsius)							
	+23.5	+18.8	+14.5	+9.4	+4.7	+0.47	-4.7	-9.4
8	22.6	17.4	12.7	7.5	2.8	-2.33	-7.4	-12.2
16	18.8	13.0	7.5	1.8	-4.2	-11.3	-15.5	-21.6
24	16.9	10.3	4.2	-2.3	-8.4	-15.0	-21.2	-27.3
32	15.0	8.4	1.8	-4.7	-11.7	-18.3	-25	-31.6
40	15.1	7.5	-0.4	-50	-13.6	-20.7	-27.8	-34.9
48	13.2	5.9	-0.9	-8.4	-15.5	-22.6	-29.7	-37.2
56	12.7	5.1	-1.8	-9.4	-16.5	-24	-31.6	-38.6
64	12.2	4.7	-2.8	-9.9	-17.4	-25	-32.5	-40.5
	LITTLE DANGER				INCREASING DANGER			GREAT DANGER

RAIN

I have already discussed running in the rain and how light rain can have a cooling effect. South Africans are lucky that, in general, it does not often rain. For this reason there are many runners who simply do not train in the rain, always aware that the chances are that by the next day the sun will be out again. The same can not be said of the UK!

The South Africans are actually missing some great runs, however. The hardest part of running in the rain is the initial period, during which you get wet. Once wet, no matter how wet, and provided you are warm, the run seems to take on a completely different aspect. I can't explain it, but I always enjoy running in the rain.

Incidentally, I have yet to find a rain suit that keeps me completely dry and allows my body to breathe to get rid of the internal sweat. No matter what happens, you are going to get wet, so why not enjoy it?

The most effective item available seems to be the Gore-Tex suit, a product that I believe was designed and manufactured in Scotland. This would be logical, since it was a Scot – one Macintosh – who invented the raincoat! Although even the Gore-Tex suit has its problems, the benefit of this type of clothing is that it keeps out the wind and helps keep the body temperature at a comfortable level.

ALTITUDE

Running at altitude was something that was completely strange to me until I went to South Africa, and my first encounter with it in 1981 convinced me that it was something to avoid. I found running very difficult and thought I was going to suffocate. It was like going back to running from scratch!

There is substantial evidence, however, that there is benefit to be had from training at altitude and then competing at sea level. The time spent at altitude increases your ability to transfer oxygen through the body and this effectively increases your VO2 max. Tim Noakes, recognising the way altitude reduces the ability to train at intensity, suggests that the ideal would be to live at altitude, train daily at sea level, and race at sea level. This, of course, is a theoretical ideal!

The use of altitude training has to be considered carefully and, once again, reactions are personal. Ron Hill relates how the British Olympic team once went to a training camp at altitude for three weeks prior to the Olympics, coming down to the Games site one week before the events. Nearly all the athletes performed poorly. However, a week later, in the annual Coca-Cola International meeting that was held traditionally, the same athletes were recording personal bests and beating many of the Olympic medallists. Obviously, this was another case of adaptation.

If you live at sea level and find yourself spending time at altitude for whatever reason, don't expect to be able to do the same amount of work or put in the same amount of effort.

Be satisfied with the fact that it will take you a while to adapt – possibly as long as two or three months. The worst time for me is the first three days at altitude, after which I gradually improve, but I never reach normal levels, although I have never yet been up at altitude for longer than ten days.

I also prefer to drive up to altitude, since flying means that I have to experience the cabin pressure of the flight, which I understand can be equivalent to 3,000 metres. Since the effect of altitude is based on blood gas pressure, it makes sense to me that a change of altitude should be as gradual as possible. Certainly, I don't find the drive as tiring as the flight.

If I am to compete at altitude I never do any exercise prior to the race once I have arrived up there. I would rather save oxygen for the race. Even at the start of the race it is important for me to take it easy and gradually adapt to the more stressful situation.

At one stage in the late '80s and early '90s I had reason to travel up to altitude approximately once every two weeks for about three days at a time. I experienced something that I have never seen any other reference to. After doing this for about two months, I found that I seemed to be able to handle the transition from sea level to altitude better and could even run some good track or hill sessions on the first or third days of my trip. I cannot say for sure that this was the effect of adaption – it could be that I had simply learned how to cope with the changes – but I must admit that I found that I ran well over that period, recording some good times in races. Perhaps regular short trips to altitude is another way of compensation.

The only athletes who seem to benefit from this move to altitude are the short-distance sprinters and field throwers. The reason for this is that the air resistance is less at altitude. Since air resistance is based on the square of the area presented to the moving object, it makes sense that the thinner air offers much less resistance.

There are certain gadgets on the American market which are reputed to help you adapt to the effects of altitude. To my knowledge, however, none has been scientifically proven to work. I have tried two of them and found that they tend to be quite awkward to use, not to mention the fact that you look like a space cadet when wearing them!

Moving from altitude down to sea level is not as much of a problem. I do feel that many runners overemphasise the advantage of this without taking care to find out just how long they need to ensure maximum benefit. I think Ron Hill's story about the Olympic team's experience highlights this.

Finally, the importance of the effect of altitude has been recognised by South African sports administrators, who no longer allow national championships to be held at altitude, a decision that I believe should be welcomed. In view of the population and financial distribution in South Africa, this must have been a hard decision to make, but it is certainly better for the sport.

This has not been a detailed or complete description of all the environmental conditions one may come across, but I hope it has been sufficient to make runners aware how conditions can affect performance and what steps they should be taking to counter adverse conditions.

CHAPTER EIGHTEEN

RUNNING GEAR

It is often said that the beauty of running is that all you need is a pair of shoes, an old pair of shorts, a T-shirt and socks and you're on your way, and strictly speaking I suppose that's true. However, this chapter will look into the question of equipment for the sport – clothing or otherwise – in more detail.

Something I would like to make clear right at the start is that I have been lucky enough to have been given several pieces of equipment over the years. I have never used anything that I didn't believe to be the best available on the market for my purposes at that particular time. There are two key points here: first, that the equipment was the best on the market at that time, and second, that it was the best for me.

What follows is my personal view of the current situation, and readers must make up their own minds about what they may find available and what works for them. I hope this won't be construed as a commercial for products that I may be associated with, but as an unbiased appraisal.

SHOES

We all know that a house needs to be built on good foundations, and the same principle can be applied to runners. The foundations in their case are their shoes. Without good foundations the runner will be unstable and can expect to suffer injury.

A small change in position at foot level makes for a large movement at knee height, an even larger movement at hip level, and so on. For this reason it is important that your feet are 'held' correctly. There is no substitute for a correct shoe (notice that I didn't say 'an expensive shoe'!).

As with training, what works for one person may not work for another. We are all individuals, all unique, all with our own variety of biomechanical problems, and the shoe we need are those that will cater for these individual requirements.

Some runners tend to look at what the top runners wear and conclude that because they wear Adidas, Mizuno, Nike or whatever, that must be the 'winning' shoe. That, of course, is not the case, it's just that that particular model in the manufacturer's range suits the athlete concerned. In some cases a top athlete may actually wear a shoe purely because of a sponsorship contract.

So the problem is how to select the correct shoe for you. The first thing to do is to go to a specialist running shop and talk to a salesperson who can tell you about the shoes. This will generally be a runner or someone who has had many years of experience with runners.

It is worth establishing beforehand from other runners just how highly they rate the advice given by a particular shop and salesperson. In addition, try to find out whether the salesperson is sponsored by any shoe company, since this may influence his or her selection of recommended shoes.

If you have been running for some time, arm yourself with a list of things you like and dislike about different types of shoes. In other words, build up the specifications of your ideal shoe. Do you like shoes with high heels and thin soles? (Normally shoes with higher heels are less stable than those with lower heels.) Normal lacing or ring lacing? Is weight important to you? Do you have a problem with pronation (too much inward rotation of the ankle, often a cause of 'runner's knee) or supination (too much outward rotation of the ankle, often associated with rigid feet that absorb shock badly)? Do you have a high or low arch? Are your feet wide or narrow? List absolutely everything that is a consideration in your choice of shoes. This will make the assistant's job that much easier, since you will have already ruled out many of the shoes that are available.

Another thing to watch for is assistants who change their recommendation of a shoe after finding they haven't got your size in stock. If they are not simply interested in making a sale, they will offer to get the shoe for you or even direct you to another shop which has it in stock. This latter attitude is the sign of good advice and would certainly result in my regarding the shop as my first choice in all future buying.

In 1984 I had a partnership in a running shop in Durban and I was amazed at some of the attitudes to buying shoes. Some examples follow:

'I'm not a top runner like Liz McColgan, Eamonn Martin or Richard Nerurkar. I don't need an expensive running shoe. I want a shoe for £35' (at a time when shoes had an average price of £50).

The point to bear in mind is that most of the top runners are at the top because of their inherited ability and physiological aptitude to running. Many could run in any shoe you gave them because they don't pronate excessively or have some other biomechanical problem. Many could run in the old gym shoe without too many problems, and thus they don't require that much protection.

But the average runner is not so lucky. Most runners have biomechanical problems with their footstrike, which to some extent probably explains why they are not as fast as the best. It is these biomechanical problems that require extra protection from shoes and this obviously involves more technology, more work and hence more money. Thus the average runner may actually be paying more for shoes than top runners, not less!

'I don't want to pay much for the shoes. They never last me
more than three months, then I need a new set . . . My dress
shoes last me longer and cost less.'

It's amazing how many people will compare the lifespan of dress shoes with that of running shoes, and yet fail to compare the type of life each has. The dress shoes are taken out on special occasions, worn for the night, cleaned the next day and put away. If it has been rainy they are stuffed with paper, allowed to dry, then polished and put away. Care is the name of the game.

Many runners have only one pair of running shoes and wear them daily in training. The shoes cover many more miles than the dress shoes and at the end of the run are packed into a kit bag along with all the other damp, sweaty kit. In many cases the shoes will stay there until the next morning's training run and so stay damp.

Such shoes never dry out, are taken on safaris through puddles, mud, gravel and sand, and have Coke and water spilt on them at refreshment stations. Is it any surprise that they don't last as well as the dress shoes? Is it any surprise that the stitching starts to rot away after a couple of months?

In truth every runner should have at least two pairs of good usable training shoes, and there is a good case for increasing that to three so that there is always another ready to move in when one wears out! In addition, a runner may opt to have a lightweight racing shoe which is kept for special races, to add that final edge to the competition. It all sounds like a lot of money, and initially it certainly is, but in the long run it's much cheaper. (Trust me, I'm a Scotsman!)

The point is that each pair of shoes is then used in rotation and thus gets a chance to dry out thoroughly before being used again. This extends the life of a shoe. This time lag also allows the runner to check the wear on the undersole and ensure that a thin film of shoe glue is spread over the wearing areas. This is so thin that it's like using a layer of cling film to protect the areas. Thus all you are ever doing is wearing down the cling film, not the sole of the shoe.

When the sole of the shoe is worn down the 'foundation' of your footstrike is totally different from when you first bought it, so the shoe can no longer be doing the job for which you initially bought it. It is therefore important to ensure that your sole is always in good condition. This sort of care will ensure that you get much more wear out of your shoes and so your initial investment will go a lot further.

It's also worth considering getting two different models of shoe for training in, especially if you are doing a lot of distance. Just as each of us has specific characteristics in our footstrike, so too each model of shoe has specific characteristics. If you are continually training in one model of shoe the 'stress' must be loaded continually on specific sets of foot muscles and ligaments. So it makes sense to change the stress slightly by changing shoes. Obviously, both shoes must be suitable for your style in the first place.

In selecting shoes, remember that there must be no compromise on fit. Many shops will allow you to test the shoe by running on the pavement outside.

Each shoe has many different features and an informed salesperson should be able to give you all the details. For this reason I will not go into detail here, but will simply list the various features, with the type of runner they suit, or the benefit they offer.

SLIP-LASTING

Most racing shoes are slip-lasted. This means that the nylon material that goes over the top of the foot is stitched together underneath to form a 'moccasin'. The lower part of the nylon moccasin is glued straight on to the midsole. If you remove the inner sole you can see the edges of the nylon stitched together. This makes the shoe more flexible and means that the upper can be re-glued easily if it comes unstuck.

BOARD-LASTING

In a board-lasted shoe, the edges of the nylon upper are not stitched together but tucked under a piece of board that is glued to the midsole. In you remove the inner sole, you can see the board. Since the upper is attached only at the edges of the board, it may pull away from the board and is hard to repair. However, the benefit of this is that it does give some extra rigidity to the shoe, which is a worthwhile feature for runners who suffer excessive pronation or supination. Board-lasting tends to be a feature of less expensive shoes. A disadvantage of board-lasting is that it requires longer to break in, since the board has to be 'taught' to bend where your feet flex.

COMBINATION-LASTING

As the name implies, this type of lasting combines the best of both worlds. Generally the board is in the rear of the shoe for more rigidity and the slip-lasting is in the front for flexibility. There have been few shoes that used the board in the front, none of which appear to have been very popular.

STRAIGHT- AND CURVE-LASTING

To determine whether a shoe is straight- or curved-lasted, look at the outer sole and draw a straight line between the centre of the heel and the centre of the toe box. If the outer sole is equal on either side of this line, the shoe is straight-lasted; if the line goes to one side, the shoe is curved-lasted. There will also tend to be a much more pronounced cut-out in the sole for the arch area.

Most racing shoes tend to be curve-lasted. Which do you require? This depends on your foot's biomechanics, but as a general rule of thumb it is worthwhile doing the 'bathroom test'. Stand with wet feet on a dry floor and leave two footprints. If the footprints show arch areas, you will tend towards curve-lasted shoes; if there is little or no indication of arches, you will tend towards straight-lasted shoes.

In the latter case you have a 'mobile' foot and thus require rigidity in your shoe, whereas a high arch indicates more rigidity in the foot, which requires flexibility and cushioning in the shoe. Typically the outer sole will mirror your foot imprint, for example the Nike Triax series tend to be straight-lasted with no 'cut away' below the arch. Compare these with the Nike Racers, which tend to have pronounced reduction in sole width and hence greater flexibility below the arch.

Beware, however; these are only guidelines. A good and experienced salesperson is what you need.

MIDSOLE

The midsole is the section of the shoe between the upper and the outer wearing sole. Typically, this is made of a cushioning material such as EVA or polyurethane (PU), or one of several substances with trade names such as Phylon. The prime purpose of a midsole is to cushion the force transmitted from the sole through to the leg. It also provides the 'shape' and height difference between the sole and heel areas. The midsole section may be a combination of materials of different densities positioned to ensure that it resists distortion under the action of pronation or supination. These differing densities are normally of different colours, thus inspection of the shoe will let you see the type and position of protection offered; however, some may be hidden inside the midsole and there are even cases where PU is mixed with EVA to give the benefits of both.

EVA is a much better cushioning substance, but it doesn't last as long as PU. On the other hand, PU has the disadvantage of being heavier. Many of the EVAs used in shoes are treated in some way to improve cushioning and/or lifespan. Puma have recently constructed shoes which replace EVA with a cellular material. This has the advantage of a longer lifespan, but initially provides quite a hard ride. Reebok have also experimented with a new midsole material which is a combination of foam and rubber. This provides a very light solution and good cushioning. For years Nike have imbedded air units into the midsole materials to provide longer-lasting cushioning. This has proved so successful that they now offer a variety of types of air units to suit different shoe applications.

HEEL-COUNTER

The rear of the upper is a heel-counter which 'cups' the heel of the foot. In very cheap shoes this tends to be made out of a card or board and is easily manipulated, thus offering little support. In more expensive shoes a moulded plastic heel-cup is provided, with additional support from leather coverings. Nowadays many heel-cups also have a plastic band on the outside around the base between the upper and the midsole, which is designed to stop the supinator or pronator from bending the cup over.

Generally, racing shoes will not have a lot of protection in this department, whereas, at the other end of the scale, a trainer for the worst pronator will have a heel-cup that is very rigid.

Your need for a good heel-counter can be established to some extent from your old shoes by placing them on a flat surface and examining them from behind. Do they lean inwards or outwards? If they do, you need a stiffer heel-cup. An inward lean would indicate that you pronate, whereas heel-cups that lean outwards indicate excessive supination. These are the hints you need to glean from inspection of your old shoes prior to deciding on your new purchase.

A typical straight-last shoe. This gives more rigidity. The air cushion is visible at the heel.

A curve-last shoe. Notice the narrowing below the instep.

The build-up at the heel-cup in a shoe like this provides extra support to pronators.

The Two Oceans 35 mile marathon, arguably the world's most scenic race. Here the author is on his way to collecting his 'blue' number for completing ten races. He is one of only a few people to have run all ten in under four hours.

OUTER SOLE

As with most things in life, your choice of outer sole involves a compromise. The higher the rubber content in the outer sole, the longer it will wear, but also the heavier it will be. Blown rubber offers more cushioning, but wears much faster. The blown rubber 'vibram' sole used by New Balance in the mid-'80s was one of the first that provided good grip, lightness, cushioning and reasonable wear. There are still companies who will offer such outer soles for repairing old shoes; look in *Athletics Weekly* or other running magazines.

Obviously attempts have been made to provide long-wearing pieces at the points of wear whilst using lighter rubber in areas not expected to wear. This should get the best of both worlds. Mizuno were one of the first manufacturers to produce shoes to have only heel and forefoot sections of rubber. The remainder is exposed midsole. This is now fairly common, and companies have designed lightweight methods of connecting the heel and sole to provide some rigidity between the two.

The tread on the outer sole is also important and will determine the amount of grip on various surfaces. Close-profile surfaces (ones in which the ridges of the tread lie close together) tend to pick up mud in cross-country events, while flat surfaces give no grip. Again, one must think about how the shoe will perform in the rain.

The old Adidas Atlanta was an excellent shoe in many regards. It was light enough for a racer, cushioned enough for a trainer, offered limited support, was hard-wearing on the outer sole but gave 'wheelspin' in the wet. A number of shoes need to be slightly worn before they provide good grip on wet tar. One of the most traditional and well-accepted all-round outer soles is the 'waffle' introduced by Nike in the late '70s and early '80s. It is still extremely popular today as it works well on most surfaces and is relatively lightweight yet hardwearing. However, the newer Nike Racers are adopting a sole where the air unit is moved out of the midsole, into the outer. In this way the low profile of the Racer can be maintained.

LACING FEATURES, UPPER FABRICS, ETC.

There are many other features that are apparent from an external inspection of a shoe and this is where the 'ideal' list comes into play. Only you know what feels good and works for you. I, for instance, like to keep my laces quite tight, so I prefer the plastic D-ring lace holes because the laces don't pull through as easily. It's all a matter of individual preference.

'TECHNOLOGICAL FEATURES'

Each manufacturer seems to have its own 'technological features' that make the shoe superior to all rivals. This is certainly not the place to knock or support these. I believe each runner must make up his or her own mind about these.

It is, however, interesting to see some of the conflicting claims. For instance, the airsole is a midsole with an air pocket running throughout, the idea being to give extra cushioning. On the other hand, the gel sole has little pockets of gel located in set positions within the midsole. Presumably this is to keep the extra weight from the gel to a minimum. However, each manufacturer claims that their product is superior.

The most common cushioning systems are: Nike air, which comes in heel, forefoot or full-length pockets and can be positioned either in the midsole or, more recently, on the outsole; Asics gel, which comes in heel or forefoot pockets; Adiprene, a shock-absorbing material put in heels or under forefoot; and New Balance 'Absorb' material, which displaces the energy of impact sideways. An absorb ball will not bounce when dropped from a height, whereas a normal EVA ball would. The success of the air units has now resulted in different types and thicknesses, such as zoom air, tensile air and visible air, each having a different application.

Reebok and Puma use honeycomb-shaped membranes to provide cushioning. One of the great benefits of this is that even if the outer sole is punctured the walls of the honeycomb continue to provide cushioning. The new Reebok 3D foam combines midsole and outer for cushioning and lightness. Brooks Hydroflow uses chambers and valves through which fluid is squeezed as the pressure of the foot is dissipated.

Most attention to cushioning has been put into the heel area of shoes, on the basis that most 'average' runners land on their heel first. Thus the runner who needs forefoot cushioning often has a limited selection. Another point of interest is that the faster you run, the more you are likely to run on your forefoot. This is another reason for having different types of shoes for speed/racing as opposed to slow distance running. This is also one reason why Nike have developed the air units for outer soles. Cushioning can be provided under the forefoot while keeping a thin and flexible shoe.

Runners who have restricted ankle flexion are likely to run on their forefoot and prefer shoes with low heel-to-midsole height. Forefoot runners tend to have less wear on their shoes, but do have a tendency towards calf injuries.

One shoe manufacturer has brought out a torsion device which allows the shoe to twist in 'the natural movement of the foot', whereas his competitor also has a torsion device to 'prevent the excessive twist of the shoe'. It has been suggested that many running injuries are cuased by too much twisting on the midfoot (beneath the arch of the foot). For this reason manufacturers have looked at methods of controlling this twist. Each manufacturer has scientific proof for his claims. The best advice I can offer is to be sceptical and ask yourself if it seems logical; if it does, it probably works! Remember that your requirements in a shoe are specific to you – don't necessarily go with the shoes that are deemed the most popular.

INNER SOLES

This is probably the most underrated section of the shoe. Since my rugby-playing days in the late 1960s I have used an inner sole that works better than anything I have found in bought shoes.

If you take out the removable inner sole from any shoe, even one that has only done 30 miles, and inspect the forefoot area of the inner sole, you will find that the toe and ball of the foot areas have lost all their cushioning. The 'bounce' at the rear may be adequate, but the forefoot will be 'dead'.

My suggestion to you is to buy a set of Spenco inners for your shoes. I feel quite justified in this recommendation, as I have yet to find a better product than this close-celled rubber inner sole. It is lightweight and yet seemingly lasts forever. There are various types of inners produced by the company and I suggest you find the one that suits you best.

I obtained a brand-new pair of Nike Duellist shoes two days before the 1989 Comrades, fitted a Spenco inner sole in place of the existing non-replaceable one, and ran a 6:07 Comrades without any problems two days later. Anyone who knows the Duellist will know that it was a racing shoe weighing only 180 grams and having very little cushioning and no air unit. I need cushioning, since I tend to be a forefoot striker. I think this story is solid evidence of the worth of Spenco inner soles.

I am able to run long distances with lightweight shoes and vary my choice between the flat Spenco inners and those which have a semi-shaped heel made out of a polyurethane shock-absorbing material. Although slightly heavier, these Spenco 'PolySorb' inners are better for when I land more on my heels in the longer events. Incidently, I also wear them in normal shoes, as I spend much of my working day on my feet and this relieves some of the tiredness. These insoles do cost about £10 a pair, but are well worth the money. A thin, flat Spenco can also be used over the top of some orthotics so that the cushioning is maintained. A second choice for inners would be Sorbuthane, but the weight of such soles is a disadvantage.

SPIKES

Road runners, particularly longer-distance runners, normally assume that they will not spend much time in track training. However, those following the recommendations of this book will find many reasons to spend time in track training, and thus make use of spikes.

Some people feel that they can do track training with normal road shoes, but I believe that if you look the part, you tend to perform better. Having the right equipment definitely helps. Another benefit for me as an ultra runner is that spikes help me get back on to my forefoot after a long event or road training, and this is the correct style for speed running.

Because road runners tend to resist using spikes, our knowledge of what type of spike to use, and in what holes, is limited. For this reason the following details, provided by Adidas a few years ago, will be of assistance to runners as a base from which to experiment. Spikes should be considered as essential when racing 5km or less on the track. Finally, bear in mind that one set of spikes will last the average road runner many years and is therefore a relatively cheap investment.

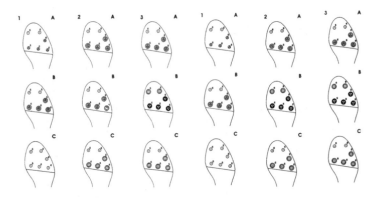

Figure 18.1 Spike types by distance

Key: 1: Body weight of up to around 50 kg. 2: Body weight of up to around 50 – 70 kg
3: Body weight of over 70 kg. A: Average track hardness B: Especially soft track
C: Extremely hard track   ⊙: Millimetre height of the triangular or cylindrical elements

⊙ : Cone element   ⊖ : Triangular element   O: 1/1 Star profile   (6 mm)

◎ : 1/2 Star profile   (3 mm)   ⬜ : Heel part (only for hurdles)

A FINAL WORD ON SHOES

A final word about buying shoes: If you believe you have a problem, it may be worthwhile consulting an orthotic specialist, ideally one who understands running. There are a number of adverts in *Athletics Weekly*, *Today's Runner* and other running magazines.

Some clinics have a treadmill and video set-up which allows runners to see for themselves exactly how their feet behave on footstrike, and they can give the runner advice on the amount of support the shoe needs to have. Even better would be to take the video to the sales assistant who would then be able to match the stride to a suitable shoe.

Determining where your foot requires flexibility and where it needs support is the first important stage of finding the correct shoe. This may change with the type of training or racing you want the shoe for. If, at the end of the day, you find an almost perfect shoe but it doesn't have enough forefoot flexibility, then you can always make some minor modifications to assist. On several occasions I have taken a sharp knife to cut some slots directly across the rubber outer sole of the forefoot. These only cut the outer sole, not the midsole. Other alterations are also possible, such as removing heel tabs that are too high, causing an irritation of the Achilles tendon. I have even cut the front part of the upper at the toe box to provide a bit of extra width. When done carefully, these alterations do not reduce the life of the shoes but do make them more suited to your requirements.

This has not been a full discussion of shoes, but I hope it will have given you some key issues to consider when buying shoes and that it will help protect you against disreputable dealers. In the same way, I would make one appeal to the runner on behalf of the salesperson. When you find a good salesperson who is willing to sit down and help you, who will, if necessary, take out every shoe in the shop to ensure that you get the best one for you, please recognise this effort and buy the shoe from that store. It's amazing how many runners will come into a shop, pick the expert's brains, and then walk miles to buy the same shoe for a couple of pounds less. They spend more than the saving in the lost time. It is worth paying more for the expertise of the salesperson; experience costs money.

VESTS AND SHORTS

These are very much a matter of personal preference, but look for the fabric and the fit that will leave you able to move freely and will not chafe you, even when wet. Think also of the weather conditions you intend to run in. If it's hot and humid, try to get as much mesh and lightweight material as possible. Also go for lighter colours, as they reflect the heat.

Top UK marathoner of the 1970s Ron Hill was the first to use a string vest in heat. Now there can be no doubt that the clothing overseas, particularly in South Africa because of its obsession with distance running, is well ahead of anything that is available in the UK for hot running. During 1991 a change in clothing was noticed on the world track and field circuit, as the ladies opted for 'boob-tube' vests. The 'shorty' vest had also made an introduction for males into triathlons. There is much to be said for using such vests in hot and humid climates. The exposure of the midriff allows for much better cooling. This is by no means the ultimate, but it is an improvement. This style of vest became adopted as official kit for the British Athletic marathon and ultra squads with the new kit sponsors in 1997. If you are going to be running in hot weather, keep looking for new ideas, as the slowing effect of heat is dramatic.

In the UK it is more likely that you will be running in cool or cold weather and be looking for warm and rainproof clothing. The best material I've found is polypropylene, which allows the sweat to move away from the body. Many companies have brought out similar products, but these are often at a much higher price. A normal T-shirt is fine in mild weather, but it keeps the sweat close to the body, which causes chafing, and gets very cold in wind or when you stop.

The key to running in winter weather is to 'layer' clothing. In the coldest weather, start with a polypropylene shirt, short- or long-sleeved, then a cotton long-sleeved shirt and finally a shower-proof jacket. In essence, what you have done is create a 'microclimate' inside the jacket. As you run the heat builds up, the sweat is taken away from the skin to the cotton shirt and condenses on the inside of the jacket. For this reason it gets very wet on the inside. However, it never gets cold. The temperature can be controlled, using the zip on the jacket. Some jackets have two zippers and hence allow alteration at both the top and the bottom of the zip. One thing to bear in mind when wearing this amount of clothing is that you will sweat as much or even more than normal. The importance of replenishing fluids cannot be overstated. With layering, too, you can always remove a layer if the weather changes or you get too hot.

RAIN- AND SHOWERPROOF TOPS

Every UK runner needs something for rainy days. These come in a variety of options, from rip-stop nylon pullovers to the fully rainproof

Gortex style. As noted above, when you are running the heat tends to result in a build-up of sweat on the inside of the jacket, so the benefit is not really in keeping dry, but rather in keeping warm. Many jackets are advertised as being breathable, but this only seems to work for walking or very light exercise.

To me one of the most important features of a jacket is to keep the wind off. It's a strange thing, but once you are out running in rain it doesn't really feel too bad. Indeed, it can be very enjoyable, as long as the wind is kept at bay. For this reason, one of my favourite jackets is a simple rip-stop nylon pullover. It can be crumpled up and put under a hat or in a pocket during a long run, so that if the wind or rain comes, it is simply a case of pulling it out and putting it on. If it clears or gets too hot, simply put it back in the pocket.

My other preference is for a pertex jacket made by View From. Not only is it relatively waterproof (and stated as being breathable), it is also covered in reflective ink. This reflection works extremely well. I regularly use this on my runs home, in unlit urban roads, as it is easily seen by oncoming drivers.

For normal running, I do not suggest there is a need for rain trousers. If, however, you consider moving up to ultra events and, in particular, those longer than 100km, then the length of the run and the lower intensity may justify their use. A full rainsuit is, however, useful for warming up, cooling down or spectating at events.

In summary, look for something bright for night running, light for ease of carrying, windproof, and in your price bracket.

SOCKS

Over the years I have tried most types of socks. When I first ran after my rugby days my preference for socks was for calf-high baseball socks. These were thick and self-supporting and did me nicely at that time. I even ran my first Comrades in 1981 in these socks. However, having realised just how much sweat they could hold, my next choice was to go without socks, as the inside of the running shoe seemed extremely comfortable – certainly in comparison to the rugby boots I was used to. As someone who sweats a lot, I soon had to end this practice because of the smell and the slipping around. This led to a well-cushioned tennis-type sock, which eventually has turned to the use of thin cotton socks. In short, I think I have tried the works and, in all honesty, you should use whatever suits you. However, keep away from the synthetic materials such as nylon if possible, since they do tend to cause sliding and hence blisters.

Bruce Fordyce once promoted the use of two socks as a guard against blisters. This may work for him, but I like the feel of as little as possible between the shoe and my feet. My personal experience is that I can take a brand new pair of socks out of the packet the day of a race and wear them without problem, and frequently do.

In 1992 I met up with American Roy Pirrung at the Spartathlon. After the 150-mile race we spent a few hours together. He had developed a pair of socks with a padded sole, and a material that takes the sweat away from the foot. These are very good and I keep these specifically for longer events. Unfortunately these have not been available in the UK, but they can be ordered from the USA at a cost.

Once again we are all different. Many runners use vaseline on their toes; I find that this is the only time I get blisters! Just as we run with different strides, so too our toes and feet move differently in our shoes. We therefore have different requirements for socks, and you need to find out what works for you.

TIGHTS AND GLOVES

When South African runners, particularly those in Durban, talk of cold weather, they mean that it has dropped to below 10°C. Arriving back in Scotland in 1995, I quickly understood the concept of 10°C summer mornings, 2°C as a good spring morning, and -2°C as a typical winter morning! The wind would add to, or more correctly subtract from, these temperatures.

It also needs stating that the weather within the UK also varies to an appreciable scale. The climate is definitely a couple of degrees warmer in the Midlands and southern areas of England than in the north of England and Scotland. This can make a significant difference to the number of layers you require.

It's all a case of dressing for the occasion, and the advent of running tights has gone a long way to making this a realistic possibility in these cool temperatures. Made of lycra, these are close-fitting, flexible and presently fashionable. Support below can be given using a speedo or suitable underwear for the ladies, and this ensures a comfortable run. If it is too cold for nylon tights, go for the new microfibre cotton lycra type, which have the ability to take sweat away from the skin and are thicker than their nylon counterparts. The other benefit of this material is that it stretches four ways. Many runners use 'tracksters'. These tend to be synthetic combinations with a two-way stretch. These are very warm, and the 'piping' down the front of the leg gives a semi-formal appearance that allows them to be worn on casual occasions outside running. The problem with them is that they do not have four-way stretch and when worn with the stirrup under the foot there is a restriction on your knee and stride action. Whilst this is of little importance in the long, slow run, it does affect higher-quality work where a higher knee action and longer stride length is required. I have found that consistent use of such tights during the winter months has even resulted in a change to my running style and I now make sure that I restrict my use of heavier two-way-stretch tights to slow (low-knee-raise) running. Those runners susceptible to knee problems may even experience a mild knee pain either during the run or the following day.

Again View From, and now others, have produced tights with sprinkles of reflective paint. These are ideal for running at night, as the legs are one of the first things that car headlights pick up on. I first used these in the 1996 Belfast to Dublin 104-mile Peace Run. It was quite amazing to see how cars on the opposite side of the road would slow down immediately their headlights caught the tights.

This reflective paint is now used on T-shirts, jackets, tights and even shorts and vests. I can recommend nothing better for any runner who runs in the dark. Add a lightweight flashing red cycle-type light on your back, and one of the headband lights or a small Maglight to see ahead with, and you should be as safe as houses on any run home.

Hands are also an area that get cold easily. Generally, I hate my fingers being covered. In the initial levels of cold I will cut the fingers off a pair of cotton gloves which leaves me with a mitten. As it gets colder, I use one of my long-sleeved shirts with the integrated gloves. This is a 'pocket' sewn on to the outer of the sleeve. When folded back over the hands it encloses the end of the sleeve, providing glove-like protection. The convenience is that as you warm up you can fold the glove away. For colder weather, it's a set of thin 'Duofold' gloves. These are thin but very warm. Finally, in very cold or windy weather, a fleece glove is the answer. I'm sure that other runners do not need such a variety of gloves, but my dislike for having hot hands has resulted in my building up a variety of options.

PROTECTION FOR EARS, HEAD AND EYES

When I first went to Scotland, my first line of defence for cold ears or head was the hood on my rain jacket. I soon found that a simple woolly hat helps. An additional benefit of this cap is that it is possible to put a thin rain top or other item under your hat to carry on the long run. As someone who often runs with glasses, I have used this convenient storage space when rain during a run has made the use of glasses impossible.

In deepest winter I opt for a good Scots invention called a balaclava, but this is a last resort for me. This is similar to the South African 'beany' but also folds down to cover the face with the exception of the eyes and nose. It's the sort of thing SAS soldiers wear during a mission, and on several occasions I have greeted someone in the street whilst wearing one. Needless to say I got no recognition from the other party – they wouldn't have been able to tell who they were looking at – but at least I was warm!

One thing to remember about head covering is that this is one of the main areas where heat escapes, and whilst it makes a lot of sense to trap this heat loss in the cold, it is also essential to ensure that the heat is dissipated in hot conditions. The ideal hat in heat is no hat at all! In heat we want to be kept cool. If you need some shade from the sun, the foam peaks that are often handed out as promotional items are ideal. The head is left open and the peak gives the required shade.

In South Africa, people often wondered why I ran with my normal glasses, and yet they would frequently see me without them at work or at functions. The reason was simple: even though I am short-sighted, I can see far enough ahead to be able to run, but my glasses were photo-chromatic, that is they also act as sun protection for the eyes. When running the distances I do it was inevitable that I would end up in the sun for extended periods, and thus I needed some protection on long runs. I held the glasses in place with a rubber band I got in Hawaii in 1984 called a 'croakie'. However, since 1988 I have used the now-fashionable triathlon glasses and now wear these virtually any time I run in the sun. There can be no doubt that they alleviate the stress of eye strain. Initially I thought that all well-established manufacturers produced similar products, but this is not the case and it is worthwhile taking time to review the whole range before investing the fairly substantial amount of money required to purchase these. Although I can also wear my contact lenses under them, and hence improve my sight, I first found a set of Bollé's that allow lightweight prescription lenses to be used. This is done by providing a small plastic frame off the nose piece. The disadvantage of this was that the weight was in the front of the frame, which did cause problems in events lasting 12 hours or more. On the positive side, it is possible to change the colour and density of the lens, which means that I now use these in Scotland when cycling or in conditions where a yellow or fog lens is required.

Technology moved on in the 1990s and Oakley manufactured glasses that could have the normal prescription put into the lense. These are absolutely ideal in consistent weather. They are light and very comfortable to wear. They are supported on the nose, and by legs along the side of the head – they do not curl behind your ear. This removes the irritation often caused by normal glasses as they move behind the ears.

You may wonder why I only briefly mention contact lenses. These are a great solution for those who can run with them, but they do have a number of disadvantages for longer distance runners. There is still a need for eye protection glasses in sunlight, and contacts can dry out and become 'gritty' during a long run. Another problem some runners experience is trying to get the contacts in on the morning before a training session or race. Contact lenses are advancing all the time, and those who can wear them should continue to experiment with the disposable options to see if they find something that works for them for training and racing.

WATER CARRIERS

If you have already read the chapter on fluid replacement then you will know my feelings towards carrying bottles and the disadvantage of this. However, fluid replacement is a critical feature of running.

In 1986, whilst involved with the organisation of the triathlon in Newcastle in South Africa, I was told how runners put water bottles behind the kilometre marks on their training route the night before a long run. It's all very complicated and time-consuming. I have yet to find or hear of a better device than the Tripper, which provides water carriers front and back. Its soft 'drip-bag' format ensures that there is no bounce as you run and it offers a lot of flexibility when it comes to choice of liquids. It comes in different sizes with the litre capacity ideal for running. Up to 500ml can be carried front and back. The canoeists prefer the one litre front and back version for the longer events, and I am sure that there is a definite place for it in long triathlons held in hot weather. In recognition of the need for fluid replenishment and the rule requiring competitors to wear a vest, the South African Triathlon Federation allow a Tripper to replace the need for a vest.

Over the years I have tried many other types of water carriers for my runs in the mountains and, in particular, for the Western states 100-miler in the USA. There are belts that carry bicycle bottles, tubes of water that fit round the waist, hand bottles shaped for holding small amounts of water, etc., but not one matches the Tripper at this stage.

WEIGHTS

Perhaps the place to start is the hand weights, and there has been much said in the past about the idea of runnng with weight in training and thus developing strength for racing. I believe these all tend to alter your running style and therefore are of little benefit. The only possible exception to this is a light hand weight, which may help improve arm-strength endurance. Three types come to mind: Heavy Hands, water-filled hand bottles and a gel-like ring.

Heavy Hands are a handgrip on to which weights from as little as 1kg to 15kg can be added. Obviously the 1kg is ample for running with; anything more is likely to make you look like a neanderthal man with your knuckles scraping the ground after the first mile! The water-filled hand bottles have the benefit of giving liquid on the run. However, they hold about 150ml and thus weigh only 150g, which is possibly too little. Finally, there is a compact gel-like ring made by Spenco which can fit over the wrists or ankles and weighs about 1kg. This seems to work quite well without much bounce and certainly would add to the stress of doing stair running, for example, if used on the ankles.

Relatively recent research has again promoted the use of a weight vest for running. Perhaps the best solution here is to use the Tripper, with the fluid on board adding 1kg (2.24lbs) to your body weight. Using the larger two-litre model will double this. A major benefit here is that it is designed to distribute the weight through the axis of the body and thus will not affect your running style too much.

On the subject of weight training, a further question that runners need to ask themselves is whether to make use of a gym or buy their own home gym. If they opt for the latter, I don't believe there is any need to equip a full gymnasium. It is sufficient to have a relatively basic machine. In the early 1980s I developed one with a Durban firm that did all the exercises I believed I needed at that time. I don't think these are still available, but I do know that other companies have subsequently developed similar types of bench. These are certainly sufficient for most runners' needs.

Weights and home gyms are also discussed in chapter nine on supplementary activities and cross-training.

CREAMS

Walk into any sports changing-room and you can smell rubbing cream. In rugby changing-rooms the smell of liniment clings to the wall. At the start of major races the scent of eucalyptus clears the blocked nostrils of runners in a ten-metre radius.

Some creams are used almost as a replacement for a warm-up, others as painkillers, or as a method of reducing stiffness; the claims are as numerous as the number of creams on the market. I certainly believe that some creams have a role in recovery from injury. They will increase the flow of blood to the injured area, and may contain a mild anti-inflammatory or painkiller.

However, their use before a run is something I would question. A runner with a problem requiring treatment should probably not be racing. Runners must establish their own preference in this regard. My only advice is to look at the contents of the cream and seek pharmaceutical advice on the likelihood of it achieving its claims.

On the other hand, there is the problem of chafing, and this is something that can affect most runners. Here there are two main types of creams: the greasy, more commonly used ones such as Vaseline, and the less well-known water-soluble ones such as Sportslube and Elastoplast Anti-Chafe. Again I believe it is a matter of personal choice. The one thing I hate about the greasy type is that it never seems to get off your fingers if you put it on during a run. You can hardly stop to wash your hands, so it gets everywhere. On the other hand, I tested the Anti-Chafe cream during my Johannesburg to Durban record run in 1985 and this suited me best. The only drawback is that it does wear off after a while and thus in long runs you need to be able to replace it along the way.

RADIOS, WALKMANS AND MUSIC

I have always found running with music to be a pleasant way of covering a long run. There are a number of problems with this, however: how do you carry a radio? What products actually work? Which products can survive sweat and bounce? Here are some thoughts.

If you are looking for a radio, cassette-player or CD-player, you need to consider the following:

Weight: Obviously you need the lightest possible. The batteries are frequently a large percentage of this.

Tuning: Many radios use a dial to tune. I find these to be a waste of time for running, as they simply do not stay on the station. The best option is something that uses digital tuning, particularly if it also has a means of locking the buttons to prevent inadvertent change.

Waterproof: Be it cold, rainy weather or hot, sweaty weather, your radio is going to get wet and thus it needs extra care after each run. I have a small polythene bag which I put it in before I put it into its carrier. Pay particular attention to the battery area, as this tends to be one of the first areas affected.

CDs and tapes: Walkmans need to be anti-bounce, otherwise the music simply stops or misplays.

Carrying: Radio headphones as a combined unit are quite a useful solution, but again rain or sweat takes a major toll, and the weight carried solely on the head can become uncomfortable.

When using a more conventional option of radio and headphone, the best solution is to go for the smallest digital radio in your price bracket and carry it in a Tune belt. This is a neoprene belt with a pocket. It stretches to fit around your waist and carries the weight in the small of your back. A small polythene bag will assist with sweat/rain protection.

One problem with using any headphone system is that the cable itself has a bounce that continually tugs at the connection to the earphones. This eventually causes a loose connection and irritation. I have yet to find a solution to this, so merely buy cheap headsets on a regular basis. The best radio I have found is a preset digital Aiwa unit about two inches in height and one inch wide, using two AAA batteries. It has lasted me for a number of years and is very light.

This said, I recently came across something even smaller that will make carrying belts a thing of the past. The radio is designed by Sir Clive Sinclair, the British inventor of Sinclair computers and bicycles. His latest addition is a small, circular radio the size of a fifty-pence piece with a single integrated earphone. An additional behind-the-ear clip assists with keeping the radio in place. As it fits in one ear, it is also safer than wearing headphones as you can still be aware of what is going on around you. There have been small radios before, but these have tended to drift off the station. Not so the Sinclair X1. Tuning is by pushing a button, which takes the listener through a range of regional and national FM stations. A wire aerial ensures good reception in most areas. The radio is driven by a small lithium cell which is readily available and easily changed. Perhaps the only two downsides are that the radio tends to go through batteries in nine to twelve hours and that there is no effective volume control. It's certainly loud enough on quiet, lonely runs, but where there is additional external noise, a few more decibels would be welcome. Weighing just half an ounce, the Sinclair X1 button radio is comfortable to wear and costs under £10.

HEART MONITORS

The use of pulse monitors is discussed in depth in chapter 15.

ICEPACKS

I have included this item because I believe that at some time every runner will have the misfortune to suffer some form of injury that needs attention. Without a medical background I don't feel qualified to say much about injuries, but from personal experience I can say that for many types of injury, getting ice on as soon as possible is one of the best things to do.

The blocks of ice formed by ice trays are not convenient for this but will do if there is nothing else. The best icepacks I have come across are the ones filled with gel. This makes them flexible and easy to wrap around any injured area. Some come complete with a pocket containing a bandage which can be used to strap them into position. These gel packs can also be heated, which is useful for those injuries better treated with alternate heating and cooling.

A cheaper version of the same thing is a packet of frozen vegetables – but the person in charge of the catering in your home might not be overjoyed!

Tim Noakes's *Lore of Running* and *Running Injuries* (the latter written with Stephen Granger) are excellent sources of advice on injury. These books stress the need to find a specialist doctor. However, when you are on the spot or heading for the doctor, there are some simple things you can do that can help a lot. The first thing you should do is to apply ice to the injured area. Where possible, raise the injured part, and take weight off it. If nothing else, this will help to stop any internal bleeding from muscle tears, will reduce swelling and may even reduce pain. (See also chapter 19 on illness and injury.)

A last benefit of ice that may come as a surprise to many is that it helps relax muscles, and so also improves stretching. This ice treatment can be used by masseurs after an event and before a massage.

WATCHES

There is a growing market for running watches, which have shown dramatic technological advances. Not many years ago the only thing you could buy was a simple stop-watch that you started at the beginning of a race and stopped at the end. Knowing your overall time was easy, but working out your time over the last kilometre of the race was a major mathematical feat.

Some watches now work this out for you. They also allow you to programme target times, memorise up to 30 lap or kilometre times, and can even be used as a running logbook.

Technology is advancing so fast that by the time this book gets on to the shelves there will, no doubt, be even more advanced watches. For this reason in particular, I do not intend to recommend any particular model, although I have found one that seems to do everything I need.

All I want to say is that a watch is a great training and racing aid, so you should buy one of reputable make, such as Citizen, Casio or Timex, and one that is designed for sport. The corresponding advances in heart-rate monitors may now result in your purchase of a single unit that satisfies all needs. Here are a few features I would want in the watch:

- stop watch
- time of day, date, alarm
- countdown timer with repeat
- min 30 lap and recall
- good full-face night light
- 10 pre-programmable target times
- easy-to-use start/stop/lap buttons
- waterproof for swimming
- not too big
- heart-rate features (see chapter 15)
- useable for work

BACKPACKS

This may seem a strange thing to include but, since many runners have to run to and from work if they are to put in all the training they need, backpacks have a place here.

The major problem with the backpacks on the market is that none has been designed for runners. Any additional weight carried during a run tends to change running style, so it makes sense to try to get something that will distribute the weight equally about the body. I have solved the problem by taking the bags out of my largest Tripper and using it as a sort of front-and-back pack for taking kit to and from work.

There is an art in packing these bags. Heavy things like shoes should be packed to lie as close to the body as possible, as this will reduce the bounce. Unfortunately, these tend to be the hardest and most uncomfortable things to have close to the body, so a compromise has to be reached.

Another problem with packs is that their straps cut into you, particularly if you make them very tight to eliminate bounce. They can also restrict breathing. My answer to this was to develop something with a local manufacturer that would allow me to breathe even with tight straps. Basically this involves a loop of elastic attached to straps so that they extend with breathing

Another problem with backpacks is that, no matter what material they are made of, they are penetrated by sweat. There is an easy solution, however, and this is to put your clothes in a plastic bag before packing them in the backpack. This is also helpful if it rains.

Finally, remember that small is beautiful. Having a small pack keeps the weight close to the body and this makes running more comfortable.

A FINAL WORD

Other things to consider buying (or putting on a list for friends at birthday time) include a sports bag, a tracksuit, lace locks which allow laces to be held in position without being tied, a reflector belt for running at night, a wrist-wallet for carrying money and/or a key, and an energy belt in which to carry your sachets. An alternative way of carrying a single key (particularly a car key at races) is to tie it into shoe laces and then tuck it under the other lacing lower down the shoe.

If you enjoy gadgets, the best way to know what is available is to look at the November and December issues of running magazines. They nearly always feature a comprehensive list of 'things to get the runner for Christmas'.

Remember that everything you carry adds to the weight you have to take with you every step of every kilometre!

CHAPTER NINETEEN

ILLNESS AND INJURY

No matter how much reading you do and how many people you listen to, there will be times when things just don't go as planned. It's all very well planning your training, but it's a lot harder to get everything just right than it is to overdo things or do something you shouldn't.

One of the failings in human nature is to think that the very principles we have learned about don't apply to us. It is amazing how easily we can, for instance, spot overtraining in other runners, but think that we have a certain invincibility about us. Overtraining is responsible for most injuries and illnesses – and it's the easist thing to do.

EXCESSIVE STRESS AND OVERTRAINING

One of the questions that I am asked by novice runners and people who don't run is 'What is the hardest part of running long races such as marathons and ultras?'. I believe the answer is easy: the period of heavy training that one has to do before the chosen major race is actually harder than the race. For ultra runners it is the period of endurance training in the final six to eight weeks. For the marathoner the endurance comes first, with speed improvement following on.

At these times in particular, strict discipline is needed, and often there doesn't seem much else in a week other than work and running. Any extra time is automatically split up between family and rest, and frequently this seems to be inadequate for both.

Indeed, the support and understanding of your family and friends can be as important as the training. The famous American running doctor George Sheehan summed it up quite neatly: 'It is not the 32km training run that causes me to be overtrained, but the stress from the argument with my wife when I get back.' The point he was making was that the damage from emotional stress can be far more onerous than the physical fatigue of running. In fact, the easy runs are to a large extent stress-relieving, if run at the correct pace.

This said, however, it is not possible to spend every waking minute running, as overtraining would be an automatic result. I repeat, training is only as good as the rest and recovery that goes with it. The secret is to find the balance between the physical exertion of the training, the physical and mental stress of your career, and the combination of a good diet and adequate recovery time. Bruce Fordyce, who won the Comrades nine times, takes on fewer speaking engagements and appearances during the final build-up to Comrades in order to be able to rest more.

Obviously, then, for the runner who has the greater restrictions of full-time employment, the backing of family and friends becomes a critical factor. The backing is usually there as long as heavy training is for a short period only, and a balance is maintained. However, even the best-laid plans often go wrong. A sudden demand on time at work, or a family problem or illness, can result in the fine balance being upset. Our natural urge is to try and battle through, keeping to our running schedule. This is a mistake. The schedule must be modified to make room for this unforeseen stress. Failure to do so will set back our training and may even result in injury or illness. It will also submit those close to us to undue stress.

Finding this balance is probably the hardest part of training, especially when the streets are crowded with runners and the word at the weekly club meetings is that this guy, or that girl, is doing 'awesome' distances in training for the same race as you.

The tendency is to start worrying that you are undertrained for the forthcoming race. However, this is the time to adopt a 'don't worry, be happy' approach, safe in the knowledge that you have the flexibility to match your training to your stress capacity and available recovery time. With this approach there is every likelihood that you will pass those 'mega distance' runners where it really matters – in the race.

IS IT INJURY OR ILLNESS?

There are two words which, when spoken in front of runners, will give rise to an instantaneous reaction. The first is 'injury', accompanied by a reaction of immediate sympathy and advice. This is normally followed by a complete account of the listener's own injury history, as if to let the unfortunate injured runner know that he or she is not alone in misery.

The second word is 'illness', accompanied by a reaction that is obvious and slightly embarrassing: the afflicted individual is left with an ever-increasing distance being put between him and the others in the group.

There tends to be an almost epidemic increase in the use of these two words over the eight weeks leading up to major events such as the London Marathon or Comrades, and one must take precautions against them and learn ways to counteract their effect.

Let's start with injuries. In contrast to other sports such as rugby or football, our injuries are, in general, self-inflicted by our desire to run. In other words, most will go away if we stop running. Of course, that is not a cure that we can consider, since it *is* our desire to run. However, the onset of an injury is normally a sign that we have overstressed our bodies in some regard. Perhaps we have increased our distance too much over a short period of time, or just started doing hill work or speed sessions without proper adaptation. Alternatively, our favourite pair of shoes may now have given up the ghost or there may be problems with our selection of new shoes. The point is that in most cases an injury has a fairly simple solution, often a period of 'running rest'.

It is known that there is a fairly fast decline in VO_2 max when we take time off. The concept of VO_2 max can be understood as a measure of our ability to transfer oxygen within our body, and in general the higher the VO_2 max the better. This sharp decline during 'off periods' has been a concern for some time, but recent research shows that the biggest portion of this comes from the fact that we lose blood volume when we stop training. As trained runners we have a greater blood volume than the average person and thus we have more red blood corpuscles, which transfer more oxygen and thus give a larger VO_2. The problem is to try to maintain this volume during enforced running rest.

In times of injury this is relatively easy, provided you are willing to modify your training. It has been shown that by doing two speed sessions per week, this volume can to a large extent be maintained. Thus, provided you are able to run a session of, say, four repeats of 400m at your best one-mile pace with as much rest as you wish, your fitness can to a large degree be maintained.

Of course, most injuries prohibit running and thus alternatives have to be found, but the same principles need to be used. An alternative would be two hard cycle sessions which will raise your heart rate to anaerobic levels for two to three minutes at a time, or a twice-weekly session of running in water to keep the heart rate and blood volume up. There are endless ways if you just sit and think them through, and thus injury need not be the devastating knockback that it has tended to be in the past.

Illness, on the other hand, is a bigger problem. This usually strikes when one least expects it, frequently after a patch of particularly good running. Runners in peak fitness lives their lives on a razor's edge. Just too much training can throw them over the top and make them very susceptible to illness, and there always seems to be a willing flu or cold donor standing in the wings waiting for such an opportunity to offload a virus.

During your build-up to a peak, it can be worthwhile getting your doctor to give you an anti-flu jab. The problem is that there are many strains of flu and this doesn't prevent the others attacking you. However, the more bases covered the better.

It has also been noted that a high percentage of runners pick up a virus two or three weeks after a major peak. This obviously indicates a period of vulnerability. It is thought that the immune system is depressed immediately after training and then super-compensates. One tip to maintain a high immune level is to supplement with zinc and vitamin C tablets. These are cheap and readily available in Boots or other chemists.

Another time of susceptibility is when travelling by plane. First, the cabin pressure is equivalent to an altitude of about 10,000ft, which most people are unaccustomed to, and, second, the air circulating in an aircraft is doing so in a closed system. Thus any virus and germs from other passengers are circulated throughout the plane – not the healthiest of situations for a runner.

If you do become ill you should seek out a diagnosis, advice and treatment as fast as possible. Don't try to struggle through by yourself for a week, only to find that you have to go to the doctor anyway. Generally, this is a week lost.

Many illnesses will require you to lay off, and this is where you face the biggest problem. Any virus that requires rest is going to result in a drop in blood volume and hence VO_2 max. This means that the pace and intensity of training must be severely reduced on your return. Failure to do this will put you into a low again and could result in a recurrence of illness. Although these are frustrating and depressing times, you can be grateful if it happens early in your build-up. It would be worse to get sick a week or so before the event.

It is important to note that there has been some research into the connection between simple flu and colds and people subsequently going down with chronic illness or ME. Make sure you are over the virus before returning to full training, or you may pay an even heavier price.

Often doctors will prescribe antibiotics for illness and it should be noted that this usually means that you should stop taking vitamin supplements during the treatment. The antibiotics unfortunately have a negative effect on certain vitamins and cultures as part of the treatment. However, it becomes important to reinstate the vitamins as soon as treatment is finished. Your doctor will be able to give you precise details of your requirements, but the use of vitamin B and a multivitamin is generally a good starting point.

So, if you do pick up a niggling injury, be grateful – things could be worse. It could have been an illness, and that takes longer to recover from!

POSTURE AND BALANCE

Balance and bite can improve your health and performance. Most athletes and coaches would agree that the more biomechanically correct sportspeople tend to gain the greatest success in their chosen sport. It is unusual to see a hunched athlete dominate a middle-distance track race. Indeed, the commentary attempting to explain the African domination of athletics, be it marathons, track or cross-country, normally relates to the easy, relaxed manner and grace of the athletes' loping style.

The same principles apply to most sports. Cycling is a sport that highlights the importance of mechanical and postural efficiency. Setting up the saddle and handlebar positions to the correct relationship has a dramatic effect on the power output of the man and machine combination. Professionals make seemingly minor adjustments over hundreds of miles to gain optimum positions.

This may be the sharp end of the sport, but the same principles apply to all sportspeople. Correcting your body's imbalances and adopting mechanically efficient styles can help you to achieve your true potential in sport. More importantly, it can contribute to your overall health and welfare.

Incorrect posture or an unbalanced style often lead to injury, as forces are transferred to other muscles or joints which become overloaded. The first reaction is to treat the point of injury, but this only treats the symptom, not the cause. In more recent years, runners have begun to accept that many injuries are best treated by looking for problems with their shoes. Worn-out shoes or shoes that do not give the necessary support (or flexibility) are often at the root of injury problems. This line of thought works on the principle that each person is individual and that shoes are selected to correct the natural imbalances of the ankle/foot mechanism. Treating or correcting postural imbalances to provide a more efficient base structure would extend this logic a step further. Possible sources and methods of such balancing may be surprising, but the results can be dramatic.

The muscles, bones and membranes of the body are totally interrelated. Movement or disposition of one part has a reciprocal effect on other areas. Tension in the neck or back can affect the rotation of the pelvis and hence leg length. That in turn affects the foot plant while running. The change in strike and push-off will put load on to different muscles from those that were previously trained and hence can result in calf or hamstring injuries. Whereas initial treatment will focus on the injury, the only way the problem will be solved is when the chain of causes have been identified and treated.

Applied kinesiology analyses body movements, strengths and weaknesses in an approach which is both insular and holistic in order to bring the whole body back into balance. This approach has been used to great effect by a number of top sportsmen, including at least two big-name athletes in the UK. In the mid-'80s there was great media hype surrounding the dwarf-like running sensation Zola Budd. Her world-conquering times were only surpassed by her South African connections and the clash with Mary Decker in the 1984 Olympics. Budd experienced a dramatic fall-off in performance through chronic hip and leg injuries. Despite attention from physios, doctors and sports-science assessment, there seemed to be no return to previous form. Back in South Africa, she met with Ron Holder, an applied kinesiologist, known to many South African ultra runners as 'the guru'.

In layman's terms, the basic principles of the analysis is to test muscle strength and movement as the athlete's body is gradually put into a balanced position. The greatest strength exists when balance has been achieved. Assessment often begins with 'rubbings'. These break down adhesions and release various membranes around the body, allowing them to 'reset' when put into the position of balance. A torturous combination of tickling and irritation, these momentary rubs provide vivid memories that patients are unlikely to forget in a hurry! The benefits outweigh the ordeal, however. The patient is then put into a balanced position using a wedge of sheets from a telephone directory. In the case of a runner this will be under a heel or on the side of the foot; in the case of a canoeist it might be sitting with half a directory under one buttock. The patient then pushes or pulls against resistance provided by the practitioner. The number of sheets in the wedge of the directory is altered to the point where the patient is able to provide the greatest resistance. The final wedge is then used by the patient over the next months. This keeps the body in a balanced position in the same way as shoe orthotics are used to put your feet into a neutral position. With the patient now training and working in this balanced position, the forces and loads are transferred to the correct muscles, which in turn start to adapt and strengthen. As this happens, the body begins to return to a natural position of balance and the size of the wedge can be gradually reduced.

The applied kinesiologist can undertake similar resistance tests to identify a lack of protein or minerals such as iron.

Procedure can be adapted to suit most sports. The canoeists, for example, are balanced at hip height so that they put the edge of their paddle blades into the water at exactly the same position either side of the canoe. This ensures that all the force is used to pull the canoe forward and effort is not required to correct the turning effects generated by strokes of different lengths.

In a runner the stride length becomes equal and this balance can be heard in the rhythmical sound of shoes touching the ground. Shoe wear will often reduce.

The logic and procedures go against the current diagnostic norms of medical practice but have sufficient effect that a household name in British 400m running ascribes his return to world-class form to Holder's treatment. Holder now spends part of each year working in London, with the remaining time outside Johannesburg. On more than one occasion the British athlete has flown out to South Africa specifically for treatment.

Personal experience of these treatments confirm their success and has allowed me to run thousands of injury-free miles. On a most memorable occasion, I took one of my athletes who had recently competed in a national cross-country competition and subsequently sustained a sciatic nerve injury which virtually prevented any walking and prolonged sitting. In a single half-hour, Holder had produced a telephone directory heel wedge that had the athlete walking smoothly, attending the social functions at night and back running, albeit a short distance, the following day.

There is also reason to balance the body from the top down. The average person's head weighs around 15lbs, being one of the heaviest parts of the body. If the head is held out of alignment, the remainder of the body needs to adjust to compensate and maintain an upright position. Every inch the head is held forward increases the strain threefold. Part of the head, the jaw, performs regular and relatively large movements, thus altering the balance. When the alignment of teeth is incorrect the muscles in the jaw compensate by torquing to bring the teeth together. This causes muscles to be overworked and hence a chain reaction of load transfer begins. There are 68 pairs of muscles above and below the jaw which determine the head, cervical, shoulder and jaw posturing. Over 50 years ago, Penfield and Rasmussen demonstrated that almost half of both the sensory and motor aspects of the brain are devoted to the dental area. Thus half the brain's 'programming' comes from the dental system. The key to this is the correct positioning of the temporomandibular joints (TMJ). These are the two joints which connect your jaw to your skull. When correctly aligned, the vertical axis should pass through the foremost part of the ear and C1 to C4 of the spine. The horizontal axis aligns with the underside of the upper teeth. Poor dental closure can cause malposturing of C1 and C2, which in turn can show as 'hump back', sidesway of the spine, rotation of the pelvis and uneven shoulder height or leg length.

It is true that the body follows the head. You can realign the whole body by moving your head backwards or forwards. Such movement can reduce your vital lung capacity by up to 30 per cent, which would have a devastating effect on aerobic sport.

Whilst we are primarily interested in the potential improvements for sport, it is worth noting that over the past 30 years more and more evidence has been amassed showing that corrections to dental structures can provide a remedy for a wide number of chronic ailments. Perhaps it is more correct to say that many chronic symptoms are as a result of dental dysfunction. Recent media coverage has highlighted health improvements as a result of removing metal fillings from teeth, underlining the connection of teeth to other body functions.

Those who have a basic knowledge of acupuncture and reflexology will know that there are points in the soles of your feet that relate to organs around the body. Similarly, each tooth has a relationship with joints and organs. For example, a painful knee can tie up with an abcess in a tooth.

The prime objective of correcting the dental closure is to build up the rear molar teeth so that they are first to close. This can be done in a temporary state using an orthotic that adds height to the rear teeth or more permanently by building directly on to the rear molars. When it is considered that we swallow twice every minute when awake and once a minute when asleep, it can be appreciated that even with a small 3lb force applied to teeth with each swallow, the total daily load on muscles is very substantial. It is not surprising that correct bite is important.

One of the simple tests that can let you see a malposition of the head is to stand in front of a mirror with arms outstretched to the side. Now close your eyes and move your head from side to side. With your eyes still closed move your head to the point where you feel you are looking straight forward. Now bring both arms and hands together in front of you. Are you looking directly at your hands or slightly to the left or right? Ideally you should be looking directly down the line of your arms.

To the athlete, the bottom line is does balancing work? What are the benefits? There can be no doubt that better posture will help you perform at a higher level and reduce the risk of injury. Top performances come from periods of consistent training. These are only available to those who do not get injured.

If these methods are so great, why haven't we heard about them before? Both applied kinesiology and TMJ work have been around for years, but may have been overlooked as they do not fall into current 'normal practice' and are not fully understood. The fact of the matter is that Zola Budd and the British 400m athlete are only two of many people from a wide variety of sports who have benefited from such work. No matter what level your performance, it is worthwhile having your posture and bite assessed. Even if this only moves you up the results a few places, it could well improve your overall health and lifestyle.

Points of contact:
Stewart Wright Dental Seminars, 38 Union St, Greenock,
Renfrewshire, PA16 8DJ. Tel: 01475 26775
Upledger Institute UK, 52 Main St, Perth PH2 7HB. Tel: 01738 444404
Dental Practice, 57A Winpole St, London. Tel: 0171 636 9933

AN INJURY CHECKLIST

As soon as you have the initial twinge or hint of an injury, put ice on the area concerned immediately after training.

- If soreness persists, make use of aspirin's anti-inflammatory properties after sessions.
- Once you are convinced that what you are feeling is not a one-off twinge, start by examining your shoes. Most injuries start at these 'foundations', even if the pain is felt in the knee, hip or lower back. Check for wear and place the shoes on a level surface to see if the heels have been bent over or tend to fall to one side. The only solution for worn shoes is replacement.
- If your injury occurred just after you bought new shoes, you probably selected the wrong model. Try to exchange them, or sell them and buy a different model.
- It you are able to run, immediately reduce distance and effort. If it is a soft-tissue injury, make a booking with your physiotherapist. Do not struggle through yourself trying your own remedies unless you are 100 per cent sure what the problem is and why it occurred. A few days' delay in getting a diagnosis at the beginning of an injury can cost weeks of training later.
- Injuries affecting joints and bones should be referred to orthopaedic specialists.

- In all cases try to select medical specialists who compete or have competed in athletics, or have a recognised sports medicine qualification. Their understanding of your needs and the problems is usually better than that of their less active counterparts.
- Be prepared to accept a short lay-off from running if it is prescribed but ask about alternative exercises that can be done to maintain your fitness level.
- Follow the prescribed treatment or therapeutic exercise with the same enthusiasm that you applied to your running. Runners are given medical advice to speed their recovery, but many fail to follow it and thus take longer to get back to training.
- When you are ready to return to training, do so at about 50 per cent of your previous level in terms of both distance and speed, and build back up over a few weeks. If you fail to do this your injury will probably recur.

PREVENTION IS BETTER THAN CURE

This age-old saying has much to recommend it. The easiest prevention for a running injury is not to run, but this doesn't really help! In addition to the recommendations above and elsewhere concerning tapering, rest and recovery, there are a few things you can do in the hope of reducing the likelihood of injury.

One of the keys has to be regular inspection of shoes. In the chapter on shoes, I recommend the use of a shoe glue spread thinly over the sole to reduce wear. This means that the shoe has the same mechanical balance properties after wear that it had when you bought it. Worn shoes cause a redistribution of stress, which can result in injury.

One of the best preventative measures for the serious trainer or the runner in heavy training is massage. A regular weekly or fortnightly massage will take the tension out of muscles, restore an even balance to the structure and highlight any 'hot spots'. Hot spots are the areas that are likely to become your next injury. For instance, if a problem with your shoe is causing you to land differently, it is possible that one muscle is being used more than normal and it might be tight after the run. If the following day you go for a faster pick-up but the muscle still hasn't eased off, the additional load of speed may cause a minor tear. This will continue to feel like a tightness until it is properly rested or relaxed. The tightness will cause you to land differently, throwing more load on to other joints and muscles. So it goes on. A good masseur can pick these things up and relax the muscle. The massage will also promote circulation of nutrient-rich blood, which assists in the normal repair of training breakdown, thus speeding recovery.

MEDICATION

Some of the much-publicised drug abuse can no doubt be associated with pre-race medication in the hope of delaying certain conditions. Such drugs include painkillers. There is no place in sport for drug abuse, but over the years there have been many promoters of vitamins and natural remedies which were supposed to improve performance or have some prophylactic benefits. Their use has been open to much discussion, but may warrant your consideration.

For years I had been using the homoeopathic remedy arnica during long runs as a means of reducing leg pain and inflammation. This and aspirin seemed to be the only legal thing that worked for me and I have gone to fairly long lengths to investigate what is available within the IAAF limits. During this search I have spent hours with a top Durban orthopaedic specialist looking for medications that do not contravene the drug rulings and are safe to use. Strangely, it seems that my original choice was in the right direction. In 1992 a product called Traumeel-S was brought on to the South African market. This contains a large percentage of arnica as well as 13 other homoeopathic ingredients and is available in tablet, drop, cream and injection form. The product is manufactured in Germany, arguably the home of homoeopathic treatments, and is available in the UK primarily through homoeopathic clinics. It can also be prescribed by your GP.

I have tried this product before and during a number of long runs, and found that it reduces the inevitable leg soreness during and after such events. One of my first attempts was during a 7:39 100km training event, and three hours after the race I was able to tackle five flights of stairs two at a time – both up and down!

Following this training race, which was in August, I competed in the 1992 International Spartathlon from Athens to Sparta, a distance of 152 miles. This gruelling race at the end of September was my major peak for the year, but included a 1,200-metre-high mountain which had to be climbed on a rock- and shrub-strewn path. As most runners know, it is the downs that cause the trouble, and there was an equally devastating downhill to be negotiated after having reached the top. This all happened after the legs had been suitably 'softened' up at 155km!

I finished this event in sixth position after 29 hours, so you can imagine the muscle damage (consider six back-to-back marathons!). By using Traumeel-S before and after the race, I became convinced that my recovery had been speeded up, or at least that the damage was limited. In an attempt to test this belief, and thus against all my other advice, I attempted another long run only 13 days later in Port Elizabeth. There, during howling winds, I completed a 100km race, finishing second. Make no mistake, the legs were sore by the end, but without the benefit of this treatment I doubt I could have got close to the marathon distance, let alone a 100km. It must be stressed, however, that I only attempted this as a test of the product for future use, and this was done *after* my peak for the year. I do not advise such action by other runners. It would be against all recommendations of this book.

ACUPUNCTURE

I have experienced anti-inflammatory and remedial benefits from acupuncture, and the Healthpoint machine in particular. This is a small, hand-held, battery-operated electro-acupuncture device which is used on point of injury and the body's node points. The Chinese have used acupuncture for centuries, and although it is hard to explain, I can only testify to its success.

Basically, the belief is that the body has a number of lines connecting joints, points and organs. Sometimes these lines of communication get blocked, which results in injury or illness. By stimulating these lines at node points, the acupuncturist breaks down the blockage and revitalises the lines. This can be done with needles or with a very mild electro-stimulus, as is the case with the Healthpoint machine. A circuit is created by holding the machine in one hand and a terminal on the relevant points with the other hand. Each of the designated points is stimulated for 40 seconds, and there are normally about four to six points associated with each diagnosis.

Does it work? I believe it does, and offer this experience as testimony. My father-in-law, Jan Strydom, is a doctor with over 40 years' experience, and also a committed member of the Dutch Reform Church in South Africa. I mention this because as a religion they do not accept acupuncture as a medical solution. As a result of my wife's involvement in sport, Jan is also experienced in sports medicine and has an open mind to finding relevant solutions. When he was over in the UK in 1997, he irritated his lower back by carrying heavy suitcases. This was not a new injury to him, but one that had given him problems over the years. One night, when all else had failed, we tried the Healthpoint on this doubting Thomas. The relief the following day was significant enough to get him using it on a regular basis, and even to consider purchasing one for himself. His view on acupuncture had been changed.

THE USE OF MAGNOTHERAPY

The use of magnets in medical treatment has gained popularity in recent years. One such use has been in the treatment of stress fractures. The limb is placed in a tunnel magnetic field several times per week. The alternating positive and negative charge is thought to activate cell movement and assist in the healing process.

My own experience of magnotherapy began in 1984, when running from John o' Groats to Land's End. As related earlier in the book, I had the unfortunate experience of having to stop running in the Scottish Borders with a stress fracture in my lower left leg. After completing the route on bicycle, the immediate concern then became to recover in time for the Hawaii Ironman competition less than six weeks later. This event would require a 2.4 mile swim, a 112 mile cycle and a 26.2 mile run. I had been loaned a small magnetic pulse machine by a company in Durban and proceeded to keep this 'bandaged' to the affected area of my leg for extended periods each day. At the same time a visit to the physio in Edinburgh saw him pull out a magnotherapy tunnel. Obviously this latter piece of equipment was more effective, purely because of size, but the principle was the same. At that stage I was unsure of how effective this treatment was; however, four weeks later I was back running and on race day completed the course. I would hardly claim that my running fitness was ideal, as it was based more on cycling and one week of load-bearing work.

The next major encounter with magnetism came when I had some knee problems and my orthopaedic surgeon suggested that a MRI scan be considered, as opposed to the orthoscope surgery, to see if there was any internal damage. Basically, MRI, or Magnetic Resonance Imagery, is a means of having an 'internal picture' of the tissue, bones and organs of the body. It's much like an X-ray, but whereas the X-ray only shows bones, MRI can handle soft tissue. In addition, because the images are stored on computer, it is possible to show pictures at different 'slices' through the injured area. The patient is put on to a bed that slides into a tunnel. The different levels of cell activation from the magnetic resonance provide the basis of the images. What is particularly interesting is that many patients say they feel much better or have improved symptoms after the MRI scan. Again this can relate to the use of the magnetism. One of the greatest benefits of MRI is that it is not invasive, whereas surgery must always carry some risk of damage as tissue is cut.

More recently, the use of magnotherapy has become available on a smaller scale in the form of bracelets. One such product comes from

BIOFLOW and makes use of their Central Reverse Polarity Technology that mimics the effects of the larger machines. On one side of the strap there is a strong magnet and there is a smaller one almost on the opposing side. The main magnet is worn over the wrist pulse point. In this way it is in the best position to affect the polarity of the cells. A wide range of benefits has been experienced, including improved athletic performance. Certainly the use of electronic pulse magnetic fields has been proven to penetrate the body and speed recovery; this is purely an extension of this practice. It is also possible to get bandages with magnets placed at strategic points. When put over the injured area, the cell activity is increased to assist repair. It is virtually impossible to monitor the effectiveness of such products because each injury is an experiment of one – everything is different on each occasion. I can only say that I feel it has worked for me on a few occasions. The overriding benefit is that it is readily available and can act as an immediate first step in the treatment of injury.

With regard to wearing a bracelet, I found that it seemed to improve my sleep pattern during periods of high stress. I still feel there is a difference between when I use it and when I don't – and whether that is psychosomatic or not is irrelevant to me. It's the benefit I am after.

WHAT MEDICATION ARE YOU USING?

There is no doubt that more attention is being paid to such homoeopathic and complementary remedies, and scientists and doctors are beginning to understand and accept their role in medicine. It should be noted that homoeopathic remedies have been around for years in Europe, first being used in Germany in the 1700s. The basic principle is to treat like with like, and this makes sense. It is the same principle used, for instance, with the anti-flu jab recommended earlier. Incidentally, there are many other homoeopathic remedies, including those for flu and colds, and they could be worth experimenting with. The place of such remedies in sport looks set, as they obviously do not fall foul of the listing of banned drugs. These products are now being stocked by many pharmacies and are losing their 'witches' brew' label.

Another product that I have found beneficial is a homeopathic 'calmer'. It is an ideal way to get some rest the day before a major event, and, of course, it does not have any side-effects. I do not wish to give the impression that I am against traditional medicine, but all athletes have to look for solutions and benefits from products that are not going to give them problems in drug testing.

CHECK AND RECHECK WHAT YOU TAKE

It's worth pointing out that South African athletes have the advantage of simply checking the Mimms book of drugs in sport to determine if any of the medicines they are using are on the banned list. This book is readily available to every runner. In Britain this is significantly more difficult, as you need to consult with not only your Sports Council but also your national federation doctor. Hopefully a book providing a more widespread listing of products will be available to all sportsmen and women soon. A list of banned substances is given in appendix four.

Don't forget that many of the over-the-counter medicines contain banned substances, and it is your responsibility to ensure that you are not using these.

LEFT: A relaxed training run back on home ground in the Great Scottish Run.

BELOW: Cresting out at 9,000 feet in the Drakensburg mountains during the Mont aux Sources 50km race – 25km up and 25km down to 3,000 feet.

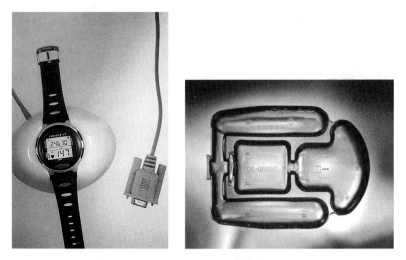

LEFT: Cardiosport heart-rate monitor which stores your heart rate during training and can be downloaded to a computer for analysis; RIGHT: A typical visible air unit for use in the heel of shoes to provide extra cushioning.

The Sinclair X1 FM radio. Weighing just half an ounce, it is comfortable to wear and costs under £10.

4

RACING

CHAPTER TWENTY

TAPERING TO PEAK FOR A RACE

When runners really want to achieve their true potential, they programme their training and racing into segments, often called macro and micro training blocks. This by necessity means that they will be peaking for only a few races. With such limited opportunities to excel, it is important to take full advantage of the training you have done during the build-up period. In the final weeks before the race you need to give some serious thought to how you are going to taper down to the race. It has to be remembered that your training is only as good as the rest and recovery that you allow your body.

Training is a form of breakdown. When the muscles repair during the rest and recovery, they grow stronger, and it is this growth that improves your performance. Few runners dispute these facts nowadays, but the question of how to taper is still one of the great unknowns in sports science.

The taper is the phase of training which allows you to recover from hard training. For a marathon the taper will probably be about a week long; for distances of 5km or 10km it may be only three or four days. However, in the 5km and 10km events there is much more emphasis on speed and race tactics, and thus it is likely that your competitive period stetches over more than one race.

Track runners, even for distance events such as 5,000m and 10,000m, use two or three build-up races in a period of about a month to peak for the major race. Thus they will have a schedule during this period which is low on distance, has lots of technique sessions, and short track sessions done at fairly high intensity with long recovery periods between the intervals. The marathon runner will also tend to reduce distance in the final couple of weeks, and will use fartlek and track sessions to get the bounce and spring back into his or her stride.

Under no circumstances must the taper period tax the runner. The biggest problem runners experience over the taper period is the tendency to test themselves to see just how they are doing. This inevitably leads to them running too fast (or too far) in some sessions and these runners, as a result, will leave their chances of succeeding in the race out on the training roads!

The taper should also be used as a period when runners can concentrate on the race and the tactics and game plan they intend to use. It is an ideal time for mental strengthening.

Whilst other types of training have been the subject of much research, until recently the taper has always been left to the individual to work out. Thankfully a sports scientist in the Netherlands has now turned his attention to this much overlooked aspect.

THE TRIED AND TESTED TAPER

It is widely known that the total quantity of your training should be reduced over the last week to ten days before a race. It is also recognised that hard runs should be kept to a minimum and that there is little chance of damaging your chances if you don't run at all over the last three days. Since the body takes seven to ten days to benefit from a training session, the purpose of the final taper relates more to active rest, circulation and psychological preparation than physiological development.

There has, however, been relatively little information on what speed you should run at in the last week, or what percentage of your total previous weekly distance you should cover. Tapering is thus a bit hit-and-miss at present, with runners sticking to the regime that has given them a good result in the past. They are unwilling to try too much else in case it doesn't produce similar results. This is further complicated by the fact that it is virtually impossible to adjudicate the variations in taper, since the conditions of each race tend to be different.

The long-term research done in the Netherlands has been able to determine what sort of training can be undertaken without muscle damage. In brief, a group of long-distance runners were monitored for a period of 18 to 20 months and their muscle damage assessed on a regular basis. In the first period the 23 runners trained lightly, averaging only 18 miles per week, with a longest run of 8 miles and a 15km racing event after six months. The second period saw training increase to 50km a week, with a maximum long run of 14 miles and a 25km road race. The final period of seven months saw an average of 48 miles per week, with a 20-mile long run and a marathon race at the end.

No runners had muscle damage after the first period of training, but

14 per cent showed damage after the 15km race (this is to be expected after a race). In the second period, 33 per cent of the runners had muscle damage both before and after the race, and in the third period this had increased to 57 per cent with pre-race muscle damage and 62 per cent with post-race damage. Thus 57 per cent of the runners had damage before the marathon!

Remembering that there are many studies that show that recovery from muscle damage can take between three and five weeks, it becomes obvious that it is necessary to reduce weekly mileage to between 20 and 30 miles per week over this final period if you are to line up with 'fresh' muscles. This would involve both an overall drop in weekly distance and a reduction in the length of the 'long' run. Professor Tim Noakes has suggested from his experiments that muscle damage begins when a long run exceeds about 15 miles. It is suggested, then, that the last run longer than 15 miles should be about three weeks prior to the race. This might seem ridiculously low, but remember that your amazement arises from previous resistance to such dramatic cutbacks and natural resistance to change.

The one aspect of the taper that has not been discussed so far is what speed this training should be carried out at, and it is here that the secret of effective tapering lies.

From what has been written in other chapters on maintaining fitness during off-periods and periods of injury, you will remember that there is much proof of the worth of speed work. It should be noted that it is distance that causes muscle damage, not speed, and the important thing is to maintain your average training speed. Within your reduced training schedule you would still keep your 5km run at 10km race pace, and your intervals at 5km race pace, for instance. This means that in fact the average training speed will probably increase as the amount of long, slow running is 'sacrificed' in the weekly distance reduction.

You may also remember comments elsewhere on the fact that the fastest fall-off in fitness comes from a reduction in blood volume and the resultant reduction in VO_2 max. It was, however, found that if one quality session of repeats of about 400m at best 1500m pace was undertaken each week, this decline could be counteracted.

From the above you will see that it is quite possible to reduce your training safely over a two- to three-week period in this way, before reaching the final week before the event. Here more research has come to our help.

The same basic principles are supported by this new work. Research in America suggests that a runner peaking for a 10km or half-marathon should do only speed work for the last week. This is certainly a relatively new view which will be dismissed out of hand by some.

Before you do so, however, consider the details of the recommendations.

The week starts with, say, 6 x 500m at best mile pace, with as much rest as you need between each. This is sandwiched between a warm-up and cool-down of about a mile. The second day requires is 5 x 500m run in the same way, the third day 4 x 500m, and so on, reducing the number of repeats until the penultimate day involves only 1 x 500m. The last day is reserved for total rest.

Compare this schedule to the normal recommendation of a longish run seven days before the race to help depletion of the carbohydrate stores before carbo-loading, then three or four days' light easy running and two or three days of complete rest. (See the section on energy replacement.)

In the speed taper there will certainly be a considerable depletion effect from running 6 x 500m. The amount of glycogen burned up increases with speed and thus it will take a shorter distance to deplete with speed work than it does with long, slow distance.

Another benefit of this taper is that we are preparing ourselves for a race, which will involve some amount of anaerobic work. The speed taper certainly falls into this category, whereas light jogging is aerobic. There should be no doubt about the aerobic qualities of a runner in the final week of training for a distance event or marathon. Running at the faster pace will make the race pace seem easy. In any case, the few miles the runner puts in during the final week will have had no positive effects by race time.

Have you also noticed how light you feel on your feet when you have completed a speed session? This not only boosts your confidence but actually seems to give a physical boost as well – which is certainly what you require before a race. By comparison, running longer distances at slow, easy paces tends to make you feel sluggish and also makes you more likely to go out and 'test' yourself again by running too hard.

But what of the muscle breakdown associated with speed? Putting in only 500m and having long recoveries causes little breakdown, as the muscles are not put under major stress. Furthermore, the total distance of the speed work in the week adds up to only about 21 x 500m = 10.5km. Add the warm-ups and we get a weekly total of 22.5km.

The only danger here is that the runner tries to set PBs in each set, or gives himself too little recovery between the 500m repeats. Limit your speed to your best mile time and allow a minimum of two minutes between each. The quantity of speed taper is recommended as being only 9 per cent of your weekly total; thus a runner doing 60 miles per week would do 5.4 miles of 400m or 500m over the full week. Provided this is done, the speed taper is available to runners of all abilities as it is based on their PB time. In other words, the only difference will be the speed and number of the 400m or 500m intervals.

Let's now compare a typical slower taper, which may look something like this: day seven, 13 to 14 miles; day six, 5 to 6 miles; day five, 5 to 6 miles with pick-ups; day four, 4 to 5 miles; day three until the race, rest. This gives a total for the week of between 27 and 31 miles, most of which will be done at slower than race pace.

The only drawback to this whole system is that I suspect it will work only for those runners who are used to doing some form of speed work, even if it's only fartlek. The speed taper appears to have many advantages, and to me it makes a lot of sense for the runner who has trained to peak for a particular race. On the other hand, the conservative method of slow and easy running and rest is a good way to ensure that you go into the race rested, but it may not take you to your peak of fitness.

My own experiences and testing of these taper methods before long events have convinced me that the speed taper has a lot to offer. The psychological boost of faster work in the last week has overwhelming advantages.

CHAPTER TWENTY-ONE

RACE PREPARATION

Some runners seem to think that if they do the training the result will automatically come. To a certain extent this is true but the longer the race, the more thought has to go into the race plan and hence the race preparation. Apart from anything else this is because the longer the race, the more opportunity there is for things to go wrong! This seems obvious, but an unusual set of circumstances in 1989 showed me that many people had not really come to terms with it.

Early in 1989 I was training for a journey run of 1,800km across Africa, which was to involve a number of large companies in the launch of the now annual Ithuba event. I planned to start my heavy training in June, build through Comrades, and then culminate in the journey race in August.

This meant that, as had been the case for the previous six years, I would train around 200km in the week of Comrades. Typically this meant a 20km to 25km run three days before Comrades; 1km repeats two days before; a very easy 10km to 12km the day before; Comrades; and then 10km very easy the following day and a rest the day after. As a result I had generally been satisfied with anything under 7:00 and had frequently run with another runner most of the way.

This year, however, I was told ten days before Comrades to hold back on the training as the journey run would be delayed as a result of negotiations with TV. So, unsure when the run would take place, I just carried on with about 100km a week and on Comrades day started out running with a group going for a time of 6:30.

Going through halfway in 3:12 I was probably placed well over 300th position, but was finding it uncomfortable to stay back with many of the runners. Without increasing my speed I actually started moving forward through the pack. By Botha's Hill I was still feeling fresh and increased the pace a bit, so by the time I met my spectator friends at Kloof I had moved up substantially – so much so that triathlon teammate Philip Kuhn almost dropped his beer!

I had left a radio with Mike Bell at Cowie's Hill and, once I had managed to tune it, heard the commentator relating that Frith van der Merwe (the leading lady, who was to set a new course record) was now in the top 20, having earlier passed Mark Page, whom I had just passed. I realised that I was now quite high up and pushed a bit harder over the last 10km, although, as anyone who saw me at the finish will testify, I was still fairly fresh. Indeed, I immediately ran to my car and went back up to Kloof to second a friend.

My time was 6:07, my position 27th, but what was most surprising was the flood of congratulations I received in the following weeks. Many of the good wishes came from running administrators, and this was very gratifying. But the time was not as good by comparison as some of my 100 mile times in previous years. I had been tested by Westville University in March and they had predicted a Comrades time of under 6:00.

The point is that a 100 mile race is twice the length of Comrades and thus there is twice as long for the weather to be adverse. It has been estimated that any race run in an effective temperature of 25°C is 7 per cent slower than the same race run in 20°C or less. The 100 mile races in South Africa that start during the day frequently reach temperatures of over 30°C. This fact had obviously escaped many of the people who had gone out of their way to congratulate me. My good time in Comrades was therefore much easier to achieve than an equivalent time in the 100 mile race would have been.

I hope this will not be construed as being ungrateful. That is not the intention, which is rather to point out that long races have to be planned. Don't fall into the trap of thinking that double the distance means a straightforward double the time.

PLANNING

Race preparation can be classified into a number of aspects, the most obvious being training, which has been dealt with. Then there is the question of fluid and energy replacement, which is covered later. But perhaps one of the most important considerations is pacing for the race. This is the product of two things. First, one has to know what is a realistic target time, and then one has to set some sort of schedule to attain it. This pacing schedule has to be flexible enough to allow for variations on the day.

The approach of the lead runners will generally differ from that of the back runners in as much as the top runners are going for a win and thus see tactics as more important than finishing time. Of course, the lead runners must still have some idea of what they are capable of if they are not to fade. The back runners, however, can concentrate on achieving a time goal, and will generally actually receive assistance from the runners around them.

Logistic planning is another area that has to be considered. For most runners this is simple: all they have to do is turn up at the start of the race with sufficient time to enter and warm up. Refreshments, routes and other important requirements are all taken care of by the organisers. Runners going for a win may organise somone to give them a time split or tactical information, but generally they can simply roll up on the day of the race and run.

In longer events there may be a need for helpers (or seconds, as they are known) along the route. Perhaps there are special drinks or food to be taken. Then there is food and drink to be provided for the seconds if it is an all-day event. Vehicles may be required, and so on. In track ultras you may be required to provide two lap scorers for the whole length of the event. It's often very hard to find people to do this thankless task, especially since they will be asked to lap-score some runner unknown to them. Peace of mind comes only with the knowledge that everything is in place.

The final aspect that needs to be considered in the making of race plans is your mental approach to the race. To a large extent, if all the other areas of preparation have been sorted out, the runner will already be over halfway down the road to having a positive approach to the race. Runners can gain great confidence by knowing that everything has been planned for and that all that is left to do is run the race.

In journey events a positive approach has much to do with having a top-class second. I have been very lucky over the years to have Andy Booth second me over many of my long runs. Andy was also my first partner for the 100 mile three-day Duzi canoe marathon and was one of the first friends I made in South Africa. He knows me so well that he can actually predict what I am going to want and frequently meets me with, say, a cup of soup at a seconding point when that's exactly what I have been craving for the last 2km.

In journey runs the runner runs, sleeps and eats. Everything else is the job of the second. If my hat blows off, the second will go back to get it, so that I will not have to travel twice the distance before moving forward. Every metre counts! With that sort of back-up, who wouldn't be confident?

Although much of the above relates to the long events, the same principles and requirements apply to shorter, more common events from 5km upwards.

SETTING A REALISTIC TARGET

Earlier in the book we had a look at the concept of each individual having a maximum oxygen-processing capacity (VO_2 max) which, when combined with the threshold-point measure of efficiency, gives an indication of a runner's potential. As pointed out at the time it is possible to improve these to some extent, but major improvements cannot be expected.

When these parameters have been determined for an individual, it is possible to estimate his or her potential time for a race of any distance using mathematical formulae. These times will be particularly accurate for distances between 5km and 30 miles, but tend to become less accurate at either end, although modification factors can be applied to correct this.

Using these principles, I have written a computer program which will allow runners first to determine their own profiles based on their previous race results, and then to predict their times for a given distance. Thus, without going near a laboratory, which is the common way of determining VO_2 max and threshold point, runners can get an indication of their potential.

In many ways this method is more accuarate than lab testing, although the figure for the VO_2 max will be a general indication only and of use only relative to other VO_2 max figures determined on the same program. However, its accuracy rests on the fact that it is based on the runner's race capacity. Running on a treadmill in a lab requires a different skill and involves having various heart monitors and breathing tubes attached to the runner, who is also working in a stationary position in a very hot and humid indoor climate. I know this disrupts my style.

On the other hand, if I run three races flat out on flat courses I will obviously be running with the same potential as when I am running the race for which I want to predict my time. If the race is over a hilly course, I should use three race times over similar courses as the basis for my prediction.

An additional benefit of the computer program is that once it has your profile you can use it to determine the time in which you need to run a distance in order to be running at 85 per cent or 90 per cent effort. Alternatively, given a distance and a time, the program will tell you at what percentage of effort you ran. Both options can be of great assistance in ensuring that you don't race in your training.

This program has been written for IBM-compatible personal computers and is discussed more fully in chapter 22 on computerised training and race prediction.

To predict:

- Half-marathon time from 10km time: double 10km time and add 5 to 8 minutes
- Marathon time from half-marathon time: double half-marathon time and add between 5 and 10 minutes
- 35 mile time from marathon time: marathon time x 1.42
- 55 mile (London to Brighton) time from 35 mile time: 35 mile x 1.71

In 1985 I compared the best marathon times of gold medal Comrades runners with their Comrades times. By dividing their Comrades (55 miles) times by their marathon (26.2 miles) times I ended up with a ratio. What surprised me about this was that, despite the fact that I had made no allowance for either the direction or the ever-changing distance of Comrades, in statistical terms the ratios were very close. I then added them up, divided the result by the number of runners and came up with an average factor of 2.42. Thus I suggested that the quickest way of predicting your Comrades time was to multiply your best recent marathon time by 2.42.

Early in 1989 I received a letter from Jan Louw in Johannesburg which informed me of a useful modification of my idea of a ratio for predicting a Comrades time from a marathon time. Jan had come up with a formula that took account not only of a runner's ability over the marathon but also of the amount of training done by the runner between January and May. This obviously makes a lot of sense, since running a 3:00 marathon in March and then becoming a couch potato until race day (which in those days was always 31 May) would certainly not give you a Comrades time comparable to your potential.

Jan also includes additional factors to make allowance for the number of years that a runner has been training, for a runner's sex, for an up or down run, and so on. The resulting table (Table 21.1) has been reproduced here with modifications to the dates, as I feel it will be a very useful tool for anyone in the UK who wishes to try a move up in distance to the 55 mile London to Brighton.

One point I would draw to your attention is that a 3:00 marathon runner need only do about 56 miles (90km) a week to be able to win a silver medal; even if this runner trained at 73 miles (120km) a week he or she would improve only to around a 7:00 Comrades. This would still be a silver medal time. Because Comrades distance varies, the route changes, the direction changes and so on, one must ask whether this runner would not be better off running for a safe silver, with as little training as possible, and saving heavy training for improving his or her

Table 21.1

TIME PREDICTION TABLE (DOWN RUN)

Copyright © J.A. Louw 1988

Current performance		5	13.52	14.31	15.11	15.50	16.30	17.09	17.49	18.29	19.08	19.48	20.27	21.07	21.47	22.26	23.06	23.45	24.25	25.05	25.44	26.24	27.03	27.30
		8	22.54	23.59	25.05	26.10	27.15	28.21	29.26	30.32	31.37	32.43	33.48	34.53	35.59	37.04	38.10	39.15	40.21	41.26	42.31	43.37	44.42	45.27
		10	29.04	30.27	31.50	33.13	34.36	35.59	37.22	38.45	40.08	41.31	42.54	44.17	45.40	47.03	48.26	49.49	51.12	52.35	53.58	55.21	56.44	57.41
Race distance (km)		15	0.45	0.47	0.49	0.51	0.53	0.55	0.58	1.00	1.02	1.04	1.06	1.08	1.10	1.13	1.15	1.17	1.19	1.21	1.23	1.25	1.27	1.29
		21	1.05	1.08	1.11	1.14	1.17	1.20	1.23	1.26	1.29	1.32	1.35	1.38	1.41	1.44	1.48	1.51	1.54	1.57	2.00	2.03	2.06	2.08
		32	1.41	1.45	1.50	1.55	2.00	2.05	2.09	2.14	2.19	2.24	2.29	2.33	2.38	2.43	2.48	2.53	2.57	3.02	3.07	3.12	3.17	3.20
		42	2.15	2.22	2.28	2.35	2.41	2.48	2.54	3.00	3.07	3.13	3.20	3.26	3.33	3.39	3.46	3.52	3.58	4.05	4.11	4.18	4.24	4.29
		50	2.45	2.53	3.01	3.08	3.16	3.24	3.32	3.40	3.48	3.56	4.03	4.11	4.19	4.27	4.35	4.43	4.50	4.58	5.06	5.14	5.22	5.27
		56	3.10	3.19	3.28	3.37	3.46	3.55	4.04	4.13	4.22	4.31	4.40	4.49	4.58	5.07	5.16	5.25	5.34	5.43	5.52	6.01	6.10	6.16
TRAINING GRID KM per week																								
May & June	July & August	Total - May to 1st week Oct																						
127	156	2600	5.15																					
121	149	2482	5.17	5.30																				
116	142	2374	5.20	5.32	5.45																			
111	136	2275	5.22	5.34	5.47	6.00																		
106	131	2184	5.25	5.37	5.49	6.02	6.15																	
102	126	2100	5.28	5.39	5.52	6.04	6.17	6.30																
99	121	2022	5.31	5.42	5.54	6.07	6.19	6.32	6.45															
95	117	1950	5.33	5.45	5.57	6.09	6.22	6.34	6.47	7.00														
92	113	1883	5.36	5.48	6.00	6.12	6.24	6.37	6.49	7.02	7.15													
89	109	1820	5.39	5.51	6.03	6.15	6.27	6.39	6.52	7.04	7.17	7.30												
86	106	1761	5.42	5.53	6.06	6.18	6.30	6.42	6.54	7.06	7.19	7.32	7.45											
83	102	1706	5.45	5.56	6.09	6.21	6.33	6.45	6.57	7.09	7.21	7.34	7.47	8.00										
81	99	1655	5.48	5.59	6.12	6.24	6.36	6.48	7.00	7.12	7.24	7.36	7.49	8.02	8.15									
78	96	1606	5.51	6.02	6.14	6.27	6.39	6.51	7.03	7.15	7.27	7.39	7.51	8.04	8.16	8.30								
76	94	1560	5.53	6.05	6.17	6.30	6.42	6.54	7.06	7.18	7.30	7.42	7.54	8.07	8.19	8.31	8.45							
74	91	1517	5.56	6.07	6.20	6.33	6.45	6.58	7.10	7.22	7.34	7.45	7.57	8.09	8.21	8.34	8.46	9.00						
72	89	1476	5.58	6.10	6.23	6.36	6.48	7.01	7.13	7.25	7.37	7.49	8.01	8.13	8.24	8.36	8.49	9.02	9.15					
70	86	1437	6.01	6.12	6.26	6.39	6.51	7.04	7.16	7.28	7.40	7.52	8.04	8.16	8.27	8.39	8.51	9.04	9.16	9.30				
68	84	1400	6.03	6.15	6.28	6.42	6.54	7.07	7.19	7.32	7.44	7.56	8.07	8.19	8.31	8.42	8.54	9.07	9.18	9.31	9.45			
67	82	1365	6.06	6.17	6.31	6.44	6.57	7.10	7.23	7.35	7.47	7.59	8.11	8.23	8.34	8.46	8.58	9.10	9.21	9.33	9.46	10.00		
65	80	1332	6.08	6.20	6.34	6.47	7.00	7.13	7.26	7.38	7.51	8.03	8.15	8.27	8.38	8.50	9.01	9.13	9.24	9.36	9.48	10.02	10.15	
63	78	1300	6.10	6.22	6.36	6.50	7.03	7.16	7.29	7.42	7.54	8.06	8.18	8.30	8.42	8.53	9.05	9.17	9.28	9.39	9.51	10.04	10.16	10.26
62	76	1270	6.12	6.24	6.39	6.52	7.06	7.19	7.32	7.45	7.57	8.10	8.22	8.34	8.46	8.57	9.09	9.21	9.31	9.43	9.54	10.07	10.19	10.27
59	72	1200	6.17	6.32	6.47	7.01	7.16	7.29	7.43	7.56	8.10	8.22	8.35	8.48	9.00	9.12	9.23	9.36	9.46	9.58	10.09	10.21	10.32	10.39
54	66	1100	6.25	6.41	6.56	7.11	7.26	7.40	7.55	8.09	8.23	8.37	8.50	9.03	9.16	9.29	9.42	9.54	10.05	10.17	10.29	10.41	10.52	10.59
49	60	1000	6.33	6.49	7.05	7.21	7.37	7.52	8.08	8.23	8.37	8.52	9.06	9.20	9.34	9.48	10.01	10.15	10.27	10.40	10.53	11.06	11.18	11.26
44	54	900	6.41	6.58	7.15	7.32	7.49	8.05	8.21	8.37	8.53	9.08	9.23	9.39	9.53	10.08	10.23	10.37	10.51	11.05	11.19	11.33	11.46	11.55
39	48	800	6.50	7.08	7.26	7.43	8.01	8.18	8.35	8.52	9.08	9.25	9.41	9.58	10.13	10.29	10.44	11.00	11.14	11.29	11.43	11.58	12.11	12.20

times at shorter distances. This in turn would have the effect of improving his or her potential at the Comrades. It's all a matter of priorities! Likewise anyone who can't manage a 3:15 marathon, assuming it's been a flat-out effort, is not Comrades silver-medal material.

There have often been stories of runners who say they were able to complete Comrades with less than the minimum 800km training indicated in the table. This is by no means impossible. A look at the table will show that a runner who has the potential to run a 3:00 marathon can expect an 8:52 Comrades with only 800km of training, and would probably be capable of finishing in under 11:00 with very little distance training. The key, however, will still be for the runner to set a realistic target in the light of the training, and to adopt a suitable pacing strategy. At present there are no awards based on time in the London to Brighton race, but there are different time standards awarded for races by the Road Runners' Club. A similar approach could be adopted for these as the Comrades gold, silver and bronze medals.

DECIDING ON RACE PACE

Even before you enter a race you should know how you intend running it. Perhaps you think that once you have a realistic target it will be easy to determine at what pace you will run. Just divide the distance into your target time and you will know your pace – right? Wrong. You must also allow for the terrain over which the race is run, and what you should be aiming for is even *effort*, not even pace.

Get all the information you can about the course beforehand. You should be able to anticipate the hills, the corners, what effect changing weather might have, and so on. Try to live the race before you run it; try to ensure that you have planned it.

Planning gives confidence, and confidence is something every winner needs. A sports psychologist has noted that the winners are the athletes who think that they can win before the race starts, and that is the truth of the matter.

In the shorter races and over flattish courses it is fairly easy to keep a relatively constant pace, and this will deliver an optimum time since it uses up energy at a constant rate. As with cars, it is acceleration that eats up fuel, so even pacing is generally the most efficient approach to racing.

COLLAPSE POINT

Table 21.2 How far can you go?
Basic Mileage Requirements   1 mile = 1.6km

WEEKLY TOTAL (miles)	PER DAY (miles)	'COLLAPSE' (miles)	MAX. RACE (miles)
10	1½	5	3
15	2¼	7	5
20	3	9	6
25	3½	11	8
30	4¼	13	10 (16 km)
35	5	15	13 (½ mar.)
40	5¾	17	15
45	6½	20	19 *
50	7	21	19 *
55	7¾	23	20 (32 km)
60	8½	26	20
65	9¼	28	marathon
70	10	30	marathon
75	10¾	32	50 km
80	11½	34½	56 km
85	12¼	37	
90	12¾	39	64 km
95	13½	41	
100	14¼	43	
110 (177 km)	15¾	47	Comrades
130 (209 km)	18½	56	

'Collapse point' is approximately three times the daily average; maximum racing distance should be slightly below the collapse point.

*20 kilometres is slightly less than 13 miles, the half marathon slightly more; 30 kilometres is just below 19 miles; 31 miles is about 50 kilometres.

Therefore, by implication, to race 100 miles:
   Weekly distance = 234 miles   = 375 km   = 54 km/day
   Even at 5 min/km = 270 mins   i.e. 4½ hours

Extract from Step Up to Racing, *World Publications, 1975*

The distance you can race depends on the distance you have been training. Table 21.2 illustrates the American rule of thumb that relates average weekly training distance to a collapse point, and hence to the maximum distance you should race.

To run, for instance, the London to Brighton according to this approach one would have to train about 190km a week at peak times.

This is a realistic figure for the dedicated medallists, but for most of us it is an impossible weekly distance. There just isn't enough time to recover. If you intend tackling a race whose distance is beyond your collapse point, I suggest that you try a run-and-walk schedule.

In 1989 I was asked to give a club clinic in Durban, where my run-walk theory was fairly well known as a result of my newspaper articles. The person who spoke before me was one of Natal's women runners, who had run Comrades around the 7:30 mark for a few years. I was horrified at her advice to aspiring Comrades runners to 'start off running and keep running until you can run no more, then walk until you can walk no more, and then crawl if necessary'.

It is obvious that the great majority of runners do not do sufficient training to enable them to run Comrades non-stop. If they try to do so, at some stage they will be forced to walk, knowing that they have used up their energy. They are condemned to shuffle painfully to the finish.

Such an approach is like tramping down on the car accelerator until the tank is on reserve and then hoping blindly that there's enough petrol left to take you to the end of the journey. Or it's like lifting too much weight all at once and then being unable to lift even the slightest load; whereas lifting a lesser weight allows you to lift the same weight several times over.

It is the same with running. Let's say your fastest 400m run is 65 seconds. If, after a flat-out 65-second effort, you tried to run another fast 400m, you would either get cramp or slow down to 80 or 90 seconds at best. On the other hand, if I were to ask you to do ten runs of 400m at 70 seconds with a short break in between, it would be easy.

This is the principle behind the run-walk theory, and it works. Club runners have used it to achieve their best marathon times, let alone London to Brighton times.

Table 21.3 shows you how to work out a run-walk schedule.

Table 21.3 Run-walk schedule

Best marathon	=	3 hr 30 min
Average pace	=	4 mins 58 sec/km
Best predicted L. to B.	=	3 hr 30 x 2.42 = 8 hr 28 min
Average pace	=	5 min 46 sec/km
Allow for walk of 3 minutes every 8 km		
Distance say 88 km		
No of walks	=	9
Time walking	=	27 minutes
Distance walked	=	2.5 km
Distance per walk	=	275 m

Time for running	=	8 hr 28 − 27 = 8 hr 1 min = 481 min
Distance to run	=	88 − 2.5 km = 85.5 km
Average speed	=	5 min 37 sec/km
Time per run	=	(8 − 0.275) 5 min 37 sec
	=	43 min 27 sec

DISTANCE	TIME	DISTANCE	TIME
8	45 mins	48.275	4:40:18
8.275	48 mins	56	5:23:45
16	1:31:28	56.275	5:26:45
16.275	1:34:28	64	6:10:13
24	2:17:55	64.275	6:13:13
24.275	2:20:55	72	6:56:40
32	3:04:23	72.275	6:59:40
32.275	3:07:23	80	7:43:07
40	3:50	80.275	7:46:07
40.275	3:50	88	8:28:00
* 48	4:37:18		

$$\frac{* \text{ MARATHON}}{\text{BEST MARATHON}} = \frac{4 \text{ HR } 05 \text{ MIN}}{3 \text{ HR } 30 \text{ MIN}} = 126\%$$

LOGISTICS

It is important, after all the effort of training, not to leave logistical details to chance. Weeks before a major race you should know how you are going to get to the start, particularly if the race is in another city and you need to book a hotel room, and so on,

If you are sleeping in a strange bed it is better to take your own pillow with you, as hotel pillows never seem to be as comfortable as your own. What about eating arrangements? Will you be able to get your favourite pre-race meal there? Must you take food with you? In short, try to ensure that you will be able to maintain your normal schedule wherever you go. It will pay off.

If the race is a local one, logistics are still important. You must make sure that you arrive with enough time to enter, have one last visit to the loo, and warm up and change for the race. Have you put out all your kit the night before? Is the entry fee ready? Anything that needs doing is worth doing the night before, if possible.

Finally, on the subject of sleeping, don't worry too much about a restless night before the race; rather, ensure a good sleep two nights before. Very few runners sleep well immediately before a race, but too many of them lie in bed worrying about it. This additional worry makes sleep less easy, and so the vicious circle continues.

If you find yourself unable to sleep, lie back and realise that it's merely the excitement of the race that is making it hard to sleep. Remind yourself how well you slept the previous night. Accept that you might not sleep much and tell yourself that you can simply lie there and relax. When you take the pressure off, you will be surprised how fast you fall asleep!

RACE DAY

Have a plan for race day. Know how to get to the start. If you are going to use the lift in the hotel, remember that there will probably be many other runners doing the same thing and that will take time. What about your position at the starting line? Do you know where you want to stand and how you are going to get into place? All these things need to be worked out.

Helen Lucre tells a marvellous story of her 1985 Comrades. Although she lived in Westville, she thought it best to stay in the Royal Hotel the night before. The starting line was right outside the hotel, so she reasoned staying there would be the easiest way of ensuring a good position while still having time to lie in late.

All went well until the morning of the race, when she opted to use the fire escape rather than wait for the lifts, which were full of other runners. When she went out on to the fire escape, the door closed behind her. A few flights down she tried to open the door to get back inside and found that it would not open from the outside. Panic! Luckily she found an open door into the kitchen, which ensured her freedom, although it gave the chefs a shock. She got to the starting line in time and went on to win that Comrades, but it could have been very different.

So, you can see that planning can be vital. You must know beforehand whether you are going to have something to eat; you must make sure you have a bottle of water to take with you to the start. Check that the fire-escape doors open!

MENTAL APPROACH

There is no doubt in my mind that one of the factors that makes the difference between a win and second place, between achieving a goal and failing, is the mental attitude of the competitor. If you think something will go wrong, you can bet your bottom dollar it will.

As a lecturer I believe that many students will reach only the level their teachers expect them to reach. If the lecturer doesn't think a student will do well in a class, chances are that he or she won't. In other words, the student senses the lecturer's assessment of his or her abilities, and proceeds to live up (or down) to it. If you know your coach does not feel you are ready for a race, it is unlikely that you will do well.

Building a positive attitude towards your goal is an important objective throughout your training. This does not mean being unrealistic, but it does mean casting aside unsubstantiated doubts and concentrating on your strengths.

The concept I discussed earlier of building a ladder to success has everything to do with this need to build a positive attitude. As each short-term goal is achieved, the runner's confidence increases.

One of the techniques that top sportspeople use in this regard is visualisation. A sports psychologist who interviewed a number of sporting greats found that all imagined themselves competing in the event beforehand: they would visualise themselves sinking a putt, putting away a backhand smash, or running a four-minute mile. It's worth trying.

In road running it is necessary to visualise exactly what you are going to do when you come to a hill, how to handle the race and, most importantly, how you feel as you see yourself crossing the line within your target time.

It has often been said that we use only a fraction of our mental ability and that it is our mental view of ourselves that restricts our physical ability. I firmly believe this, and I need only relate the story of the mother who lifted a truck with one hand to free her trapped son to show what our bodies can do if the desire and drive are great enough. The same principle prevented people from running sub-four-minute miles until Roger Bannister proved that it was not impossible. Within a few months many others had also broken through the same barrier.

When I was at school I was always last in the 100-yard dash, and last around the rugby field. Even my first 7:09 Comrades 'showed' me that I had endurance and not speed! Then Richard Turnbull suggested that I did have speed as well and eventually I started to believe it. Now that I know I have a lot more speed than I previously thought, my times over the shorter distances are coming down.

Even as I moved into the veterans' category (40 plus), I recorded times that were better than those I managed when I was years younger. I know that when I give up the longer distances and concentrate on the shorter distances I will be even faster, because I not only have speed, but believe that I have it. It was only my attitude that slowed me down in the past. I may not set any records, but I shall still improve my times, and that will make running worthwhile.

On the other hand, it is important to realise that there is a limit to one's concentration-span; thus to focus on one goal for months on end can actually become detrimental, since it can result in unbearable anxiety by the time the event occurs. What is needed is a balance between desire and anxiety.

Anyone who has seen *Chariots of Fire* will remember the scene in the changing-room after Harold Abrahams had won a gold medal. One of his team-mates wanted to congratulate him and give him some champagne but the others stopped him, saying that Harold should be left alone because he had just won a gold medal.

This might have seemed strange to some people, but I didn't find it strange at all. When you are aiming for something like a major win, your whole life becomes directed towards it. At the time it seems that achieving your goal will be the only thing that will ensure another sunrise. As soon as you do achieve it, however, you experience a sense of anti-climax that can be very hard to bear. Behind it is the realisation that in fact the sun would not have failed to rise even if you had failed. At the critical time, however, it was that exclusive focus and mental determination that made the difference between a good effort and that special 110 per cent race.

INCENTIVE

The driving force that we talk of is implicitly linked to your 'need' to compete, and this frequently results from some success-linked incentive.

There can be little doubt that South Africa is one of the best countries in the world for training and racing as an endurance athlete, partly because the climate is extremely conducive to training each day. I also firmly believe that South Africa's return to international racing will eventually prove that they have the world's best at every distance from 10km upwards. Not all of these runners have come to the fore as yet, but with the sort of talent that put 11 South Africans in the top 15 fastest 15km runners in 1990, and a world best from Elana Meyer in 1991, the indications are there. There are many other examples to substantiate this claim.

On the other hand, the isolation of the past had to some extent robbed many of the top runners of the incentive to achieve their true potential. After all, racing at major events was always against the same competitors, and most had very predictable tactics. Matthews Temane was known to wait to use his kick, a tactic he passed on to his protégé Adam Motlagale, the 1991 15km champion; Xolile Yawa used surges;

the Tsebe brothers destroyed the opposition as a team – there were few dark horses to really create challenges. Could it be that the reason the 10km and 21.1km records fell in 1989 was that Colleen de Reuck was challenged for the first time for some time by Elana Meyer? Prior to that Colleen had dominated unchallenged and, as we all know, when it really gets tough out there it's easier to cruise in if there is no one else to challenge you. This is not to say that Colleen or other athletes had consciously put in anything less than a 100 per cent effort, but that extra 10 per cent that sets records comes from the incentive of a challenger.

For this reason I didn't believe that we had seen the best of Colleen or many of the other top athletes, and this view seems to be vindicated by results since South Africa returned to tackle the opportunities of international competition. De Reuck and Meyer have both competed in the Olympics and World Championships at 10,000m and the marathon, Joshua Thugwane won the Olympic marathon in 1996 and set a new South African record of 2:07 for the marathon in 1997. Ezakiel Sepeng not only broke the long-standing South African 800m record, but also medalled in a number of top international competitions. South Africa arguably did as well or better than Britain in the Olympics and World Championships. Why the sudden upsurge in South African performances? Greater challenges and greater incentives.

How does this affect the majority of runners? The point is that incentive and challenge are essential to achieving top performances. Incentives can be anything – money, trophies, silver medals, even prizes not connected to the race, such as a meal out with family or friends. Thus, if you are aiming for a best performance in an event, let your family and friends become part of the challenge. This will benefit you because it will force you to make a public commitment to your goal. This awakens in you the need to do what you have said you will, and that in itself can be a great driving force.

Another benefit is that this involves the people close to you in your sport, making them view the time you spend training more sympathetically. Suddenly you can find that you are competing with them as your support team, and success or failure is something you can share with them.

No matter how long the race, if we are running to our potential we all have to bite the bullet over the last quarter. In a 10km race this is only for six to ten minutes; in a marathon it's up to six miles, or about an hour; in 100 mile races it can seem forever. The support gained from friends, the need to run for them, the need to gain that incentive, the 'prize' – all of these keep you going.

Another way to improve you chances of achieving your ambitions is to select other runners who you know will run roughly the time you are aiming for, and then set out to beat them. Evenly matched training partners can be good in this regard, but so can a runner who is consistently just ahead of you over your target distance.

It's probably safer to pick a couple of these runners, in case one decides not to run your target race. Your 'incentive' can then be to beat one or more of these runners. When the going gets tough, you can draw on your competitive element to pull you on and you will have someone in particular to get ahead of. Careful selection of this person should also give you your personal best time.

Perhaps the best recorded use of this method is Roger Bannister's attack on the four-minute mile. Training and racing in a highly competitive group assisted him through the historical barrier. What is also of interest is that, despite the fact everyone said it was impossible, once it had been achieved once, the four-minute barrier was broken a number of times in the following months.

These strategies cannot be improvised at the beginning of a race, but are rather planned in the same way that you plan your training to culminate at the race. You must determine your incentives, challengers and goals weeks in advance and then visualise and live your success during your training. Come the race, the incentives, correct training and the looming rewards of achieving your goal will take you through the darkness of the last quarter.

The incentive of large cash prizes, international competition, appearance money, recognition and so on resulted in the highest number of runners breaking 7:00 in a single 100km race in Stellenbosch in 1989. It also resulted in a world record. Similar prizes have resulted in many South African records over the years, and in major upsets in many Olympics. The rewards may not be the same for the average runner, but use of incentives and competition can do much to help you achieve your goals.

So now you are ready to race. You have planned the training with a set goal in mind, and intermediate goals along the way. You have trained concentrating on your weaknesses and with an eye on the specific requirements of the challenge. You know what time you are aiming for, you know the game plan you are going to use to reach your target during the race, you know how you are getting to the race, and you are mentally attuned and prepared for the challenge . . . it's in the bag! All you are doing now is reliving it all. The race is the easy part. Good luck!

CHAPTER TWENTY-TWO

COMPUTERISED RACE PREDICTION

This chapter is about the computer program that I have written to assist runners in predicting a realistic target time for any race they wish to enter. The program may also be used to establish training paces and efforts. Both facilities use performances previously recorded by the runner. The program may be obtained from Penprint c.c., PO Box 642, Durban 4000, South Africa.

WHY THE PROGRAM WORKS

Earlier I discussed the concept of an athlete's ability being related to physiological characteristics such as VO_2 max, and noted that these characteristics could be measured in a sports laboratory and used by a sports scientist to predict an athlete's potential time. I also noted that an improvement in these measurements could be expected as a result of training, and that this would be linked to an improvement in time.

There are many drawbacks to this approach, however. First, it means going to a specialist laboratory and spending about an hour running on a treadmill. At set intervals expelled air and blood samples will be taken for analysis. This procedure involves discomfort from pipes that have to be attached to the mouth and from the needles used to draw blood.

Second, the fact that the runner is tested on a treadmill means that he or she is not running with a natural action. In addition, there is no wind and thus cooling is a problem. On the other hand, the 'conditions' are identical for everyone, and this is a good basis for scientific comparison between runners.

The third difficulty with this method is that running in a stationary position with no variety in scenery can have a negative psychological effect on the runner. Sure, some runners may be determined to compete against the machine, but the boredom of the treadmill may alter the performance of others.

So if the objective is to compare one runner with another in controlled conditions, the laboratory offers the best method, but if the objective is to predict a runner's performance, I feel my program has more to offer.

The program constructs a 'model' of the runner on the basis of three past performances at any distance, and from this it determines the potential performance of the runner at any other distance.

The advantage of this is that it takes into account the runner's actual running style and the mechanics that he or she used while running previous races. Because it is based on previous performances, it automatically allows for any competitiveness or anxiety that improves or detracts from the athlete's performance.

One can also use the program to predict performance in a particular race by using data from performances over similar courses and in similar conditions. Thus one can take into account the runner's like or dislike of hill running, the ability to deal with heat, and downhill running.

The program can be used to mirror fairly accurately the conditions that can be expected to prevail in the race and so provides an accurate assessment of potential. Everything on which the prediction is based is related to actual racing conditions.

The flaw is that the program uses a mathematical model to extrapolate a time from one distance for time over another distance, but since the scientists do the same, this drawback is common to the laboratory too.

PREDICTING A RACE TIME

Access to the program is protected by means of a password. Thereafter three past performances over any variety of distances can be entered. When this is done three VO_2 max values will appear on the screen. These values are in no way related to the value of VO_2 max that would be determined in the lab; they are simply 'comparative' figures for performance.

If, for instance, the top VO_2 max figure was 58, the second 60 and the third 57, it would indicate that the runner's performance in the second race was the best, while the first performance was superior to the third. In other words, these VO_2 max figures give a relative rating for the entries.

This can be of use in itself. If, for example, entry one were a 21km race, entry two a marathon and entry three a 10km race, then the VO_2 max figures in our example would suggest that this runner's training needed to emphasise speed, since it appears that the speed endurance here is high in comparison to the ability to use pure speed, i.e. he has an affinity for distance events.

If, on the other hand, entry one were a marathon, entry two a 10km race and entry three a 56km race, it would suggest that the runner was lacking in endurance and that his or her training should include more long, slow runs.

The program then computes a working figure for VO_2 max which is used to predict a time for the race. The proposed race distance and a rough estimate of time are then entered, followed by the percentage of effort. Obviously, for a full race this will always be 100 per cent, but this facility is of endless help in writing training schedules, as will be seen below. The computer will then return the predicted time in minutes.

This output is then followed by a number of other questions which allow you to vary the percentage effort, and a pacing chart for the race will result.

This program has been used quite extensively in South Africa and has proved to be accurate to the minute in a number of cases, from 10km events through to Comrades, for both the gold medallists and the back-markers. It was used to predict Frith van der Merwe's 1990 marathon record to within a second and Elana Meyer's 1991 record to within five seconds – so it certainly has a track record of note.

WORKING OUT RACE PACING

Another feature of the program is its ability to give a race pacing chart for any race distance. Two methods are used here. First there is the run-all-the-way method of pacing for those who wish to run the entire race. It incorporates information from research about slowing down during long races (slow-down quotient). Second, there is a method of pacing for those who want to incorporate some walking.

These are straightforward systems which can print out paces, times and average speeds for any number of splits in a race.

DETERMINING TRAINING EFFORT

After entering your performance for three previous races, you can select an option that allows you to determine just how hard a run has been in terms of your previous race performances and fitness. When you input the race distance and time taken, the computer will give the percentage effort used for the run. This, of course, will be over 100 per cent if you have improved beyond your previous fitness level, and will be below 100 per cent if you held back.

Frequently the problem for the runner is to decide what is an easy run and what a hard run. We are told, for example, to do a training run at 85 per cent effort, but few of us have any idea of what that is. This program solves the problem.

All you have to do is to choose three races over courses comparable to that of the training run that you intend doing, and enter a 'race prediction' format. When asked what effort you want to use for the run, enter 85 per cent, and the computer will tell you how long your training run should take and the average pace at which it should be run.

This can be done for any distance, irrespective of whether the entered race times are for a similar distance or not. Thus a whole week's training schedule can be detailed in terms of time, distance and pace, and can still be modified to cater for daily fluctuations in how you feel.

A FINAL WORD

The program is not particularly sophisticated in computing terms, but I believe it has a lot to offer. It is certainly more accessible than a laboratory when you want a race prediction or help in drawing up training schedules.

5

ENERGY AND FLUID REPLACEMENT

CHAPTER TWENTY-THREE

ENERGY PRODUCTION IN EXERCISE

A key part in understanding the need and use of energy drinks and foods lies in understanding the energy systems incurred during exercise. It can be described in layman's language.

ATP AND CREATINE PHOSPHATE ENERGY

Very short, intense exercise up to a couple of seconds in duration (sprint starts) is fuelled by ATP, a chemical that exists in the muscles, allowing them to contract. This does not require oxygen. From here to 45 seconds the body relies on a combination of ATP and creatine phosphate for fuel.

In sprinting terms this will take an élite athlete around a 400m track. You may have recognised the name of creatine, the major constituent of a number of new supplements on the market. Again no oxygen is required, but the process produces lactic acid. Lactic acid is not the 'baddie' that some people would have you believe. Your body only has the capacity to process (metabolise) lactic acid at a particular rate, and when it is produced faster than it can be metabolised, your muscles are unable to function properly as they are too acidic. This explains why 400m track runners are often seen to 'tie up' as they come down the home straight towards the finish line. The example of a runner is used because the effects are more visible, but the same process happens in cycling, swimming and other continuous sports.

An important point is that this will be at the same time, not the same distance – in other words, after 40 to 45 seconds of flat-out effort in the sport concerned. Your capacity to cope with high levels of lactic acid can be increased to some degree by training.

PREDOMINANTLY CARBOHYDRATE ENERGY

The next energy process relates to periods of flat-out exercise lasting 45 seconds to about three minutes. The amount of oxygen required increases as the time of exercise increases. This is used in the conversion of glycogen into ATP and hence energy as before. This is a very efficient method of fuelling exercise and can be compared to a high-octane petrol. Thus this section uses energy derived from processes without oxygen, anaerobic, and those requiring oxygen, aerobic. As the time increases, the proportion of anaerobic exercise decreases and the amount of aerobic exercise increases. For example, a 1,000m race is about 50 per cent anaerobic, 50 per cent aerobic. By 5,000m (typically 14 minutes' flat-out exercise) this is around 10 per cent anaerobic, 90 per cent aerobic; and a 10km (30 minutes) is around 5 per cent anaerobic, 95 per cent aerobic. The higher the percentage of anaerobic work, the greater the build-up of lactic acid.

As the race distance increases to the half-marathon, the amount of lactic acid produced reduces to a level where it can be metabolised, thus there is no build-up. This balanced level is called the lactic threshold and for a runner it tends to occur around the one-hour mark. Running as far as you can for one hour is a good way of determining your lactic threshold pace, which is one of the key training paces for most endurance sports.

Carbohydrate is stored as glycogen in both the muscles and the liver. Muscle glycogen is used for exercise, whereas liver glycogen is primarily used to maintain normal blood sugar level. Blood sugar is the vital fuel for powering the brain. Liver stores deplete all the time, even when sleeping. The maximum liver stores are around 150 grams, which deplete at a rate of about nine grams per hour when resting. Thus people who exercise or work in the morning without eating may only have 50 per cent or less of their liver stores remaining before they take their first step!

Muscle glycogen stores are sufficient for about 90 minutes of continuous exercise. After this the blood sugar is faced with the dilemma of trying to assist muscle energy and the brain's requirements. This often results in a difficulty in concentrating or doing simple calculations in your head, which is a sign of low blood sugar. This is referred to as the 'bear' or the 'wall' (different sports use different terminology). Exercise that lasts beyond this time, or is of a lower intensity, makes use of a combination of glycogen and blood fatty acids. The less intense the exercise, the higher the percentage of the energy that comes from the blood fatty acids.

FREE FATTY ACID AND CARBOHYDRATE AS ENERGY

Blood fatty acids are a very 'low-octane' fuel, as they first have to be converted to glycogen and only then into ATP and energy. Deriving energy from fatty acids takes an additional 10 per cent of oxygen. This two-stage process means that energy cannot be produced fast enough to keep up with the demands of high-intensity exercise. You are thus prevented from running or cycling at a high speed. Fatty acids become an important energy source to those who race for two or more hours. Lactic acid is produced in these processes; however, the rate of production is low enough that it can be reconverted to useful energy.

If your body has already been depleted of glycogen, then blood fatty acids will become your prime source of fuel. In theoretical terms, most people have an extensive supply of blood fatty acids and will never have insufficient stores of this for most normal events – you probably have enough to power you halfway around the equator! By comparison, you only have a limited amount of glycogen stores, and once these have been exhausted they need to be replaced. Doing this during exercise becomes difficult. The ability to replace energy depends on the variety and content of the food or drink taken.

From the previous discussion on liver glycogen it will be clear that it is important to keep blood sugar levels up so that normal brain function can be maintained.

LACTIC ACID

Lactic acid is blamed for all manner of ills during exercise. In fact, at low intensities (i.e. below the lactic threshold) lactic is metabolised and used to provide energy. At high intensities lactic acid swamps the muscles, reducing their performance.

The point where the amount of lactic being produced equals the amount to be metabolised is the lactic threshold. This is the highest intensity of exercise which can theoretically be maintained for extended periods, provided sufficient fuel exists in the muscles. It is, however, possible to run faster than this, but the amount of lactic acid will gradually increase in the bloodstream until it reaches a capacity where normal performance is impossible. For many people this is around 21 litres of lactic acid.

In an ideal competitive situation you would want to exercise at a high intensity that resulted in your lactic capacity only being reached one metre past the finishline!

SUMMARY

In a simplified form, energy production can be classified as follows:

FUEL	Time of intense exercise
ATP	0 to 3 seconds
ATP and Creatine Phosphate	3 to 45 seconds
Glycogen	45 seconds to 3 minutes
Glycogen & threshold	+- 60 minutes – approx anaerobic fatty acids
	+- 90 minutes – depletion of glycogen stores

** As time increases, percentage from fatty acids increases
** As exercise intensity drops, percentage of fatty acids increases

It can be seen that carbohydrate plays an important role in all exercise and is essential if blood-sugar levels to be maintained.

Although these fuel systems will tend to interrelate, the primary source of energy will be determined by the level of intensity of exercise and the length of time of exercise (not distance). Thus a two-hour marathon runner (26.2 miles) uses the same energy systems (say 80 per cent glycogen, 20 per cent blood fatty acids) as a two-hour half-marathon runner (13.1 miles). The two-hour half-marathon runner would take about 4 hours 15 minutes if he attempted a marathon and would use, say, 60 per cent glycogen and 40 per cent blood fatty acids. It is clear, then, that for the same distances the fuel requirements are different, but for the same time of continuous flat-out exercise the fuel requirements tend to be the same.

CHAPTER TWENTY-FOUR

THE PRINCIPLES OF REPLACEMENT

Success in any sports event is a combination of many things: training, mental preparation, logistical preparation for the event, logistics at the event, and energy replacement – the process of putting back the energy you use, which is vaguely referred to by some as 'nutrition' Replacement of the fluid lost through sweating is also essential.

This is a book for winners. That is not to say that it's for event or competition winners, but rather for sportspeople who wish to maximise their performances, whatever their standard. The issue of energy replacement affects all sporting performance to some extent, and if you use the advice given in this section, modified to suit your individual needs, you will eliminate one possible source of misfortune in competition.

Correct energy and water replacement will lead to better recovery after training, hence more effective training, hence better training results, hence better competition results. Correct energy replacement in competition leads directly to better results. Thus this section can help you improve in two areas simultaneously.

This is not another book that tells you that you must eat x or omit y from your diet in order to become a champion. The objective of this section is to give you advice, based on my own experience, on the 'how, when, what and how much' of the products available on the market.

The need for changes in your everyday diet is outside the scope of this book. Although I personally believe that there is a need for most of us to modify our eating habits in order to return our energy intake to the equivalent nutritional value of the traditional 'three balanced meals a day', there is sufficient literature on this subject for most sportspeople to be able to come to terms with their own requirements.

However, the same cannot be said about the use of sports drinks and energy products. There is overwhelming scientific evidence that supports the use of such products. The value of carbohydrate-loading as a method of improving performance in endurance events is well-catalogued. (Carbohydrate-loading, or carbo-loading, is the practice of eating food that is very high in carbohydrates shortly before a sporting event. It is sometimes preceded by a period of carbohydrate depletion – that is, of cutting down drastically on carbohydrates. This is discussed in more detail in the next chapter.) The need to keep blood sugar levels up during endurance events has been witnessed by millions who have seen disorientated marathoners and ultra runners stagger blindly towards the finish, oblivious to the crowds.

The need to be able to recover from an event has been felt by every social and competitive athlete who, on the high of a recent success, wills his or her body back into training for the next challenge.

The main problem is that knowledge about how to manage one's energy replacement is passed on either by word of mouth, by general product instructions written to cover a very wide market, or by books which gloss over the details. This section of the book aims to give the necessary practical and detailed assistance to every sportsperson.

Although most of the sports drinks currently available seem to have been developed through the sport of running, and latterly triathlons, participants in most sports can benefit substantially from the correct use of such products before, during and after their event.

To understand where the benefit is to be found it is necessary to have a very basic knowledge of where and when carbohydrate is used. The account which follows has been kept very simple. Anyone requiring a more detailed description should read Professor Tim Noakes's book *Lore of Running*.

Essentially, we have two carbohydrate fuel tanks: the liver and the muscles. The liver uses glycogen (stored carbohydrate) to keep the blood sugar levels up and this supply primarily fuels the nervous system and the brain. Only a small amount of this fuel can be used for muscle energy. The muscles have their own carbohydrate but, once these stores are depleted, the muscles have to find an alternative source of energy in order to keep working.

The liver is constantly emptying itself of glycogen (since it is always working). Even asleep, you will be burning about nine grams of glycogen per hour. Typically, your liver has a capacity of 150 grams and thus, if it were not refuelled after 16 hours of sleep alone, it would be depleted.

Under the stress of exercise or anxiety this depletion obviously happens much faster. The small amount of liver glycogen available to the muscles will be used very fast. As a result of this liver glycogen depletion, a person competing in any sport that requires large amounts of nervous energy, including brain power, will benefit from the use of energy drinks.

This also indicates the importance of ensuring a good carbohydrate store in the liver before examinations, and thus the importance of eating a good breakfast. Many sportspeople find eating breakfast before events an impossibility, and this is another instance where sports drinks fill a need, since the body absorbs them easily.

The muscle stores of glycogen are essentially available only to the muscles in which they are stored. In other words, glycogen stores in the upper limbs cannot be used to fuel the legs, although the driving of your arms will help you keep your legs moving to some extent. Thus there is some benefit in ensuring that all muscles are loaded to their maximum.

In general terms, muscle glycogen cannot be used to fuel the nervous system, and liver glycogen can not be relied upon to fuel the muscles.

Assuming an average Western diet of about 40 per cent carbohydrate, and assuming that the participant has rested for at least a day before the event, the normal muscle glycogen stores will last for about 60 to 90 minutes. The rate of use of the glycogen will vary with the intensity of the exercise (e.g. speed). Thus a person involved in a series of sprints will burn glycogen faster than someone exercising at a more uniform rate.

So depletion of the muscle glycogen stores is likely in sports such as rugby, soccer, hockey and basketball, where players are involved not only in general movement for 60 to 90 minutes but also in a series of sprints. The same applies to cyclists, runners, triathletes, canoeists and so on who want to perform at a more constant rate over events lasting longer than 75 to 90 minutes.

Whilst the liver stores of blood sugar can be supplemented during an event, the muscles stores do not accept significant supplementation during exercise. The implication of this is that events in which muscle store depletion is likely require the participant to use carbo-loading techniques to maximise the stores in the muscles. These stores can be increased two- to threefold if loading is done correctly. People participating in events in which liver glycogen may be depleted benefit from a combination of carbo-loading and energy supplementation during the event.

Clearly, these principles apply to many events that previously have been ignored in terms of usage of sports drinks. Consider the high concentration required by the seven-day motorcycle triallist, whose skilled muscle movement and tension can bring on a bout of cramps similar to those that afflict the marathon runner. Or consider the moto-cross rider who competes in several high-intensity heats that challenge mind and muscle throughout one day. And what about the rally driver?

Thus the principles of sports nutrition apply to any event where there is high concentration and the participant is unable to have normal food intake (resulting in the problem of liver depletion); and to any event where muscles are being used either for several short, very intense efforts, or one longer, continuous effort.

This means, I believe, that just about every sportsperson can benefit from sports event nutrition when seeking a peak performance.

MORE CAN BE TOO MUCH

I have said that there is substantial scientific evidence that many sports energy products work to the benefit of the athletes. Why, then, do we hear of people for whom experiments in this area have been disastrous?

If we consider a field of runners at any road race, all of whom are trying the carbo-loading and energy-replacement techniques for the first time, there will be several different outcomes from these experiments.

This is not to say that the runners will not have tried these solutions in training. I would never advocate a first trial in a race situation. Like it or not, however, people's approach in a race is totally different from their mind-set in training and thus one's race reaction can be totally different from any training reaction. Race anxiety has an influence, if nothing else.

In our field of runners there will be a few for whom there is an allergic reaction to the products making up the energy drinks. They should already have discovered this during training, though. The complex carbohydrate molecules used in many sports drinks come from maize products which can cause an allergic reaction in a small number of people.

Others in the field will have felt no benefit from the energy-replacement techniques. They may have been too cautious. They may, for instance, have opted to use a much lower carbohydrate-loading scheme and may have reduced the carbohydrate content of their drinks during the events. Whilst they will still have benefited to some extent, they will not have noticed it, since they will still have 'hit the wall' at some stage. These runners will write off the energy-replacement techniques and products as being of no use.

Finally, there will be those who believe that if the prescribed dosage makes you fast, then double or triple that amount will make you a world champion. This is definitely not the case. Whilst 'overdosing' on these drinks is not physically dangerous, it is very likely to ruin your sporting performance.

Sports products should be approached in the same way that a cyclist sets saddle height. There is a rule of thumb which determines the saddle height from the centre of the crank, and initially the saddle is set at this height. Then, after miles and miles of riding, the cyclist becomes attuned to the bicycle and makes a change to the height of a few millimetres. After more miles in the saddle another slight adjustment is made, and so on, until the cyclist's own optimum saddle height is determined. This process takes a long time, but the final saddle height is only fractionally different from the rule-of-thumb height used in the first place.

The same applies to use of sports drinks and carbo-loading techniques. Initially you should use exactly the recommended amounts; then, gradually, you can make small adjustments to the quantities to tailor them to your needs.

The runners who have understood and successfully adopted this approach will make up the majority of the field in our example. The over-loaders will probably have been left behind in the bushes!

Remember, use only the amounts directed. Overuse is abuse!

CHAPTER TWENTY-FIVE

REPLACEMENT BEFORE THE EVENT

It is said that prevention is better than cure. You now know that, in the case of depletion of muscle glycogen stores during an event, there is no cure. The only solution is to prevent depletion by using a technique known as carbohydrate-loading.

Before discussing the technique, however, I must remind you that, even if we can expand our body carbohydrate stores to two or three times their normal capacity, there will still be events in which this will not be sufficient to see you through to the end. Also, remember that the amount of glycogen you require will vary with the intensity and the length of the event.

An average runner who is competing in an event longer than 15km is likely to benefit from carbo-loading, but the effect of time can be seen if we consider the marathon distance.

Runners who complete the 26 miles in under 4:00 will find their performance improved by increased muscle glycogen stores. But runners slower than 4:00 to 4:30 face the problem of liver glycogen depletion, since they will be burning a higher percentage of fat to fuel their muscles, and thus the full carbo-loading diet will be of little benefit. There is a shorter version of carbo-loading that can be used to ensure liver loading prior to the event, and these runners may also benefit from loading on the run. Not all runners follow the carbo-loading regime, however. There are runners who believe that they are actually better off following a normal diet before the race.

Obviously, the same principles will apply to ultradistance events. Your main concern here will be with ensuring a full liver store before the event, and with organising enough food and drink to maintain blood-sugar level during the event.

Figure 25.1 gives an indication of the speeds and distances where carbo-loading diets would be of benefit.

The top runners may find this table less than accurate at both ends, since one of the reasons they are top runners is genetic endowment, which may include an enhanced capacity to absorb and store muscle glycogen.

Figure 25.1 Carbo-loading benefits

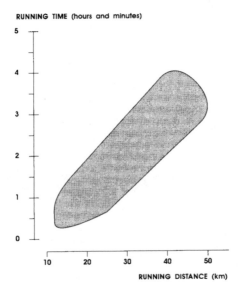

The distances and running times (speeds) which can be improved by carbohydrate supplementation. Source: Francois Pèronnet, Guy Thibault, Marielle Ledoux and Guy Brisson: *Performance in Endurance Events*

MAXIMISING MUSCLE GLYCOGEN STORES

The original carbo-loading diet went as follows. Participants depleted their existing muscle stores by performing their sport for an extended period of time (about 90 minutes), at a medium to high intensity (below competition pace), seven days before the event.

With its stores drained, the body 'craves' carbohydrates. It has been found that it is when this 'craving' is at its greatest that the muscles can synthesise glycogen best. Thus, in order to maximise this craving, a diet extremely low in carbohydrates was undertaken for a further three days.

Another reason for this three-day diet was that it meant the last long depletion effort could be moved further away from the competition to give more time for recovery.

A point to think about at this stage is that the better competitors will actually be performing this depletion routine on a regular basis during their training, although they will be replacing the carbohydrate straight away each time. This will lead to improved efficiency in carbohydrate storage and thus they may be able to load even better than their less well-trained colleagues. Such a situation will obviously improve their performance and their ability to recover after training.

Several years ago it was proved that trained runners did not need to carry out this depletion phase, since their normal daily training would deplete their carbohydrate stores sufficiently. Indeed, this depletion was found to be so effective that in countries of the former Eastern Bloc it was deemed necessary for athletes to take a full day's rest after each three days' training. Failure to take this rest was found to leave the athlete unable to train effectively on the fourth day because of depleted muscle glycogen stores. We now know that the depletion phase is not necessary before an event since normal training depletes carbohydrate stores.

The traditional carbo-loading diet continues on the fourth day with a change to a very high-carbohydrate diet of around 70 to 85 per cent carbohydrate. This results in the satisfaction of the 'craving' and super-compensation of glycogen in the muscle stores, so that two to three times the normal quantities can be stored in the muscles over a period of three days.

Achieving these high percentages of carbohydrate in one's diet is a major problem, since most high-carbohydrate foods are bulky, particularly the unrefined ones. Thus the difficulty is that we feel full long before we have taken in enough to satisfy our loading requirements.

The high carbohydrate content of sports drinks that contain long-chain carbohydrate polymers are ideal for this situation. Typically a litre of these products mixed at 10 per cent solution (i.e. 100 grams powder to 1 litre liquid) delivers just under 200 grams of carbohydrate. This allows competitors to indulge in a diet that still resembles their normal eating regime.

It should be noted that this diet was never intended to be 100 per cent carbohydrate, and that there is still a requirement for both fats and protein during this phase. Unfortunately, the human tendency to overdo things has led some competitors to concentrate solely on loading carbohydrate, and this has resulted in gastric problems and discomfort.

Another practical problem that faces most competitors is

determining just how much carbohydrate they need to take in during the loading period. This can be determined by calculation and an example is given below.

HOW MUCH CARBOHYDRATE DO YOU NEED?

Table 25.2 Carbohydrate loading

Runner's weight 65kg	=	7% body fat
Muscle weight 26kg		
Maximum glycogen/kg muscle	=	36kg
Therefore, total 'loaded'	=	26 x 36 = 936g
Liver depletion for 3 days	=	9 x 24 x 3 = 648g
(60 mins) Allowance for light exercise	=	60 x 3 = 180g
Total requirement	=	**1,764g**
Say 600g/day		
100g potatoes or bananas	=	19g therefore 30 per day
100g pasta	=	23g therefore 2.8 per day
Typical long-chain carbohydrate sports drink e.g. Maxim, Hi Five, Leppin FRN		1 litre = 195g

Whilst this is one method that can be used for running, a second method is given below.

Your carbohydrate requirements during loading are based on several considerations. First take your resting requirements, and here we will allow 40 kilocalories (kcal) per kilogram of body weight. Thus you will require your body weight in kilograms, times 40, times 3, for the loading phase.

Rest requirement = weight x 40 x 3

Then we need to know what weight of muscle is involved in your sport to determine your muscle storage requirements. We look at the predominant muscles only. In running we are concerned with the leg and hip muscles; the arms are ignored. Your muscle weight is split equally between your lower and upper limbs. Your total muscle weight can be calculated, provided you know your percentage of body fat. This will need to be calculated for you by a doctor or at a good gym.

Fat weight = weight x % fat divided by 100
Lean weight = total weight – fat weight
Total muscle weight = 50% of lean weight (for runners)

Your total muscle weight is approximately half of your lean body weight, and from this you can make an assumption about how much muscle is used in your chosen sport, i.e. active muscle. In running this would be about 50 per cent, i.e. half your total muscle weight.

Now, allowing 36 grams of glycogen per kilogram of active muscle, the amount of glycogen required to ensure super-compensation is 45 times your active muscle weight.

Glycogen need = active muscle weight x 36

Since there are 4.23 kcal per gram of carbohydrate, the total kcal required for this section are:

Muscle kcal requirement = glycogen need x 4.23

Finally we need to add these two amounts together to get the total required over the three days. This total is then multiplied by 0.9, since 90 per cent of this must come from carbohydrates. We divide this by 4.23 to convert kcal back to grams and, finally, divide by 3 to arrive at the daily requirement.

So, the equation would be:

Daily carbo = 1/3 x 1/4.23 (muscle kcal + rest) x 0.9

These are very easy calculations. It is worth noting that competitors with a low percentage of body fat have to take in a larger amount of carbohydrate per kilogram of body weight than their 'fatter' colleagues.

To get an idea of the problem that you face in meeting this requirement, divide the daily total by 20 and you will have a number which will relate roughly to the number of 100 gram potatoes that you would need to eat in one day! Remember that these are baked potatoes with no sauce or butter.

Clearly, carbohydrate-loading in this way would be a full-time occupation and is totally inappropriate since there would be no room left for the other essential ingredients of your diet – fat and protein. This difficulty is the reason some people have failed to find the carbo-loading diet satisfactory. But it is a difficulty that can be overcome by using sports energy drinks, which are low-bulk and provide just under 200 grams per litre. One and a half litres per day will cover around half

of most runners' requirements and allows the remaining requirements
to come from a more balanced high-carbohydrate diet.

REFINED OR UNREFINED CARBOHYDRATES?

In recent years there has been much debate about whether refined
carbohydrates, such as jams, syrup, white flour and so on, or unrefined
carbohydrates, such as beans, apples and potatoes, are better from a
loading and energy point of view. The debate continues, in the absence
of conclusive evidence.

Having read whatever I can lay my hands on, and tried the
alternatives, my suggestion is that you use a combination. The
theoretical optimum would appear to be to start with a predominance of
refined carbohydrates, and end the loading with more unrefined
carbohydrates.

The matter is to some extent further complicated by something
called the Glycemic Index. This is an expression of the rise in blood-
sugar level after the consumption of a particular food. High blood-sugar
levels trigger a rise in insulin and, it is thought, promote the storage of
energy as fat. Dr Michael Colgan, author of *Optimum Sports Nutrition*,
recommends that preference be given to foods with a lower glycemic
index. For example, use rolled oats, apples, oranges, lentils and
wholewheat bread in preference to bananas, raisins, honey, white
potatoes, white bread and white rice.

It should be noted that unrefined carbohydraetes, such as rolled
oats, release their 'energy' over a longer period than refined
carbohydrates, which tend to cause major surges in the system. As with
everything, however, moderation should prevail.

BEWARE OF THE ENERGY SURGE!

As one would expect, the body has many systems – safety valves, if you
like – to ensure that it is never overloaded.

Such a system exists for blood-sugar levels. When we take a simple
(refined) sugar, such as a commercial fizzy drink or even a glucose
tablet, the sugar is absorbed directly into the bloodstream and
dramatically raises the blood-sugar level. The body's blood-sugar
regulator registers this dramatic rise as above normal and counters it
with the hormone insulin.

Insulin is often called the 'anti-exercise' hormone, for the following
reason. It ensures that the blood-sugar level is reduced; however, it

doesn't bring it back to normal, but reduces it to below normal by almost the amount of the increase it was countering. This low blood-sugar level is obviously not conducive to exercise.

Unrefined carbohydrates, on the other hand, tend to be released more slowly and thus there is no major surge in the blood-sugar level and therefore no major release of insulin.

It has also been found that fructose, the sugar found in fruit juice and honey, can be ingested without insulin surges, but there are two drawbacks to its use. First, fructose is considerably sweeter than simple sugars and even small amounts are too sweet for some people to take. Second, a number of people cannot tolerate fructose.

Fortunately, it has also been found that long molecules called glucose polymers or long-chain carbohydrates are absorbed well by the stomach and also don't result in an insulin reaction. In addition, research has proven that glucose polymers at higher dilutions than simple sugars can be tolerated during exercise, and this has great benefit during the event.

It is the sports drinks that contain these glucose polymers that are particularly useful. The polymers come in different chain lengths (chain length referring to the number of molecules linked together), and it has been found that the longer the chain length, the better. The one drawback of glucose polymers is that the energy they provide is not instantly available, so the better drinks will also include a small percentage of fructose, or maltose, to cater for this (and improve the taste). Be careful in your choice if you react to fructose.

Remember: owing to the energy surge, taking simple sugars immediately before the start can slow you down!

WHEN TO START LOADING

Since the body absorbs carbohydrates best when the demand for them is greatest, it is obvious that the best time to start loading is immediately after exercise. So, on the morning that loading is to start, undertake a shortish, medium-intensity training session and start loading when you have finished.

It has been shown by research that absorption is best in the first 15 minutes after training stops. Many people find it impossible to eat so soon after training, and once again this is where sports drinks with long-chain carbohydrates come into their own. It is very easy to swallow a pint of fluid, which in turn is delivering just under 100 grams of carbohydrates to your system. An hour or so later, loading can continue with solid food.

Once you have worked through this section it will be obvious that to load carbohydrate effectively you will need between three and four drinks of a 10 per cent carbo-booster solution each day for the three days of loading. Each drink should be just over a pint (500ml) in volume.

THE FINAL DAY

We have now determined the amount one needs to carbo-load, the type of carbohydrate to take, when to start, and that loading must go on for three days before the event. What to do on the final day will vary, depending on the starting time of your competition.

Often this will be early in the morning and thus for many contestants their last meal will be the night before, since anxiety, pre-race nerves and the desire to feel 'light and mean' make any form of solid food out of the question on race morning.

The problem is that your liver doesn't know that it has to store glycogen for the competition so, even as you rest (if one can rest the night before a major event!), you are burning up at least nine grams of your 150 gram liver store every hour.

A quick calculation will show you that if, for example, your event starts at 9.00 a.m. and your last meal was at 9.00 p.m. the night before, you will be starting the event with only 42 grams of glycogen in your liver. In other words, your liver will be three-quarters empty.

So it must be topped up. Often the temptation is to take a carbohydrate drink such as Coke or Lucozade or a glucose tablet immediately before the event. After all, sugar gives us go – isn't that the message?

This may be true generally, but it is not a wise move immediately before the race. Ingesting simple sugars will result in the insulin reaction mentioned above, causing us to start the event with a low blood-sugar level – the same as if we had been competng for about an hour already.

If this is the practice that you have been used to in the past – and most people seem to have been advised to do this, even by school gym teachers – then try the approach that follows and you are likely to experience an improvement in performance.

There are two alternatives. First, you can get up early enough to have a meal, which should be a light but high-carbohydrate meal. An example would be cereal, toast with jam or honey and fruit juice or water to drink. This meal must be timed so that, despite your anxiety, you are able to digest it, allowing sufficient time for the blood-sugar level to return to normal before the event. You should eat probably three to four hours before the start.

The second alternative is to get up later and to recoup your overnight carbohydrate depletion through the use of a large glass or two of carbo-booster. Being fluid, and a glucose polymer, this can be absorbed easily and will not result in the insulin reaction. Ideally this should be taken about an hour to an hour and a half before the event starts. We calculated that your liver would have been depleted by about 110 grams overnight, so one to two pints of the drink prior to the event will satisfy your requirements and ensure that you are topped up for the start. Even if you have taken an early meal, a half-pint drink of carbo-booster an hour before the start will be good insurance.

One final thought: in events that last longer than six hours one cannot go without food. It is totally abnormal for most people to go this length of time (plus the time since their last meal) without some form of solid food.

If you think of a typical day, you start with breakfast, go on to mid-morning tea, lunch, afternoon tea, supper, and often a snack to round it off. Yet we seem to think that on the day of an ultra competition we can survive on fluid and, at best, some sort of sugar intake in the form of drinks.

While this may be sufficient for shorter events, even up to a marathon lasting five hours, I seriously doubt that we can survive without nourishment in longer events. I therefore suggest that, if you are running in a longer event, the first alternative of taking an early meal is a necessity.

Furthermore, since these longer events tend to be of a much lower intensity than shorter ones, your need to be fully carbo-boosted is less critical since much of your energy need will be supplied from fats. It stands to reason, then, that a more substantial meal will be required before longer events. Indeed, Wally Hayward, the famous South African runner who set bests at 100 miles, 24 hours and London to Brighton and won Comrades five times, used to eat a steak three hours before the race.

This practice used to be adopted by rugby and soccer teams before matches, but most people (except the most stubborn schoolteachers!) have realised that for most normal events it is carbohydrates we need, rather than protein and fats.

Ultra events are the exceptions, and any pre-race meal should include some fat and protein. During long events you will experience a craving for 'substantial' food, normally of the savoury variety. Your body has a marvellous habit of letting you know what you need, and my own experience suggests that slow runners need a meal before longer events which should be similar in kind to the meal before ultras. As I have said before, the slower pace of such races allows digestion of the meal.

CARBO-LOADING AND WATER

One of the perceived drawbacks of carbo-loading is the additional weight that one puts on before the event. This happens because each gram of carbohydrate requires three grams of water to be stored with it. Thus you can work out just how much extra weight you are likely to pick up when you have loaded properly by multiplying your daily requirement by three and by three again to allow for three days. This is also a useful guide for ensuring that you are fully loaded.

For some sports, this extra weight may seem like a disadvantage, and certainly in most cases useless weight detracts from performance. However, in events where you are subjected to heat and need to be able to cool through sweating, this additional water supply at the start can be of obvious use in extending your on-board cooling system.

Remember that your performance drops off substantially when you lose over 2 per cent of your normal body weight in sweat, and a greater loss can see you decline into heat stroke and exhaustion.

When you consider the points that have been made about the energy surge associated with drinking or eating simple sugars before the start of an event, it is obvious that the correct thing to be drinking in the last hour is water. It has been found that this is best absorbed when it is at a temperature of about 10°C and this may require you to put a couple of bits of ice in the bottle before you drink it.

FAT-LOADING DIET AND FAT BURNING

Sports science is a funny thing: it seems to operate according to a kind of vicious circle. By this I mean that sports scientists do research to tell the athletes what they think will work, and the athletes gradually move towards this advice, but by the time they get there the scientists have modified the advice, requiring the athletes to make a further change to their approach! On the other hand, the athletes spend their life in search of methods that work for them, then the scientists take on the challenge of proving why their methods work. This pattern seems likely to repeat itself with the issue of fat burning in long-distance events. By long I mean anything over four hours in duration at race pace for the runner under consideration.

In 1986, on the eve of the Durban launch of Tim Noakes's first edition of *Lore of Running*, he and I spent the night in a local gym taking tests as I ran over 100 miles on a treadmill. The object of the exercise was to determine what fuel I was burning in long runs. In his first book, Tim made note of Arthur Newton's 1924 observation that he needed a meal when he raced over 40 miles, and the carbohydrate content of the meal was highlighted. My experience of such distances told me that I needed something more substantial, but I could not put my finger on exactly what that needed to be. I did know, however, that one of the last things that actually appealed to me was the thought of more sweet food. The treadmill test confirmed in my mind the need for more fatty and protein foods during these longer runs, and indeed, closer inspection of Newton's 1924 recommendations confirmed that his meal was significantly high in fat.

More recently scientists have suggested trying a 'fat-loading' diet for a period of two weeks or so in the final preparation for races of 50 miles or longer. These recommendations are targeted, I believe, at the more élite runner, and I am sure that this advice will be proved to apply more to the length of time spent running than to the distance run. Thus we will find that fat-loading will be beneficial for any race requiring a runner to compete for over four hours. This means that a slow marathoner, a Two Bridges runner and a London to Brighton runner face the same problems as the élite runner in 50 mile and longer events.

The purpose of the high-fat diet is to train the runner's energy system to mobilise fat into energy, and this appears to fly in the face of all previous advice. However, it should be remembered that whenever you run for more than about four minutes at race pace, your energy comes from a combination of glycogen and fat. The longer you exercise, the greater the percentage of fat. When this percentage increases you are forced to slow down, since the conversion of fat into energy is a two-stage affair: fat is changed first to glycogen, then to energy, thus using fat is less efficient than using glycogen. It is obvious, then, that if you can make this energy system more efficient, the slowdown effect of it will be minimised. This is the purpose of suggesting a two-week high-fat diet: it forces the body to adapt to training without readily available carbohydrates.

This research is still in its very early stages and thus many alternatives have to be tested, but I am not entirely convinced that this is the only way to achieve such adaptation. It has already been shown that heavy training on consecutive days can cause a significant reduction in glycogen levels, and indeed, the failure to ingest carbohydrate within 45 minutes of completion of exercise will delay the replacement of glycogen. If you study my recommendations for training for the truly long events you will find that there are two recognisable features. First, established runners follow a 'quality first, endurance second' approach in their build-up to the race. This means that during the final six weeks or so the emphasis in training is on relatively low-intensity work and higher weekly distance. Second, during this period alternate weekends tend to have long runs and back-to-back runs of around 25km to 35km. Because of the short recovery time between these runs, and the increased total weekly distance, I feel that you will find that you are partially depleted for much of each week. Recovery of the carbohydrate stores is only really achieved during the rest day. I feel that during such a time I probably achieve a similar adaptation to that of the high-fat diet. Of course, the only way to be sure is to try both methods and make a comparison.

The one aspect of fat-loading that worries me is that such sudden changes to the composition of meals may cause gastric reactions. An interesting facet of this research is that the two weeks of high-fat eating are thought to be necessary only about two to four weeks before the event, after which a 'normal' diet can be resumed. If this is the case, is it not possible that a runner who specialises in long ultra races will be able to forgo such dietary manipulation, since his or her system will be almost permanently adapted to such efficient fat burning? The answer to this will no doubt take another few years to determine; in the meantime we must continue to play around with this idea. There is, however, no doubt that for the longer runs there is a need for substantial food intake and that some of this must come from fats as well as from carbohydrates.

CHAPTER TWENTY-SIX

REPLACEMENT DURING THE EVENT

You will remember that we have two kinds of glycogen store: the store in the liver, which primarily fuels the nervous system and our ability to concentrate, and the store in the muscles, which fuels the muscles in which it is contained.

For events in which the normal muscles stores would run out before the finish, we must carbo-load in the three days before the competition. There is very little advantage to be gained by ingesting carbohydrate during the event in the hope of increasing muscle glycogen, since the carbohydrate cannot be absorbed through the 'muscle filter'. This 'fact' is, however, a subject of some controversy, and more recent research seems to suggest that there can be some absorption by the muscles, but that this is limited.

Thus, in any event where you have amassed sufficient muscle glycogen and will not be depleting your liver stores totally, there will be no advantage in taking energy drinks *during* the competition and thus your efforts should be focused on replacing water lost through sweat.

Research has suggested that most runners prefer a water temperature of about 10°C. This may be because they feel that cool water is more refreshing, but in normal weather conditions the temperature is not too critical. In adverse heat, cool drinks are preferable.

Fluid is required at a rate of about half a pint (200–250ml) per half-hour. A very low concentration of minerals added to this water will aid absorption. This can be achieved by adding about one gram of salt to two pints. Alternatively, making up a very dilute solution of one of the commercial rehydration products available from chemists seems to work for me.

The next type of event is the one in which normal muscle stores are sufficient but liver stores may deplete. Such events are those of long duration, such as moto-cross, rallying, motor racing and even, I suppose, exams. Under such circumstances the taking of energy drinks will be of great benefit since the levels of blood sugar can be topped up by drinks during the competition.

The third type of event is the one which requires both muscle and liver stores to be greater than normal. This, I suspect, is the most common, but you will be able to evaluate your sport more accurately for yourself. In this category I would certainly include sports like rugby, soccer and hockey, assuming that the participants are playing at a high level of performance.

I know that the world rugby XV who toured South Africa in 1989 were given the opportunity to use sports energy products during their tour and, by all accounts, found them to be of assistance in ensuring that they did not tire as much in the late stages of the game. The use of energy and fluid-replacement schedules have became a regular feature of southern hemisphere rugby and other team sports. However, the same cannot be said of many British teams. It seems that many think that the climatic conditions mean that this is not as important. Nothing could in fact be further from the truth.

The 1997 tour by the southern hemisphere rugby teams to Britain highlighted the difference in approach. The visitors' support teams camped out on the touchline, getting water bottles on to the pitch at every opportunity. The substitutes continually warmed up and stretched. Not so the home-country teams. Indeed, Scotland's inability to get a replacement winger off the bench and on to the pitch cost them a try against South Africa and was arguably the turning point in the game. In any sport, being professional is not about receiving money, but about planning training and implementing a strategy that covers all aspects of the competition.

When normal muscle-store depletion is expected, there is a need to carbo-load in the days prior to the event. Carbo-loading will also ensure that your liver stores are at a maximum at the start.

Where this regime is not deemed necessary, it is possible to ensure that the liver stores are full by adopting the approach detailed under the heading 'The Final Day' in the previous chapter. In particular, a carbo-boosting drink should be taken around an hour before the event.

WHAT TO TAKE AND HOW

There are normally two requirements to be met during a competition. The first and most important is proper fluid replacement. Remember, no one ever died in an event through lack of energy – in such cases you simply grind to a halt. However, extreme lack of water, dehydration, can result in heat exhaustion, heat stroke and even death. So, put fluid replacement at the top of your list and energy replacement in second place.

I gave some guidance on water requirements in the last section, and this will hold good for most conditions. The only thing to be added, I feel, is that you should drink long before you feel you need it.

In the case of team games, where it is often impractical to come off for water during the play, take a good measure of water in the hours leading up to the match, and also make sure that there is cold water available at half-time. In hot conditions, consider soaking your vest or shirt in water before you start. It may not look too smart, but I'd far rather perform better because I had ensured good cooling than look good as I went on to the field.

It amazes me that, even with the professionalism of some sports, attention to basic details which could ensure that players reached peak performances is so poor. It is almost as though people relish the 'tough guy' approach of not ensuring enough water or energy for the players during a match. Many officials defend it on the basis that they didn't need it in their day. This is not to be applauded; it is sheer stupidity.

So, if you are involved in a sport in which insufficient means or time are being given for either water or energy replacement, take it up with the authorities. Get the rules changed. Sport is meant to be a challenge, not a compulsory flirtation with avoidable injury.

ENERGY DRINKS

Where there is a need to supplement blood-sugar levels during competition, a high-carbohydrate drink can be consumed. However, the amount of carbohydrate in such drinks varies with composition, since absorption can vary.

This can be a fairly complicated subject physiologically, but what really matters to the sportsperson is its practical application. Again, anyone wanting to delve deeper should consult Tim Noakes's *Lore of Running*.

We know that cold water is the liquid best absorbed from the stomach, although recent research suggests that a very small amount of minerals and salts may speed absorption up slightly. If a carbohydrate is added to the drink, the absorption rate will reduce, and when the dilution of the solution goes above 5 per cent there is a considerable reduction in the rate of absorption. Hence you may not be getting the amount of fluid replacement, i.e. water, that you require. Thus you will dehydrate and your performance will drop off. There are exceptions to this, however, and it has been found that a higher dilution of complex long-chain carbohydrates can be taken without adversely affecting the rate of absorption. This is why the glucose polymer sports drinks were developed.

When it was first launched in 1984, Leppin FRN Enduro-Booster was a world first, and has since became the industry leader. It soon became available in powder, syrup and instant-energy sachets. Many other products have subsequently been developed and put on to the market.

So the answer for athletes in competition is a solution made up of glucose polymer, a small amount of simple sugar and a 'hint' of salt. Recent research suggests that a slightly greater dilution is possible, but start with 10 per cent and try for yourself.

For the powder, a dilution of 10 per cent means using 100 grams with a litre of water. If you choose to use another fluid as a base, remember to reduce the amount of powder by the amount of carbohydrate already in the other fluid. Also remember that if the base fluid is a simple sugar, it will slow down the absorption rate from your stomach if it provides over 5 per cent of the carbohydrate in the solution.

Mixing the powder is not difficult but some people get frustrated by the inevitable lumps. The trick is to put the water into the bottle first and then add the powder slowly. In this way the powder 'folds' into the water and is easily mixed. Of course, using a blender is the best solution. Many manufacturers have recognised this problem and now provide the drinks in a concentrated syrup which is easily mixed with water to give the 10 per cent solution. Both powder and syrup come in different flavours.

These drinks can be handed to participants at frequent intervals throughout the competition, providing a constant supply of both water and energy.

In some events such as road running and triathlons, it is impractical to carry bottles of energy replacement fluid with you and, because you are travelling long distances, it is impossible to leave energy drinks beside the road or along the route.

It is for this situation that sachets of concentrated syrup were developed, since it is possible to carry several sachets which can be diluted by the athlete during the event at appropriate refreshment tables.

Before exploring energy replacement further, let's look briefly at what happens when you increase the dilution above your limit (normally about 10 per cent).

OVERDOSES

As mentioned earlier, carbohydrate ingestion does not follows the rule that if one dose is good, double must be better, but quite the reverse. The reason is fairly obvious.

You will remember that it has been found that, in general, a solution in which sugar constitutes more than 5 per cent severely limits the absorption of fluid from the stomach. However, recent research has suggested that a solution containing as much as 20 per cent glucose polymer may be absorbed at relatively normal rates, provided that some fluid is constantly kept in the stomach.

The implication of this is that the athlete should maintain a steady intake of fluid at short intervals throughout the race. Thus it is better to drink several small drinks at short intervals than larger drinks at greater intervals. A side-effect of this, which may or may not be acceptable to the athlete, is that there will be a tendency to suffer the discomfort of having fluid swilling around inside during the race.

What does this have to do with overdoses? Well, consider the available carbohydrate 'syrups'. These are highly concentrated syrups in small sachets, which allow you to carry them between stations. They are typically made up into 25 grams of carbohydrate, which needs to be diluted with about 250ml of water. The problem is that many of them are very thick and viscous. Try this experiment for yourselves.

Take a sample of the different types of syrups available and pour each of them into an empty glass. Now add the stipulated amount of water, normally 250 ml, and see how well they mix.

This is quite a good representation of the way in which many people take these syrups during competition. They bite the tops off the sachets and then swallow the contents. This is followed by an amount of water. Frequently they fail to take the minimum 250ml of water, thereby decreasing the dilution ratio considerably.

Some people suggest that the body's activity during the event will have some mixing effect, so now take each glass and turn it upside down, with your hand sealing the top, and see what happens. In most cases there will still be a large blob of syrup stuck to the bottom of the glass. This is not the desired effect, as ideally you want a well-mixed solution.

Clearly, it makes sense to select a free-flowing or runny syrup that is going to mix well with the water you swallow after it. The alternative is to take the syrup in to your mouth in small amounts, hold it there, and then take some water and make a mixture in your mouth before swallowing. This may be possible during less intense races such as an ultramarathon and possibly even a marathon, but it will destroy the breathing rhythm of most runners in something more intense, such as a half-marathon.

When the syrup is not properly mixed, a blob like the one you saw in the glass will sit in your stomach, and you will therefore have a very highly concentrated solution in your stomach. At the very least, this can cause discomfort. This can be further exacerbated by insufficient water consumption. The body senses that there is a 'meal' to digest and thus absorption of fluid drops dramatically, and blood is diverted to the stomach to aid digestion.

If the concentration is high enough, the absorption of fluid may stop totally. Either way, fluid is no longer making its way into the system at the correct rate, but it is still leaving the system through sweating. Dehydration is the next step. There is also the possibility of nausea and a series of 'pit stops', depending on the individual's reaction to a very sweet solution.

At the time it is unlikely that athletes who make this mistake will realise what is going on (otherwise presumably they would not have made the error in the first place), and thus they will often try some more of the solution, since they are now experiencing tingling and a fall-off in performance, which they attribute to low blood sugar. This compounds the problem.

The ideal way to take an energy drink, then, is in a solution of about 10 per cent (possibly 20 per cent, if the latest research is right), provided it is a glucose polymer. This is best done by placing pre-mixed bottles of the solution at stages throughout the event. If this is impractical, use the syrups but look for a runny one and take it in small amounts, ensuring that you take sufficient water with it on each occasion.

There are a number of commercial products on the market which claim to be energy drinks. It is easy to identify those which are of use. Look at the table of ingredients. The carbohydrate content per 100ml should be close to 10 grams; there should be zero or negligible protein and fat; and there should be a minimal amount of electrolytes. Some electrolyte drinks are mistaken for energy drinks. In Britain many runners perceive Isostar to be an energy drink, wheras although they do have a carbohydrate product, their most high-profile product is actually an electrolyte drink. This is best as a post-event drink or for use in longer events or hot and adverse conditions.

HOW MUCH ARE YOU DRINKING?

The importance of taking water with energy drinks has been emphasised, but do you actually know how much you are taking during an active event?

Try this. Take two glasses, one full of water and the other empty. Take a swallow of water from the full one and hold it in your mouth. Now spit it into the empty glass and measure the volume. You will find that your mouthful is only about 30ml. So even if you pick up a full bottle of water during an event, you probably only take three or four mouthfuls, which amount to a total of about 100ml. At the time it will seem as though you are drinking a lot. However, in real terms you may be drinking substantially less than you need with the syrups, and this explains why some people have problems with them.

By all means use syrups – but follows the instructions!

It cannot be emphasised enough that the first and most important concern is fluid replacement. Since you will not have a measure with you as you run, use the amount you swallowed in the above test as a guide. Let's suppose that was 25ml. We need 250ml per 30 minutes. If you know the distance between water points, which in the London Marathon may be 1½ miles, and your target speed is, say, eight-minute miles (3:30 marathon), you will pass a table every 12 minutes. You require 100ml at each table, which equals four mouthfuls. Use this as a guide to ensure you drink enough. Remember, a 2 per cent drop in fluid can cost you a 10 per cent drop in performance! It is interesting to see that 2:11 marathoners take seven and a half minutes between tables, need only 62.5ml of water at each table (= two mouthfuls) and hence don't appear to be drinking much when we see them on television.

CARRYING SACHETS

The next problem in events that cover long distances is how to carry sachets with you. In most events that rely only on your own power, such as running or long-distance swimming, any additional weight is a disadvantage, and now we are considering taking a store of syrup along with us.

One solution is to buy one of the commercially available carrying belts that fit round the waist. These are made of non-chafe material and will hold up to 12 sachets, which is sufficient for an event of up to nine or ten hours. This is calculated on the assumption that you need one sachet per 40 to 45 minutes. For shorter events it is possible to put a couple of sachets in a wrist strap and even in the pocket in your shorts. I don't suggest more than one in the shorts, however, or you will find that the weight may cause a 'lowering of your standards' – which is likely to prove embarrassing for both you and the spectators!

Another way to carry your energy replacement which is gaining popularity, particularly in hot climates, is the Tripper fluid-supply system. The system comes in different sizes, with a special runner/triathlete model which holds 500ml at the back and the same at the front. These two flexible fluid bags are on a specially designed harness that ensures the weight is transferred directly down through the vertical axis of the body. Because the bags are flexible they mould to the body and thus there is no bounce. They are also insulated and use separate supply pipes, which allow the use of two different fluids – perhaps one hot and one cold – at one time. In some countries the Tripper may be worn in place of a vest in triathlon and canoeing events.

MINERALS

For many years there has been controversy over whether there is a need for minerals in replacement drinks. Calculations of the amount of potassium, salt and magnesium lost during an event show that, under normal conditions, it is unlikely that any mineral supplementation is required. Indeed, some people have argued that since amounts of water are being lost in sweat, the concentration of minerals in one's body actually increased.

The situation in ultras is such that I personally believe that a small amount of salt is required. But this is not the case in events lasting up to, say, five hours. A few years ago, however, it was found that better absorption was obtained with energy-replacement drinks that offered small quantities of minerals and electrolytes, and this is something that you should be looking for in your drinks. If your favourite brand doesn't contain these, then you can quite simply add some yourself from an electrolyte product. My preference would be Rehydrat at a dilution double to triple the level recommended. If you are using only salt, about one gram to every two pints (one litre) should do the trick. See also 'Supplementation in the Ultradistance Events' on p.257.

If your chosen event is the marathon, there has been some research to suggest that ingesting two grams of choline chloride prior to the race and again at halfway will assist the muscle performance and reduce the fatigue in the latter stages of the race. I have found this to be of benefit, but suggest you experiment with it in training on a long run.

CHAPTER TWENTY-SEVEN

REPLACEMENT AFTER THE EVENT

As competitors we gear ourselves up for the big event, we compete to the best of our ability with an attention to detail and thoroughness of preparation that would put the armed forces to shame, and then, when it's all over, we forget everything! If we are building ourselves up to a peak with the correct foods to compete, then surely it stands to reason that we must be depleted of these foods after the event and should be replacing them?

The sort of food we need will depend on the type of event we have competed in and, strange as it may seem, our bodies will tend to tell us if we are taking in the right nutrients. Our bodies tend to 'crave' the carbohydrates, proteins or fats we need, and to be repulsed by the things we don't need.

This said, however, after most normal events the one item that we definitely do need is carbohydrate, since it is the first line of energy supply and, of course, the liver depletion of carbohydrates will have been quite substantial in most events.

You will remember that glycogen synthesis is most efficient when the demand for glycogen is greatest, and this will generally be within 15 minutes after the finish of the event. For this reason, have an extra bottle of a carbo-boosting fluid available for immediately after the competition, and make a point of getting your hands on it early.

If you have been involved in an ultra event or a marathon, your desires may well stretch to a steak or another high-protein or high-fat meal. Even if this is not your usual desire, there is nothing wrong with it under these conditions, since you will probably have become depleted of these nutrients and this is your body's way of getting the necessary fuels for recovery.

Another interesting point to think about is the type of drink that you have been using in your event. Many of the drinks we take are of a slightly acidic nature, so by the end of the event we have an acid build-up. It is worthwhile considering having your first couple of drinks in a more alkaline form. Milk and Rehydrat fall into this category, and water, of course, is neutral.

To determine what you should be taking, remember that energy used should equal energy replaced.

AFTER TRAINING

Since your ability to recover from a training session, and hence your ability to perform in the next session, is related to the recovery of your glycogen stores, it is obvious that a similar approach should be used after all training sessions.

Failure to do this can result in a gradual depletion of stores over a number of days and the result will be that your training becomes less and less productive. There can be few more frustrating things than ineffective, or non-productive, training sessions.

There is an Olympic coach who makes his athletes carry an apple with them to their training sessions as this allows them to start 'loading' straight afterwards. Why would he do this?

During times of heavy training runners have the ideal opportunity to experiment with various methods of maintaining their energy stores during the run, as well as with carbo-loading procedures before the race. The training sessions, however, are only stepping stones in their climb to their goal; hence their objective is to recover from the stress of the long run as soon as possible. There are tricks which can be used to ensure that this happens in the shortest possible time.

Remember that in the original method of carbo-loading there was a depletion phase, when carbohydrate intake was dramatically reduced for the first three days of the week before an event. This depletion made the muscles 'crave' carbohydrates and so when loading began on the fourth day, the carbohydrate was devoured by the starved muscles. This led to super-compensation. We now know that trained runners don't need to carry out this depletion phase, since their normal day-to-day training provides sufficient depletion of the stores.

Since glycogen is the prime source for muscle energy, it makes sense to replace it as soon as possible after exercise.

The quest for the best recovery method has resulted in research proving that if some carbohydrate is not taken during the first 45 minutes after exercise, the replacement of normal glycogen stores may take up to 48 hours. The rate of replenishment is also a function of the carbohydrate composition of food intake. Hence, faster glycogen absorption will occur with a higher carbohydrate content.

The practical result of this is that international athletes can now be seen consuming apples or commercial energy drinks almost immediately after they have finished their training. In this way they are already concentrating on their desire to recover for the following day's training. Obviously, the better they recover, the better they are able to handle a more intense training session. This gives some idea of the importance attached to this new practice.

To underline the point, consider that the sole reason for endurance athletes to become involved in the illegal use of steroids is their desire to get their muscles to recover faster so that they can undertake either more training or more strenuous training. This unnatural manipulation of the body by means of drugs is justly illegal and must not be promoted. Nevertheless, athletes risk life suspension in this attempt to make gains in recovery. Surely it makes more sense to make use of every legal opportunity to speed recovery?

Three rules of thumb to follow:

- Consume some high-carbohydrate food or drink not later than 45 minutes after stopping exercise (ideally in the first 15 minutes). The higher the carbohydrate content, the faster stores will be replenished. It has been found that drinks composed of long-chain carbohydrates are most efficiently absorbed.
- If you are feeling particularly jaded during a training session, look back over the previous few days of training and eating to see whether you could be a victim of a progressive depletion of carbohydrate stores. If so, take a day's rest and some carbohydrate drinks.
- Likewise, in the joyous aftermath of the next race, or after the next sweat-drenched training session, make a beeline for a cup of the carbo-boosting solution you used for loading before the race. In this way you will be preparing yourself for the next day and the next challenge.

CHAPTER TWENTY-EIGHT

SUPPLEMENTATION

VITAMINS

Do we actually need vitamins? This is yet another contentious issue in the worlds of sport and nutrition. One argument says no, because the average person gets enough from three well-balanced meals a day. But the training athlete burns much more, goes the counter-argument, to which the reply is that this is more than met by athletes' additional food intake.

However, I would argue that there is a case for supplementation. If you consider that, for example, Britain sent a team of athletes to the Olympics which represented something like 0.0003 per cent of the population, it is hardly reasonable to equate them with the 'average' person in the country, whether in diet or anything else!

What sort of vitamin or other supplementation would I suggest, then? This needs to be answered on an individual basis, especially as most people have strong likes and dislikes when it comes to food.

A good starting point for most sportspeople in heavy training is a multivitamin pack. This can act as an insurance policy. It will cover most needs and the majority of excesses will be urinated away at the next opportunity. When there is a need, however, it will be satisfied.

Assuming that you follow the basic instructions on the pack, the only danger of vitamin 'poisoning' lies in taking the fat-soluble vitamins such as A and D, but such large amounts are needed to reach the toxic levels – much more than is contained in a multivitamin pack – that this danger can be discounted.

To follow such an insurance regime for the six weeks before a major event makes a lot of sense to me. Notice that I am suggesting that for the normal club runner this is only required during heavy periods of training.

Another area which requires some thought is your preferences in eating. If, like me, you tend to steer clear of red meat and have a strong liking for vegetables and cereals, you may easily find yourself short in some areas, including protein. This can be redressed by an additional intake of amino acids and B-complex vitamins.

The real problem in evaluating the power of these potions is that no one can tell you whether it is the supplement that is working or the fact that you believe it is working. I really am not concerned which it is. If it makes me feel better and puts me in a better condition to train, that's fine.

The regime you need to follow is something that only you can develop for yourself, although you can always go to a nutritionist to get a breakdown on your intake of various components for a week and then assess your needs. These needs may change during different periods of training and in different weather conditions, so they need to be assessed on a regular basis.

Every summer morning in Durban I watched the thermometer slowly creep up, starting from sunrise just after 5.15 a.m. With it also came the escalation in humidity. With February a notoriously hot month in Durban, those who are involved in endurance training such as running leave themselves open not only to the problems of dehydration but also that of mineral depletion. This can be a slow, virtually unnoticed process.

Ironically, about the same time of year in Britain runners can create the same type of conditions for themselves. The December to February period can be extremely cold and icy, and in such conditions many runners put a rain jacket or similar protection on top of their running gear. While this keeps out the wind and rain, it also creates a very humid micro-climate inside the jacket. This reduces the amount of sweat that can be dissipated. The removal of sweat is the prime method of cooling. This means that the runner tends to sweat more than normal, and hence greater quantities of fluid and minerals are lost than in the spring or even the summer!

Let's immediately agree with the scientists that the average person does not need supplementation if he or she is having three well-balanced meals a day. This has been proved. The question is, however, does the 'average' person train for marathons or other endurance competitions? Does the average person go out training in adverse weather conditions? In addition, to my knowledge, the research backing the assertion about the adequacy of three meals has not been done in the wide variety of possible training conditions: hot and humid conditions, extremely high mileage, or other forms of heavy training.

The prestigious British Miler's Club warns its members and coaches that the one factor that separates the average person from the runner is that the runner will sweat between seven and fourteen pints of fluid in a week's training. These figures apply to a middle-distance athlete in the UK. However, it is a basic truth that anyone who eats the four basic dietary components each and every day is at little risk.

The components are:

- One meat meal or its protein equivalent in milk, cheese, dried beans, nuts, etc.
- Five cups of fruit and vegetables
- Two pints of milk (including all milk in tea etc.)
- Five slices of bread and a plate of wholegrain cereal

The question is, how many athletes can be sure that they manage to eat all this in a day, let alone every day? What with work and training, as well as other chores, many runners have little more than one and a half meals a day, let alone three. The need for supplementation then becomes more serious, particularly in adverse climatic conditions.

Let's consider the most common mineral losses.

MINERALS

CALCIUM

Calcium is listed as being indicated for people suffering from allergies, joint pains, lead poisoning (have you run in traffic recently?) and a lack of vitamin D, amongst other problems. Another important factor is that absorption of calcium, even if you are taking sufficient quantities, is greatly hampered by phosphorus, which is found in all soft drinks.

For example, 12 sufferers of chronic shin soreness were all found to be calcium-deficient even though their intake was adequate. All drank on average three litres of soft drinks a week. (Many runners will drink that in a single race in those countries where Coke is provided as a sugar drink on refreshment tables.) The absorption of calcium is also hampered by a high-bran diet.

POTASSIUM

When Steve Ovett collapsed in the 1984 Olympics, his heart was racing and he was heading for a cardiac arrest. It was subsequently found that he was potassium-deficient.

Potassium is required for correct heart function but a lack can also be indicated by poor appetite, mental fatigue and apathy, depression and muscle cramps. An American track coach monitored his team over a season and noted a monthly decline in both potassium and performance. One of the best sources of potassium is pure orange juice.

MAGNESIUM

As with calcium, absorption of magnesium is hampered by a high-bran diet, particularly in conjunction with highly processed and refined foods. Magnesium acts like a pump within the cells and distributes calcium, potassium and sodium in the body. Thus a magnesium deficiency also affects these other minerals.

In many areas, the problem of magnesium deficiency is exacerbated by the low magnesium content of the soil. This results in foods which are normally prime sources of magnesium themselves being low. This, for example, is the case in Durban, where bananas have a lower magnesium content than one would expect.

Magnesium is also involved in glycogen metabolism in the muscles, and is thus of immense importance to those needing to carbo-load or compete in endurance events. A deficiency has also been associated with cramping.

Only five members of a 14-strong French football squad were found to have normal magnesium levels. After supplementation, not only were their stores replaced but their recovery times and match results improved.

ZINC

Over 2,500 learned papers have been written on the subject of zinc deficiency, which has been linked to a multitude of problems from dandruff, ME ('yuppie flu') and delayed healing to hair loss and even impotence. Amazingly, it has been estimated that only one in 1,000 coaches is aware of these papers or their influence on performance.

Inadequate zinc absorption and loss has been associated with those who eat high-bran diets, strict vegetarians, people taking penicillin, those suffering from chronic blood loss, people taking drugs to release water retention, and those who sweat profusely. Zinc is found in egg yolks, split peas, nuts, oats, parsley, garlic, wholewheat bread and potatoes.

Zinc and vitamin C as a combination is believed to be one of the best treatments for the common cold. My own experience in recent years in Scotland suggests that a regular intake of this combination significantly reduces the risk of such infection.

IRON

Iron can become depleted for a number of reasons, and has a devastating effect on performance due to its links with the production of red corpuscles – the oxygen-carrying portion of blood. Vegetarians and runners in heavy training are particularly susceptible, as are women as a result of menstruation. It is worthwhile having a blood test two or three times a year to ensure you do not become depleted, but go to a clinic which understands running, as a normal haemoglobin count is not sufficient. Due to the increased blood volume generated by running, a false picture results. The test needs to include serum ferriton. If results show low iron, get a prescription for a supplement and reduce training for a week or so.

This should give you an idea of some of the more common minerals that you need to think about, particularly in the 'hot' months of training or in the conditions which promote a high degree of sweating. 'Hot' according to Dr Steve Browne, author of a book on the subject, is when the effective temperature is above 25° C. However, a more expressive guide can be found in the 1990 New York Marathon entry form, which details time incentives for runners. Incentives are paid to runners breaking 2:12 for the marathon distance under normal conditions and to those breaking 2:18 when the temperature is above 19.5° C and humidity is above 65 per cent. In addition to the $23,600 prize money the winner gets a new Mercedes, and if he sets a new course record he receives a further major bonus. If the weather is classified as 'hot', this incentive is increased by $10,000.

The influence of heat on your training and your body cannot be highlighted any better than this, and it underlines the need to avoid long training in times of adverse conditions. Although a single long run in heat and humidity is not that much of a problem, putting a number of these together in continuously poor conditions will take its toll.

Many major championships such as the Olympics and Commonwealth Games are now being held in very adverse climates, particularly for endurance runners. It was made clear to me that some team managers have little hands-on experience of the true effect that these conditions can have on the runner. It is one thing reading up on the science; it is a totally different matter to be exposed to it as an athlete for three to four weeks.

AMINO ACIDS

Amino acids are at the centre of a new controversy, one aspect of which sees them quickly becoming a popular alternative to anabolic steroids. It has been suggested that certain amino acids are responsible for increased circulation of the human growth hormone, and/or increased levels of free fatty acids. The theory is that if you supplement with these specific amino acids, you will derive these benefits. Thus, by increasing your intake of arginine, for example, you are supposed to increase the levels of free fatty acids in your blood and thus make this a higher percentage of your energy supply at the start of an event, so saving some of your glycogen stores until later in the race.

Similar claims are made for other amino acids which, when taken on an empty stomach at night, are alleged to increase the circulation of the growth hormone and thus assist in recovery and muscle building, which in turn allows you to train harder.

Members of the medical profession tend to doubt that these amino acids in pill form can be absorbed into the system and therefore doubt the claims made for them. In my own case, I believe that there is some benefit to be had from certain forms of amino acids. I feel that supplementation has assisted in countering possible deficits arising from my tendency towards a vegetarian diet and helped me to recover from long ultras such as the Spartathlon.

To sum up this whole issue of supplements, then, there is definitely a place for supplementation of some sort, even if the benefit is purely mental; but the kind and degree will vary from person to person.

SUPPLEMENTATION IN THE ULTRADISTANCE EVENT

Most of the above applies to the type of events which I consider to be of 'normal' duration, in other words, events ranging from a few minutes to three or four hours. Events such as a 100km or a 100-miler are not what I call 'normal'. These have abnormal requirements in that they are usually greatly in excess of our normal training distances or times. They have special requirements because they require us to think about how they alter our normal day.

Consider, for example, an ultra of 100km. For average runners this distance will take between nine and eleven hours. If these runners followed the recommendations set out above, they would take only water and energy drinks for this length of time. In a normal day, however, they would probably have something like three meals and two or three snacks in the same period of time. There can be no training to get used to this 'abnormal' regime and, for some unknown reason, the competitors seem to think that their bodies will be willing to accept this abuse without grumbling on race day. This makes no sense at all!

In my view, any event which requires constant effort over a period of more than seven hours requires the competitor to give significant thought to some substantial form of food. The longer the event, the more reason for more substantial food.

I cannot claim that this is my idea, but I can't imagine why it had to be reinvented, given that the great Arthur Newton wrote in 1924: 'If I race over 50 miles I need something substantial to eat around 40 miles.' Why do we keep ignoring lessons from others?

As you increase the length of the event, the number and type of 'walls' that you experience becomes greater. It is said that the 'wall' in the marathon is at 20 miles. In reality it is at about two hours in any endurance event. There is another at around four to five hours and others as you move beyond 100 miles.

This was highlighted when the top South African runners first graduated through to 100km races, despite their exceptional talents over the gruelling 90km Comrades course. Typically they could finish Comrades in 5½ to 5¾ hours, but the 100km race required them to run for another 45 to 60 minutes. In reality, they finished Comrades just after they had reached the 40 to 50 mile wall that Arthur Newton identified. In this case they were able to 'hang on'. However, in the 100km race they still had around two hours to go, and therefore could not continue at the same pace, as they had ignored the different energy requirements of this longer event. This became patently clear in the World 100km Championships of the early 1990s, when the South African team often dominated the race up to around 50 to 55 miles, only to grind to a halt. The other top runners, who had been taking on board some food between 30 and 40 miles, then had the sustenance to move through to take the lead.

One of the greatest short-distance ultra runners of the 1980s has to be South African Bruce Fordyce, who won Comrades nine times and London to Brighton three times, and set a world best for 50 miles and 100km. One of the attributes that made him so great was his ability to listen to what others had to say, whether they were novices or experienced runners. He would then evaluate each piece of information as it related to him, throw away the rubbish and modify his approach to training and racing in the light of what remained. He was constantly able to learn and keep abreast of what was going on. His preparation for an event was thorough. That is what we have to strive towards, no matter what sport we wish to excel at.

In ultra events this ability to learn from others can be critical. The longer the event, the more that can go wrong, and the greater the role that elements such as weather, crowd support and seconding can play in the outcome of the competition.

So, the fact that some runners seem to manage 100km without eating does not mean that they, or you, cannot perform better by including some substantial food. For a top runner who will finish in under 8:00 it may be sufficient simply to add a liquid food such as Complan along the way, but for a 9:00 or 11:00 runner it may mean a few sandwiches and soup, which is one of the meals that Arthur Newton used.

Remember that in low-intensity events – which ultras tend to be – the tendency is for a greater percentage of your energy to come from fatty acids and less from carbohydrates. Also, after substantial lengths of time you will also be experiencing protein breakdown. Doesn't it make sense that some of this has to be replaced in long events?

One of the major problems is that most scientific research has focused on shorter events, marathons at the longest, and in general mostly on the élite runners, with a view to gaining insights that will help produce more élite runners. This doesn't help the average runner or ultra runner who has to find out by trial and error what is right.

I suggest that one way of looking at the problem of energy replacement is to compare performances according to time. In other words, your requirements as a six-hour 35 mile runner would be similar to Bruce Fordyce's requirements for 50 miles. Likewise, an 11-hour 100km runner would do well to look to the eating and drinking of the top 100-mile runners.

Obviously, the same principles apply to cycling, canoeing, surf paddling and triathlons. In the longer events, take advantage of the opportunity to eat. In some of these sports eating is not the problem that it is in running, since there is less bouncing and therefore less stomach discomfort. In a triathlon, for instance, it makes sense to eat early on the bike since you have an ideal opportunity to digest the food before the rigours of the running leg. Of course, sense should prevail in as much as any food you take should be as easily digested as possible. The less energy wasted in digesting, the more is available for competing. Select foods that you know will not disturb your stomach.

DRUGS

I have little doubt that some runners have experimented with drugs as performance enhancers, and no doubt many of these runners have got away with it and the resulting prize money.

There is no doubt that this practice should be stopped, but the problem is that it can only be deterred through thorough testing procedures. Britain has certainly been at the forefront of the battle against drugs, with its random testing programme. It is only to be hoped that other countries will adopt similar programmes, in addition to the measures initiated by the IAAF.

There still seems to be a perception that the drug problem only relates to top sportspeople. I am not so sure. In South Africa there was a suggestion that the greatest abuse was actually in the school rugby teams, where parental, peer and teacher pressure was such that attempting to make the top team would drive many to seeking chemical assistance.

The use of the small pocket drug awareness card that has been produced by the Sports Council is to be commended, but new and more effective means of distribution need to be evolved to ensure it gets to every sportsperson, parent and teacher – and to the chemists. Only in this way will people truly understand just how easy it is to fall foul of the laws, since many of the over-the-counter cold, cough and flu remedies contain substances which are banned. A copy of the listing on the drug awareness card is given in appendix four. Take this to your doctor and your chemist the next time you need something for an ailment. Ask them to make sure that you are on the right side of the law.

It is a pity that the IAAF have now reduced the penalty for being found guilty of drug abuse. However, it is understandable that with the advent of professional athletes, the IAAF would not be in a position to defend too many legal battles in cases where athletes claim that their right to work has been taken from them. This has made the whole drugs issue much more difficult to enforce.

Whilst most of the attention seems to focus on the athletes, I feel more worldwide attention should be given to the suppliers and those who write the prescriptions for these drugs. After all, it is necessary to treat not only the symptoms but also the source of the problem.

SOME FINAL THOUGHTS

It would be impossible to list the requirements for each event and specific details of the ideal drinks, amounts, consistencies and so on for each and every sport. For one thing, what works for me or you will not necessarily work for the next person. However, in general, the advice given in this book is a good starting point for all sportspeople.

It is now up to you to plan for your requirements in your sport, whether that means getting drinks brought on to the rugby field at half-time, putting a sachet or drinking bottle at the front of the squash court, or carrying a Tripper full of fluid with you on your next orienteering competition.

One thing is certain: if you attend to your energy and water requirements in a more professional manner than you did before, your performance and recovery will improve, and that means better training and better competition. I believe this is the goal towards which all sportspeople strive.

Several suggestions need to be modified for your individual needs. For example, the principle that glycogen synthesis is greatest when the demand is greatest should lead the reader to deduce that in an event consisting of multiple heats or multiple efforts, it will be important to take a carbohydrate-boosting product as soon as possible after each leg of the competition. In this way the competitor can recover in time for the next leg, even if it is on the same day.

Another point that has to be made is that what has been written here must not be considered as the final word. There is so much more still to be learned in this area that you need to be constantly on the look-out for updated material. Although the basics may not change, newly discovered subtleties can make for the slight improvement in performance that can make the difference between winning and losing, whatever that means to you.

It is important to put winning into perspective. Winning is not necessarily about those who cross the line first or take home the trophy. Winners by my definition are people who achieve their targets and ambitions in sport by reaching their potential within the limits that they find themselves. Whilst the Boris Beckers, Bruce Fordyces, Peter Elliots and Gary Players of this world can afford to be professional sportsmen, the majority of us do not have the same opportunities, nor the same skill. Instead we have to shoehorn our sporting interest into a lifestyle which has priorities of work, family and social life. We can, however, strive to be the very best we can be.

6

AN INTERNATIONAL PERSPECTIVE

CHAPTER TWENTY-NINE

THE PROBLEMS OF BEING A WORLD-CLASS ATHLETE

It is very easy to recommend a certain approach to training, racing and preparation in athletics. It is even possible to do some of this without ever having taken part in the sport, and indeed there are some coaches who do this. The truth of the matter is that the recommendations for race preparation contained in this book are only the starting point. They form only a source of a trend which you must develop to cover your own particular needs. Preparation is everything; the outcome of the race is to a large extent predetermined, and your participation becomes the fulfilment of your preparation. This truth was highlighted in a discussion I had with former world-record-holder Sebastian Coe in 1991 on the simple matter of flying.

FLYING WITH SEBASTIAN COE

As more and more opportunities exist for athletes to compete internationally, and as more events are being held outside a simple two- or three-hour flight from home, one is entitled to ask, 'Do the athletes really know what they are letting themselves in for even before they reach the stadium?' This was a particularly relevant question for South Africans in 1992, when the international sporting ban was lifted and sportsmen and women strated to return to the international arena.

To Sebastian Coe in his glory days, flying was something that had to be carefully managed to ensure that its effect on performance was minimal. While the average traveller views flying as something between an exciting experience and a relaxing means of getting around the world, the same journey was to Coe something requiring substantial planning. In a world where performances and records are measured in hundredths of a second, being rocketed across time zones, no matter how comfortably, can have a devastating impact on one's chances of achieving a goal that one has trained for for over four years.

Take the 1984 Olympics, where Coe faced a seemingly easy flight, along with the rest of the British team, from London direct to California on the west coast of the United States. In all, the journey involved a relatively minor eight-hour time change, which many business and holiday travellers regularly handle with ease. For the dedicated athlete in search of Olympic titles in the cut-throat battleground of the 800m and 1500m, however, this was not the case.

Coe broke this flight up into smaller, more manageable sections by stopping over in the north-eastern city of Chicago. Then, after four weeks of full acclimatisation and training, he tackled the shorter flight to Los Angeles – but still left a further two weeks to recover before taking on the best the world could throw at him. It is history now that such an approach helped Coe become the first man ever to retain the Olympic gold in the 1500m. There can be little doubt that a similar detailed approach to competition helped Coe set four world records within a space of 41 days.

Now that he has retired from international athletics, the rigours of such preparation are things of the past. However, the softly spoken Englishman went on to embark upon a political career, and continued to fly as much, if not more, than he did in those memorable days of the '70s and '80s when he captured not only world records and gold medals but also the imagination of millions. Coe became the hero of a nation, kept schoolchildren up late and was every mother's ideal son-in-law as he raced to victory on the tracks of the world with apparent ease. In truth, however, the attention to detail that preceded such victory was awesome. Coe became closely involved with Atlanta researcher David Martin, who was studying the hormonal changes caused by flying. He had discovered, for instance, that flying caused minor changes in the hormone balance of long-haul travellers which could last for up to six weeks. This was of no consequence to the average passenger, but to the athlete in search of the slightest edge on the competition, it was vital.

While most air passengers are desperate to sleep, Coe would take pains to stay awake throughout the flight in order to avoid a drastic change in his waking and sleeping routine. Allowing his routine to change gradually would lessen jet lag. Even the timing and quantity of meals had to be considered. Soft drinks and water were chosen in preference to the pleasures of wines and other alcoholic beverages to ensure that the dehydrating effect of flying was minimised.

Coe, who is involved in a few business ventures over and above his political ambitions, is now able to take a much more relaxed view of flying. His basic requirements of air travel are still the same, though, he says with typical humour: 'The first priority is that it must stay up!' However, like most of us, he wonders why passengers are ushered aboard a flight at the scheduled time, only to be told that there will be a 50-minute delay. Why aren't we allowed an extended and relaxed stay in the more comfortable airport lounge? In the old days such annoying delays could have upset Coe's preparations considerably.

The other thing that puzzles Coe is the universally uttered 'Enjoy your flight' before take-off. 'What does it mean?' he muses, with a glint in his eye. 'I understand "Hope you had a good flight" and "We trust that you had a comfortable flight", but "Enjoy your flight"?' There is no answer from the man who has obviously come to terms with spending many hours in the sky.

CHAPTER THIRTY

A PERSONAL PERSPECTIVE ON SOME OF THE WORLD'S CLASSIC RACES

The following pieces were written immediately after I had completed the races concerned and they are faithfully reproduced here to retain the authentic atmosphere of the events. The intention is to enable the reader to experience the races as I did. As with everything, time changes views and blunts the memory. I therefore leave the reader to form his or her own judgements from these short reports.

Here, then, is a journey through some of the more unusual racing challenges in the world. Sit back and enjoy the tour . . .

THE WESTERN STATES 100, 1985

The Western States 100-mile (160km) endurance race represents an aspect of running that is new to most South Africans. The best way to describe it would be to say it is a combination of the intensity of the more popular mountain races with the trails and remoteness of some of the more obscure Duzi portages, and that the whole experience is located in an extreme version of the Drakensberg, where canyons, valleys, climbs and tracks allow only two directions – straight up and straight down.

Two more aspects that militate against rapid running are prime ingredients of the Western States 100. First, there is the altitude, which tops out just below 2,700m within three miles of the start at 1,860m and remains above 1,800m for the first 33 miles. Second, there is the footing, or rather the lack of it.

Apart from short stretches of road, which in total make up no more than eight miles of the course, the race route follows a twisting, narrow trail. It is booby-trapped with loose rock and exposed roots, and runs across rocky outcrops that require hand-over-hand climbing. It is said that there is not a flat section on the course longer than 250m. Even the final lap of the track is only 300m, as if too much flat surface would detract from the character of the race.

The Western States 100 certainly has character and atmosphere, and it is this that brings a hard core of runners back to its challenge year after year. Even seasoned runners sometimes have difficulty completing the course: the 'Western States Parachute Club' is probably bigger than in any other event. Some 45 per cent of the field recorded a DNF (Did Not Finish) in 1985, the year that two-time winner Jim Howard, a regular entrant since 1978, failed to pass halfway for the second time. Bruce la Belle, a regular since 1981, was reduced to a limping shadow of himself by the time he withdrew at 32 miles.

When this can happen to the best-prepared athletes in the race, it is little wonder that there is more than the usual pre-race apprehension as the entrants line up in the dawn in Squaw Valley. The gradual lightening of the sky emphasises the dominance of the three massive peaks facing us. The seconds, friends and loved ones take more time and care than usual in giving their charges the normal farewells. Perhaps the thought that they will not see the runners for at least 20 miles and more likely 60 miles has something to do with it. Possibly it is the knowledge of all the things that can go wrong – if the course doesn't get you, the bears and rattlesnakes will. In 1985, a very dry year, runners training spotted a record number of snakes. And then, for those who are allergic like me, there are also bee stings to worry about.

Despite all these perils facing the entrants, there is still a spirit of celebration at the start, a carnival atmosphere which acknowledges the fact that those present have survived the training and managed to make it to the start in one piece. If Comrades has its pre-race injuries, the training for this event could fill field hospitals in wartime. Almost all the runners can tell of falls, twists and pulls from their last training run over the course. Photographs taken at the start are evidence of participation; many won't make it to photographs at the finish.

There is no relief greater than the release of nervous energy resulting from the crack of the 12-bore that signals the start of the Western States 100. As in all ultras, the main core of the entrants chatter, joke and cheer during the start, but the immediate steep ascent (810m in 5km) soon brings silence.

For all the difficulties in the race, few sights can match the view of the world spread below as one crests Squaw Peak. The runners have little time for the view save to check on the next yellow ribbon that guides them on the course to Auburn. The ribbons and small metal 'WS' markers are the only trail markers and the race organisers wage an all-year battle with conservationists bent on removing the ribbons.

It is this battle of opposing interests which stimulates the organisers to announce that there is no guarantee that all the ribbons are in place on race day! This year, as the race director marked the first 10 miles (16km) of the course on the day before the race, a conservationist followed behind, removing the ribbons.

In some barren areas there is nothing to tie the ribbons to, so they are secured under loose rocks. By the end of the trail one has become accustomed to searching for the ribbons, some high, some low, but still there are long stretches where doubt enters the mind – how long since the last ribbon? Many runners have been lost on the trail. In 1983 Jim King was lost for 40 minutes, regained the lead, and finally lost the race to Jim Howard by just 31 seconds!

Then there have been controversies over distance. In 1985, after several measurements made on mountain bikes, the previous course was found to be eight miles short. Four of the easier sections were extended to make up the distance but, in true Western States spirit, care was taken not to bypass any of the steep or rough sections!

In the same way that the early Comrades competitors were looked upon with awe yet considered a lunatic fringe, so too are the Western States competitors. Each year more lunatics are ready to challenge the mountains and the race is slowly coming of age.

The Western States is considered the ultimate challenge to ultra runners and many a well-known star of road or track has come to the race expecting to win, only to be humbled and forced to withdraw. The second-fastest man in America over 50 miles (behind Bruce Fordyce), Barney Klecker, lined up in 1984 but withdrew at the first medical station. The world's number one ultra man, Yiannis Kouros of Greece, entered in 1985 but apparently thought better of it and failed to show up at the start. A rumour that Kouros had asked for appearance money and had been turned down by the organisers flew about in the two weeks prior to the event. But this race, like Comrades, is a race about challenge. To run is to challenge the course, not the other competitors; it is not about lining one's pockets.

The advice I received from an experienced Western States 100 runner on my arrival in the United States stayed with me during the run: 'The race is not against man or time, it's you and the mountain. Be flexible, work with the mountain.'

I became very close to that mountain during the many hours we shared.

THE JOHN TARRANT MEMORIAL 50-MILER, 1985

Many older runners in South Africa will remember the name of John Tarrant from the early 1970s when he came to run the Comrades. Others will better recognise him as the 'Ghost Runner', a nickname he earned because he was not allowed to run officially in international events as a result of having received a £3 prize for boxing some years earlier. It was during his visits to South Africa to run the Comrades – without a number – that he received the nickname.

During the late 1960s and early 1970s John Tarrant was arguably the best ultradistance runner in Britain, having won all the major ultra events, including the London to Brighton. In both of his attempts at Comrades he finished in the top placings but his name was neither announced as he crossed the line nor recorded in the results. However, he was not ignored by the runners behind him, who all passed their medals up one position, thereby ensuring that John received the gold he deserved.

John died of cancer at an early age and on 16 June 1985 an inaugural 50-mile race was held in his memory. It was appropriate that the course should be around the roads of Hereford, as this was his training area. The organisers had contacted Dave Box, one of John's friends in South Africa, asking him to see if anyone from South Africa could participate and so continue the connection. The four-lap course was described as undulating over a scenic route with two minor hills and a bit of city as well.

Since I was training for a 100 mile race early in July and was able to stop in Britain en route to the United States, it seemed an ideal opportunity to put in a final long training run.

I was extremely pleased when Paula Newby-Fraser and her boyfriend, Dave Alderton, both Savages members who are living in England at present, offered to second me. Paula is a winner of the Durban Carling Triathlon and five-times winner of the Hawaii Ironman. They met me at Heathrow on the Saturday and we spent the rest of the day driving to Hereford.

The next morning, at the very civilised hour of 8 a.m., I reported for registration and was warned to drink frequently and pull out if I 'felt dicky'. The risk of dehydration did not bother me too much since I had a good seconding crew; in fact, we were more concerned about the cold. Although the sun was visible, it shone with as little warmth as on a bad winter's day in Durban. Meanwhile the locals were muttering about the stations being over two miles apart.

A glance at the list of entries, which numbered 50, showed that most of the previous year's top 12 in the London to Brighton, including the familiar names of Martin Daykin, Mark Pickard, Peter Sugden and Bruce Slade, were participating. There were also three women entered, including Christine Barrett, the 37-year-old from Gloucester who holds a mass of records from 72 hours to 400 miles, and Lynn Fitzgerald, the current 100 mile record holder.

At 8.55 a.m. the runners lined up and my thoughts rolled back to what it must have been like to run Comrades years ago. There were no massive check-in procedures or crowds, no TV, no worries about getting a good start, and everyone seemed to know just about everyone else.

We observed a minute's silence and the race was blessed in memory of John Tarrant. At 9.00 a.m. the race began and the runners moved off at a conservative pace in what could easily have been mistaken for a club training run on the Comrades route a few weeks earlier. There was no rush for the TV or press and it was only after the first mile that the leaders increased the pace to something approaching respectability.

The course ran along the main ring road, which I remembered as the one Kenny Craig had run down the previous year on his way to breaking the Jogle record, before heading for the quaint and picturesque villages of Lower Bullingham, Holme Lacy, Mordieford and Hampton Bishop. As the route returned to Hereford the leaders went through the ten-mile mark in 58:09. Already making his mark on the race was Peter Sugden, and by the end of the first lap he was leading from a bunch that included Mark Pickard and Martin Daykin.

The format of the race followed that of other ultras, with those who had started off too ambitiously returning to their true positions, or worse, by the third lap. The course description had been fairly accurate and one wondered what Bruce Fordyce and other top runners could have done to the course and records.

My very professional seconding team kept me constantly informed of the goings-on, including the fact that a large percentage of the field was dropping out as a result of heat. Frankly, this was surprising, as the weather was taking a turn for the worse and my problem was trying to keep warm. Obviously I have missed the glory of a British summer for too long!

Sugden had been recording consistent five-mile splits and went through the 40-mile mark in 3:56, followed a couple of minutes later by Daykin and then Pickard. The gradual climb from the 40-mile mark back to Hereford took its toll on the fourth lap and there were a number of place changes in the last 12 miles.

Obviously Sugden had also had his problems in maintaining the pace and finished the race in 5:01, taking 64 minutes to cover the last ten miles. Daykin followed him in 5:11 and Pickard was third, with Andrew Battee running through to fourth.

Both of the leading women were having problems and, although separated by only two minutes, were only starting their final lap after 5:55. Having witnessed the strength of Helen Lucre running Comrades two weeks before, and bearing in mind the course differences, I am convinced that the world 50 mile record would have been broken had Helen run this race. The record at that time, depending on your source, was given as either 6:20:42 or 6:02, but both sources credited it to Leslie Watson from Scotland. Helen Lucre went through the 80km mark in Comrades in 6:11.

The prize-giving was held early to allow competitors time to start their long journeys home. The prizes were presented by Edie Tarrant, John's widow. I finished seventh in 5:56.

THE HAWAII IRONMAN, 1984

The Ironman has become a pilgrimage for an ever-increasing number of endurance athletes who seek the challenge of pitting mind and body against consecutive distance races in three sports. This, the original triathlon, was conceived by Commander John Collins and his military mates over a few beers. In an attempt to determine which sport demanded the greatest fitness, a race comprising a 2.4 mile (3.8 km) swim, a 112 mile (180km) cycle and a 26.2 mile (42.2km) run was developed. The distances were enough to tax the fitness and endurance of any self-respecting athlete, but, to add further spice, it was decided that the event would be held in the claustrophobic heat of the Hawaiian islands.

So it was that in 1978 a small field of 15 athletes pioneered what has become the premier triathlon event. It has been estimated by the Triathlon Federation of the United States of America (TriFed USA) that there will be 1,500 triathlons involving 60,000 triathletes in the United States this year. On 3 October 1984, the Federation of International Triathlons, suitably abbreviated to FIT, was born. It brought together the national bodies of 12 countries, happily including South Africa.

In 1981, when entries grew too numerous for the original Ironman course in Honolulu, the event moved to the lava-covered island of Kona. This move has resulted in an enormous tourist boom on the 'Big Island', which lists the production of marijuana as its main industry. The Ironman 1984 was worth $4.2 million to the island.

The cycling course allows the more casual participant to view four towering volcanoes, some still smoking. The closest and smallest is Mount Mualalai, which the cycle course contours around. In the north is Mauna Kea and in the south Mauna Loa, which is a million years old and still growing. Mauna Loa's last eruption sent 16 miles of lava flows over the island, threatening Hilo, the county seat of the Big Island.

Near the turnaround point on the cycle course is the Mookini Heiau, a temple believed to have been constructed around AD 480. According to legend, the walls were constructed between sunset and sunrise of a single night by over 15,000 men who formed a human chain to pass the stones from the Pololoa Valley 12 miles away.

The base for the triathlon is the town of Kialua-Kona, a lush oasis at the start and finish of an open and desolate course.

For the three weeks prior to the event, triathletes arrive at Kona airport, which consists of a small series of thatched shelters. For many the task is to adapt to the tortuous heat baking down and being reflected off the grotesque lava forms. For some, being here is the culmination of months, if not years, of training. As the race date approaches, the competitive atmosphere brews. There is no discussion of definite target times and commitments remain personal secrets. Every physical and psychological advantage is sought over each of the other competitors. The American dream does not allow competition for competition's sake. This is Olympic year!

A walk to the bay in the morning in the days before the race reveals an endless stream of red bathing caps bobbing along the course in the clear blue Pacific. The water is warm and allows a view of the marine life of Kialua Bay. Even the fish have become accustomed to the annual intensification of activity and no longer dart out of sight.

The Queen Kaahumanu Highway is crawling with cyclists from Kialua to Hawi in the north. The infamous Mumuko winds, together with the long hill, defy the cyclists to reach the turnaround mark, much as they did when King Kamehameha's warriors were sent to run in the winds for strength training. Only the very best, says the legend, passed the test of the churning winds that seem to blast from all sides.

As the clouds assemble in the late afternoon, activity moves to Alii Drive. Runners skulk from one area of shade to another, avoiding the heat as best they can. Survival is reaching the next watering point.

The daily ritual proceeds with greater enthusiasm as race day approaches. Final tune-ups or emergency repairs ensure that the local cycle shops are financed for another year. Every business has an Ironman special: carbohydrate-charged meals, souvenir T-shirts, race clothing, jewellery, even haircuts! Water and air are free – everything else has a price.

The last two days before the event are marked by calm. There are fewer swimmers, cyclists and runners to be seen. Instead there is registration, check-in and cycle inspection. Energy is being conserved; the air smells of competition. Battle-scarred T-shirts from the world's hardest events are paraded at every opportunity, each announcing that the body inside has accomplished some gruelling physical feat, each intended to 'psyche out' the opposition,

The carbo-party is held in a pair of marquees and features anything that sounds, smells or looks like carbohydrate, accompanied by copious supplies of Bud Light, the American beer. Considering that this event was conceived in a pub, if is fitting that Bud Light should sponsor it.

The 1984 Ironman had competitors from 38 countries and 48 states of the USA. Each had a story to tell. For Joan Joesting, who had won a struggle against alcohol, drug addiction and her husband's physical abuse, the 1984 Ironman was a triumphal celebration. *Women's Sports* magazine declared: 'If a 46-year-old mother can leave a battering husband, recover from multiple addictions, cycle 13,000 miles alone in a strange country [she had already cycled round Australia], write a book and become a triathlete, what can be impossible?'

Michael Russo made history by being the first deaf participant in the event. Then there were the 50 or more who were full-time triathletes, fully financed by one or more companies. These athletes, male and female, knew only days filled with running, swimming and cycling, with periods of rest liberally spaced throughout. For them a good performance would entail the lure of further product endorsements and invitations to foreign shores. Also present were the many who shoehorned training into a day already full with eight hours of work, personal commitments and that essential training ingredient, sleep. Their goal was to prove themselves against their own specific targets and thereby achieve the best possible position in the professional-amateur international field.

There were also three South African entries: David McCarney, Moira Hornby and myself. McCarney had won the trip as first prize in the 1984 Durban Triathlon. He was no stranger to international competition, having been a member of the successful London to Paris Triathlon team, and having come eighth in September 1984 in the Nice Triathlon, which has the richest prize money in the sport and so attracts many of the top professional triathletes. David, who is not married, had resigned in May from his work as an attorney to allow himself time to train for these events.

Moira Hornby, like McCarney, won the trip as first woman home in the Durban event and made a similar arrangement with her employers to allow her a more flexible training schedule. A veteran of the 1983 Ironman, Moira had been in California and Kona for three weeks before the 1984 event in the hope that this would help her improve on her 1983 performance of 12:19 (position 299).

I had come second in the Durban event, captained the London to Paris team, and had shortly before attempted with Ken Craig the John o' Groats to Land's End record sponsored by *Squire* magazine. Five weeks before the Ironman event I suffered a stress fracture of the fibula after 305 miles of the Jogle run, which I then completed on an old borrowed bicycle. Once more *Squire* stepped in to assist me with a sponsorship to the Ironman, and I arrived in Kona the week before the event.

Race day eventually arrived. 'Good morning, Kona,' said the radio. 'It will be very hot, with a high of 97 degrees. Clear skies are forecast with no cloud build-up and winds between 10 and 20 miles per hour.' The prayers of 1,200 triathletes had not been answered.

When final check-in procedures were over, we awaited the gun that would release us from the penned enclosure of Kialua Harbour. The front markers were mysteriously held back by a line of overhead flags. At 7 a.m. we swam off in a sardine-like shoal on the 2.4 mile out-and-back journey.

Dan Madruga, the Brazilian 1500m Olympic finalist, churned through the Pacific in a new record swim time of 47:48. Three-time winner Dave Scott emerged in fifth position and was soon powering his way over the cycle route. McCarney was the first South African out of the water in 15th position, followed by Hornby and then myself in 1:06.

Mark Allen, the top money-earner in triathlons that year, led in the bicycle leg. Dave Scott and Scott Tinley were moving through to second and third place but there was to be no catching Mark Allen, who appeared to be opening the gap.

McCarney was cycling well against strong opposition and was still in the top 20 at the cycle turn. Having completed my weakest event, I now moved through the pack, passing Moira when we were 22km into the 180km ride. The sun was shining down at full force from a cloudless sky, just as promised. The winds were more amenable than they had been in 1983 but, as always, the headwinds for the 12 miles to the turnaround point drained the strength of all but the strongest.

For the last 55km of the cycle we rode into a constant headwind, a condition that is not usual, since riders can normally expect a tailwind for the last 25km. The road ahead of us shimmered in the heat. The only distractions were the helicopters of ABC World of Sport overhead, and the messages written in white pumice stone on the lava.

Mark Allen reached the run stage having taken 4:58 for the cycle leg (another record time). Dave Scott followed, with Scott Tinley in third place. In the women's section, Jennifer Hinshaw had won the swim leg, coming in among the top 20 men, but now had the Puntous twins, Sylviane and Patricia, rapidly narrowing her lead. Hornby completed the cycle course in just under 6:30.

McCarney and I took 6:00 and 5:51 respectively for the cycle but we had both been drinking too much and were feeling bilious. In addition, my shoulders and arms were cherry-red from the 97°F (45°C) sun and too little acclimatisation.

Using ice to relieve the pain, I tried to reduce the burning but the sun was still high in the sky when we started the run. It was at the five-mile mark that David and I met. We were both having bad runs and walking at the aid stations, seeking the maximum amount of water to pour over ourselves.

Up front, Mark Allen was dying and Scott passed him at 27km. From then on the result was a formality and Scott broke the tape in 8:54:20 – 11 minutes faster than his previous best and breaking the 3:00 barrier for the first time ever.

Scott Tinley was second again, having passed Allen in the run. Sylviane Puntous broke the women's record to hit the tape in 10:35, with sister Patricia in second place two minutes behind.

McCarney and I began to recover at the turn in the run and completed the course in 10:59 and 10:52 respectively. This positioned us 73rd and 51st. Hornby finished in 11:07, 84th position overall, and was the fifth woman home.

There are several ways to qualify for entry into the Hawaii Ironman event, one of which is coming in the top 100 in a previous Hawaii Ironman – so the three South Africans were assured of places the following year.

Moira Hornby's remarkable improvement is an example of the results one can expect from knowing the course and from proper acclimatisation for the event. It is worth mentioning that she won her age group (30 to 34), that Dave McCarney came 30th in his (25 to 29) and that I ended eighth in mine (30 to 34).

THE TWO BRIDGES ULTRAMARATHON, 1986

It is common knowledge that the London to Brighton race that is run in October each year is the British equivalent of the South African Comrades; what is lesser known is that we also have an equivalent for their Two Oceans, which is held about two months before our prestigious 54-miler.

The Two Bridges Road Race was inaugurated in 1968, two years earlier than its Cape Town counterpart, and has always been run over a course of 36 miles and 185 yards which circles the Forth estuary in central Scotland. The race starts in the Fife town of Dunfermline, winds its way along the north bank of the river which it first crosses at Kincardine, and then returns along the south bank before recrossing at the Forth Road Bridge to finish at Rosyth.

Like the Cape Town race, this is considered to be one of the best-organised ultra races, and competitors come from all corners of the country to make up one of the biggest fields in the UK. However, it is probably here that the similarities end.

There are no distance markers at 1km intervals; instead, times are shouted at five-mile intervals. The Cape's plentiful refreshment stations and sponging points at 1.8km intervals offering everything from Pepsi to chocolate are replaced by picnic tables holding a few plastic cups of water or diluted orange, spaced at regular three-mile intervals. And, just to make sure that the 140-strong field has spaced out enough, the first table is set up at least 11km into the race. Gone are the enthusiastic, encouraging, supporters who line every hill of the route; instead a few locals glance at the runners as they wait for the pub to open.

Despite the rule against seconding, in 1986 all the regular runners had their own crews, and a constant stream of cars leapfrogged their way down the course from three miles out. I never thought that it would be possible to dehydrate in the cool climes of Scotland, but the restriction on the water was such that I managed it. With only two miles to go I startled a local petrol attendant by downing his watering-can of water before continuing on my way.

If I have painted a bleak and dreary picture of the race, that was not my intention, because there is just as much excitement and apprehension before the start of this race as there is before Comrades.

The big names are all entered: Don Ritchie, holder of many records at distances from 50km to 200km; Calvin Woodward, former 100 mile record-holder; Dave Dowdle, 24- and 48-hour record-holder; Mark Pikard; and a certain Ken Shaw, who is the only person to have completed the race in every one of the 19 years it has been run.

If the on-course facilities are spartan, the Scots value for money is lavish. In return for an entry fee of £2, each entrant receives numbers, a programme, a bus trip to the start line, a meal after the race, and a certificate and results at the finish.

The 1986 race started at the Dunfermline Glen park gates as usual. After a short trip along the narrow, winding park paths, the lead pack of about ten broke away. Wayne Evans of Tipton Harriers moved straight to the front, going through five miles in 27:54. The following pack of five included Ritchie and Woodward. Woodward was chasing his sixth win in the race, whilst Ritchie was after his second.

What was surprising about Evans was that until recently he had been a middle-distance runner, with only one outing over the marathon distance in 2:40. Despite this, he was comfortably leading the race and held on to the pole position until just after the marathon, recording splits of 57:12, 1:26:39, 1:55:22 and 2:25:17 for the 10-, 15-, 20- and 25-mile marks respectively.

By the time the race reached the Kincardine swing bridge, the field had stretched out and runners were alone on the twisting country roads, without sight of those in front or behind.

The route on the south bank took the race through the oil town of Grangemouth and into Boness. At the east end of the town lies a steep 2km hill and, as if to make life harder, the water station is positioned at the very start of it so that any hope of a good drink is ruined by the desire to get a rhythm set for the hill.

By 25 miles Don Ritchie had left the chasing pack and was closing on Evans. Shortly after the marathon, it was all over; Ritchie had opened the gap and the fight was left for the minor placings.

From the top of the hill the towers of the Forth Road Bridge can be seen, but they are many miles off and seem to linger teasingly on the horizon for hours. Eventually the road runs down to the 2.4km bridge, which has its own special hill as a result of the suspension cables. A strong wind inevitably buffets runners on their journey across the river and the only consolation is that it affords a fine view of both the Edinburgh and Fife coastlines.

Dramatic changes were occurring down the field as legs began to seize up from the early pace to the marathon mark. Woodward had dropped back to tenth place, Dowdle had moved through into eighth and Evans was hanging on grimly to seventh. Local hero Mike McHale, encouraged by his seconds, was challenging Richard Dalby for second place. Further down the field, Morag Taggart was leading the women to take the honours in 4:40:25, 16 minutes clear of her nearest rival.

Ritchie took the title in 3:36:37, and in doing so also claimed first vet and first Scot. It is indicative of the friendliness of the race that Ritchie asked that his vet's prize be handed on to the third vet (second vet receiving an official award). Alan Evason, who had won fourth prize, second vet and part of the Tipton Team prize, then asked that his vet's prize be awarded to Wayne Evans who, by finishing seventh, had missed out on the awards.

Each entrant had been handicapped so that even a back marker could win the race in this section. Grading was set by the race referee, the basic principle being 'the less we know about the runner, the shorter the handicap'. This prevents outsiders hustling a win. However, it didn't prevent regular entrants like Dave Atwell from making full use of his

50-minute advantage to add the handicap prize to his prize for sixth place and Ritchie's gift of third vet's prize. It appeared that no one wanted to walk away with three prizes, because Atwell then handed on his prize to the vet in tenth place.

Whilst it is possible to laugh at the scarcity of the watering points, the marshalling (I almost took two wrong turnings) and other on-course facilities in this race, where else can you see runners handing on their hard-won prizes?

THE FIRST FAT-ASS FIFTY, 1989

> *'Here is an ancient solitude that mocks a light and feckless mood. Here is a sense of mystery and a strange solemity. Here can a man stand still to pray, for the world seems far away. If weather smiles or weather frowns, there is a magic on the Downs.'*

> PATIENCE STRONG

These few lines could have been written specifically for the approximately 30 ultra runners who entered for the challenge of the 'Recover from the Holidays First Fat-Ass Fifty-Miler Finishing in Farnham'. They had been forewarned by race director Alan Firth, who openly admitted to 'importing the race under exclusive contract' from Joe Oakes of Los Altos in California. The pre-race literature stated that the race was guaranteed to be disorganised and proclaimed, 'No entry fee, no aid, no awards and no wimps!'

So it was that on the 13th day after Christmas we set off at 7.00 a.m. from the Dunton Green railway station near Sevenoaks in Kent, heading for Farnham in Surrey to run the Fat-Ass Fifty trail race across the North Downs.

As my overnight accommodation had been in Sevenoaks, I jogged the 4km to the start, where I was furnished with six pages of directions to Farnham. I had expected the route to be adequately marked, but this was obviously a luxury the race organisers couldn't afford.

Amongst the entries were Hilary Walker, who had set world records at 100 miles for both track and road distances, as well as establishing new records at most distances in a 48-hour race; Richard Browne, who had broken the Land's End to John o' Groats record in August; and Nigel Robson, who had considerable experience at trail races and was attempting the grand slam of trail 100-milers in America in 1992. Many of the other runners were in training for the Milton Keynes 24-hour race on 18 February and were keen to make use of this early 'time trial'.

Equipped with a light backpack which contained only a rain suit and a few Leppin squeezies, and wrapped up in tights, long-sleeved shirt and gloves, I settled into the lead pack, aware that many of the others had had the direction sheets for over a week and therefore, I presumed, would have a better feel for way ahead. The notes indicated that the first crew access point for seconding was at 14 miles until that until then we were on our own. As we turned off the road after 4km and climbed over the first stile into a mud patch, the reality of the challenge began to emerge.

Although the UK was having an unusually warm winter, there was a lot of mud, and the paths were not well-marked. For much of the early going it was a case of following the deep hoof-prints of cattle. One poor chap had to retrieve a shoe from the quagmire before proceeding.

The lead bunch consisted of five when we ran 'past the church' and turned 'right to follow the path'. This led us to a security gate of a manor house, at which point it became obvious that we had taken the wrong route. We retraced our steps, found the correct turning, and realised that we were now the hunters in the second or third pack.

As we climbed and descended the hills my legs went in all directions – I felt like Bambi on ice. Since the race had been an afterthought for me, I had only a pair of Nike Air Mariahs. This is an excellent and very comfortable shoe for road races, but its ultra-smooth orange outer sole offered no grip on the slithery mud paths. Paul Simon's song 'Slip-Sliding Away' immediately came to mind, and would stay with me for the rest of the race!

Three of us worked together to catch the lead bunch, and briefly pulled along Hilary Walker, who then fell off the back. Crossing another stile into another field, it became evident that at least one runner had done his homework, as he ran along an adjacent track to overtake the whole lead pack, who were struggling through the mud. The pace dropped to allow the pack to benefit from his experience for the next few miles.

Another couple of wrong turnings and much discussion amongst the pack convinced me that my decision to stick with the leaders had been wise. In any case, I had decided that one scalp I wanted was Richard Browne's, as minor 'revenge' for his removal of Ken Craig's name from the Land's End record.

At last the first crew point loomed, and while many grabbed sustenance from their seconds, I filled up the two 125ml hand bottles I had been running with and quickly caught up Browne and Robson, with another Scot, Rab, just behind us.

Through woods and over stiles we went, checking directions,

picking a route through narrow, muddy, cattle-trampled paths, over more stiles – the routine had been set. Intermittently I could look up to appreciate that here on the small island of Britain I could find the solitude, mystery and magic of the Downs that Patience Strong wrote of. Too soon, however, I was brought back to the reality of the task in hand by another fallen tree, stile or decision by my legs to slide away to the left when all other parts of my body intended going forward.

At the next support point Richard, Rab and I clocked in. While they restocked their backpacks from their crew, I bought a cool drink and a piece of cake from the kiosk in the car park. We left together and the direction became clearer as we headed for the Box Hill check-point. The track became more distinctive and, in places, almost dry.

As we climbed the hill, a squadron of mountain bikes, the latest UK craze, wove their way past. I decided that this was the time to make a break and by the time I reached the Box Hill check-point, I had a six-minute lead.

The support crews awaited their runners while I filled the hand bottles and then departed for the steep downhill to the river crossing. The pattern was the same as that of the Western States 100-miler I had done in 1985, but there was no altitude and the route was not as well marked.

Another climb took me to almost 29 miles. As I looked up to the crest I could see a recognisable figure bekoning me. Ian Champion, previously the London to Brighton organiser and a great promoter of South African running, had come down the path to meet me and would now offer me support over the remaining 20 miles. Ian had offered to come down to second me when I was staying with him, but since neither of us knew the exact route we left it as a flexible arrangement, and I had prepared myself for the possibility that I might see him only at the finish so that I wouldn't be disappointed if things didn't work out. But, as his many friends in South Africa will testify, Ian is as reliable as the Rock of Gibraltar and now relieved me of the backpack and a few unnecessary kilograms of weight.

This equalling of my conditions with those of the other runners, plus what was then about a 15-minute lead, spurred me on and success now rested on my ability to find the correct direction.

Richard Browne had mysteriously missed the Box Hill check-point and, although he had been in third position after the previous check-point, had pulled through to second by the next support stop, leaving fellow Scot Rab in third. As the time approached 4.00 p.m. and the North Downs Way threaded over hill, through forest and eventually along a river, I raced the falling of darkness.

Feeling the effects of mild dehydration from the early part of the race, as well as my energy dropping, my legs splaying, and the ever-present mud slapping at my feet, I had to pick up pace again if I was to beat the 9:00 mark and the dark.

Emerging from the track past quaint cottages and on to the final 400m of tarred road, my legs queried this sudden, solid footing as the final target of Farnham railway station loomed close. As I passed the car-park barrier, the clock stopped at 8:59:47 – by no means the fastest 50-miler I've done, but certainly one of the most challenging and interesting.

Richard Browne and Raymond Ball tied for second place 33 minutes later, but Browne seemed to have taken another wrong turning, as he approached the finish from another route!

Hilary Walker, as expected, finished well up the field to take third place with another 24-hour exponent, Bob Musgrave.

Results:
1. N. Williamson 8:59:47
2. R. Browne, R. Ball 9:33:21
3. H.Walker, B. Musgrave 10:00:20
5. B. Clayton-Jolley 10:31:45 (13 finishers)

THE NATIONAL CLASSIC, 1991

There is something about travelling from Pietermaritzburg to Durban that seems to 'call' every endurance sportsperson. The runners have the Comrades, the canoeists have the Duzi – so it came as no surprise that the third annual *Natal Mercury* Pick 'n' Pay Hypermarket National Classic was oversubscribed within five days of entries becoming available. By 1992, in fact, riders would have to qualify for this cycle race by completing other recognised races with an average speed of over 25km/hr.

In three years the race has grown from a field of 150 to 900 accepted entries, and this limit, which allows for 'no shows', was imposed to ensure that all 750 places allocated by the traffic authorities were taken. Already the field could be two or three times the size if entries were not limited.

In the first race the top 12 places were reserved for professionals, and the country's best entered the event. Mark and Gary Beneke, Steve and Alan Wolhuter, Willie Engelbrecht, Robbie McIntosh, Theuns Mulder, Lourens Smith, Johnny Koen, Rodney Fowler, Jannie van der Berg and Graham Cockerton all lined up to compete for generous prize money and 'hot spot' and 'king of the mountain' bonuses. Then there were licenced cyclists and non-licenced amateurs, many of whom had travelled the distance before as runners or canoeists.

The 95km course is as long and taxing as the name of the event, and the swift north turn in Pinetown to a road aptly named Mountain Rise left many gasping.

The race up front was swift, with a group of 30 together until Cato Ridge, 38km out. Then a devastating break saw Gary Beneke and team-mate Wille Engelbrecht forge ahead with Robbie McIntosh and Johnny Koen, but this two-time winner couldn't hold the pace and dropped back. From here on the triumvirate led the race.

Beneke, who won the hot spot and hill sections in the Rapport Tour, took the first king of the mountain spot on Inchanga as well as the Hillcrest hot spot. McIntosh tended to hang in behind, but produced the effort required to win the second king of the mountain on Mountain Rise, and Engelbrecht earned the third bonus for the Pinetown hot spot.

As they sprinted for the finish, Beneke edged out Southern Sun/M-Net team-mate Engelbrecht by half a wheel, with McIntosh third. Beneke's time was 2:24:36.

But this race is one for the people, and crowds lined the route, particulary at the hills, to see the cyclists struggle!

Numerous well-known runners and sportsmen were in the field: Comrades and 100-mile veteran Dave Box; triathlete Russell Dyer, who has also a top 20 Comrades to his credit; Springbok triathlete Manfred Fuchs; jockey Brian Strydom; Natal runner Athol Dand; Springboks Trevor Strydom and Gary van Wyk; Comrades number one Clive Crawley. The list goes on . . .

At this end of the field the objective was not the top prize, but the competitive spirit was there as small clusters tried to make breaks from the large bunches 'taking a free lift' in the slipstream, whilst those up front battled the inevitable headwind that prevailed for most of the way.

The runners were evident too by their tactics, taking things easier on the gradual but constant climb up to Radnor Farm before making any move.

The whip of the wind and the whir of the gears was occasionally broken by the sound of steel and flesh on tar, and steel on steel, as a miscalculation or pot-hole brought riders down. There was no stopping, though. The fear of being dropped off the bunch, left to face the wind by oneself, and the time schedule for a 2:50 minute gold certificate kept the pressure on.

Even those who came adrift found the motivation to get right back on their saddles: witness the gutsy and blood-stained Russell Dyer, who came unstuck within 10km of the start but caught up to the front of the second major pack and was fighting for a break. Even the cut that would later require four stitches couldn't stop him.

As the over-enthusiastic fell off the front bunch, they were swallowed up and often sat out at the back of the chasing bunch.

Hills galore: up to Lion Park, then Cato Ridge, Inchanga – 20km/hr up, 70km/hr down. How many forgot Alviston? Their numbers were etched in sweat on the tar as the bunch headed for Kearnsey College; time to make up average speed down Botha's Hill, speed climbing to 70km/hr and more.

The climb to Hillcrest lost some more fellow travellers, but nothing could separate the bunch as they sped to Kloof and then down Fields into Pinetown.

Passing through one of three watering points, cyclists were thankful for the new diluted FRN energy drinks packed in booster bags, but many were unable to grab these life-giving packages as they sped past at 50 to 60km/hr.

Another attempt at a break failed as they left the Comrades route and headed for New Germany and the hill that is the stuff of legends. Finally, a right turn took cyclists down to the Palmiet river, a sort of calm before the storm. But a pot-hole just before the bottom took out two more contenders just before the sheer 1km climb facing riders.

Tactics differed. Some charged the hill, almost willing the momentum of the short downhill to see them far enough up the other side. But no, a frantic search for levers and the gnashing of gears reduced them to an almost stationary bundle, with feet hitting the ground.

Some selected their easiest gear from the start and got left to face not only the hill but also the wind and loss of contact. But it was the few with less sense of panic and more control who eventually dominated as they stood on their pedals, shifting full body weight from side to side to the encouragement of the crowd, who lined the hill to watch.

The cyclists struggled up that last 400m. Cresting out, there was hardly time to spare to change from bottom to top gear – don't let the bunch re-form! Then the final long downhill and flat wind-hammering pull to the finish at the Hypermarket; another wheel to wheel and two more dropped to the back, with bruises to prove they were there.

A short climb, which felt to your drained legs like another Inchanga, a left turn, and sprint for the line – it was over.

This ritual was repeated over and over again for the next two hours, as licensed, amateur, leisure and would-be cyclists conquered the course. Recovery was quick once the legs touched Mother Earth, and already there was talk of improving the next year . . .

The National Classic is certainly an event every Comrades runner and Duzi canoeist should compete in. In case you need an incentive, those who have completed all three are regarded as having completed the Ultimate Triathlon and can earn a ceramic beer mug to prove it.

Now, if only they could organise a swim from the Duzi start to the ocean – or, perhaps, roller-skating?

THE INTERNATIONAL SPARTATHLON, 1992

Over 2,500 years ago, a Greek messenger ran from Athens south-west to Sparta to request help in defending Athens against the Persians. History tells us that he arrived 'the next day', which means he took somewhere between 24 and 48 hours to complete the 250km journey. Due to religious beliefs, the Spartan army could not leave Sparta until after the full moon. So, having delivered his message and rested, he later returned to join his army as they marched to the plains of Marathon, some 46km east of Athens. The Greeks were able to beat off the Persian invaders and it is thought that the same messenger, Pheidippides, was then ordered to run to Athens to tell of the victory. With over 500km already under his belt, Pheidippides became the first known victim of over-racing, as he struggled to Athens, shouted his message of victory, collapsed and died!

This last leg has been credited with being the inspiration for the marathon, an event commenced at the first modern Olympic Games held in Athens in 1896. Fittingly, it was a Greek who won this race, although the exact distance of 42.2km was not fixed until the London Olympics, for which the start was moved to outside the Queen's palace window.

Little had been made of Pheidippides' exploits until 1982, when a British air commander, John Fodden, researched the route used by Pheidippides for his run and, with a group of colleagues, completed the same course. This led to the initiation of the annual International Spartathlon 250km race in 1983. As in the original run, athletes must arrive in Sparta the day after they leave Athens; thus a 36-hour time limit is enforced.

Traditionally only about 35 per cent of the field have ever completed the course, but in 1992 that increased to 50 per cent. Although the organisers receive many applications each year, the field is curtailed by their selection panel to include only those likely to complete the event. There is no prize money, nor any commercialism allowed in this event. The true spirit of amateurism is maintained from start to finish. It is an event that is entered into because of the challenge, the history – and because of the amateur ideals.

The organisers encourage athletes to bring messages from their various community leaders, so that they are running with messages in the same way as Pheidippides did in his run. In 1984 they gave completion certificates only to those who had carried messages.

I had not been able to run the race until 1992, when my application as a South African was approved for the first time. Dreading the thought of not having my completion of the race officially recognised, I arranged to carry three messages from South Africa: one from the President of the National Olympic Commitee of South Africa, one from the Mayor of Durban and one from the South African State President. These would provide the essential incentive when the going got tough.

Last-minute sponsorship by a benefactor who shall be known only as 'Nic the Greek' and SAA in Athens saw me fly out of Jan Smuts on Tuesday morning, to be met by one of the race organisers at 9.00 p.m. that night.

The next day I moved into the Olympic Village with the other athletes and was joined by my wife Karin, who had had to leave a day after me but would provide my seconding where it was allowed.

The atmosphere in the village combined friendship with anxiety. We all knew the statistics, the 65 per cent drop-out rate, we all knew that we were competing first against ourselves, then against the course and only finally against each other if we got past the 200km mark. We knew all of that, but each of us wanted that finish desperately.

Greek administration seems to operate in a different time zone, and 9.00 a.m. meetings run into 2.00 p.m. meetings; all meetings will happen 'shortly'. The novices show frustration as the vests and shorts we are all to wear fail to make deadline after deadline.

Spare time, what there is of it, is taken up with preparation of seconding items, resting and the occasional walk round the massive Olympic complex built for the failed bid to hold the 1996 games. Four is the lucky number: four synthetic tracks, four swimming pools, four tennis arenas. Add to this a railway station, two bus and car parks, a 'police village', two diving pools, a cycling track and a massive indoor hall, and you have the beginnings of the Olympic structure. The shops were selling off many items marked 'Athens 1996' at bargain prices, mourning the successful bid by Atlanta.

Ten hours to go and the running kit arrives, greeted with a flurry of scissors and needles to amend the errors in size. A fleeting meeting with my bed brings me to race day and the dark bus journey to the old Stadium and the 7.00 a.m. start.

Hilary Walker, the diminutive UK record-holder at 24 and 48 hours, is swamped by the blue Spartathlon vest; American Roy Pirrung is psyched up and going for the win. Friends from previous ultras wish me luck, as the experienced hands watch the rookies in their nervousness.

We line up across the entrance steps of the original 1896 Olympic Stadium, regimental trumpets blow, a gunshot is fired and we are under way.

Four lanes of traffic obligingly stop as we enter the centre of Athens and head west. Even in this early light, one can begin to taste the fumes. It takes us 20km to get out of the main stream of traffic, but even the undulating coastal road that reminds me of the Bantry Bay run in Cape Town is poisoned by industrial and traffic fumes.

Small picnic tables form oases along the route, with the selection of refreshments varying as the route proceeds. The harbour, after 60km, heralds the smell from the oil refineries. Ahead is the Corinth Canal at 80km, and the first meeting with your second.

As we cross the bridge, the pace slows as we marvel at the deep, clean cleft that has been gouged out of the rock to form the famous Corinth shipping link. By now the pollution, in unseasonably overcast and humid weather, has taken its toll. A nauseous feeling never quite reaching the point of discomfort is an ever-present shadow.

From the climb to the seconding point we drop through the vineyards and on to crushed shell tracks that weave their way through the countryside: only two Comrades to go!

Fresh grapes are added to the menu at the roadside tables, as this lonely period of running allows the mind to dream back to 496 BC and the journey of the messenger whose footsteps we are following. The hills became mountains as both they and the darkness begin to close in. The climb out of the plains became steeper and a car draws close to hand out torches to the runners.

The seconds are able to see their charges at 10km to 15km intervals now, and most of these meetings coincide with the small villages we run through. The greetings from the residents standing outside the local watering hole become more vociferous. Often children act as lookouts, warning of the approaching runner.

As I turn a corner I can hear the carnival atmosphere of the next refreshment point, but a steep 200m climb separates us. Clapping pulls me up the hill to the reward of hot soup and biscuits. I depart, to be swallowed by the darkness: 150km gone, *and now for the worst part*. Soon I am following a tarred road with hairpin bends that climbs the side of a mountain, on which I think I can see the next seconding point . . . why is it moving away? The beam of the torch is not strong enough to allow me to see my surroundings properly. Eventually I step off the tar on to a gravel road. Only metres ahead it ends in a parking area and I am greeted by Karin and an army officer who insists that I can't change in the car. He points upwards and I strain my neck, eventually seeing a small light on top of a pitch-black ridge against a darkened sky.

I had imagined that there would be a track and understood that we would be led over this section, but no such luxury. No track, no leader – just fluorescent bars at turning points along a rock-strewn ascent that seems to have no distinct direction. The instructions are simple: make your way between the markers on each corner until you reach the top! In the darkness, hand-over-hand climbing and careful picking out of a route see me on my way.

A voice with a heavy accent shouts 'Are you OK?' and my legs turn to jelly with shock at this cry out of the darkness. It is one of the four or so soldiers who are stationed in the bushes on the ascent, just in case of problems. The precautions are justified as one runner breaks his leg on this section later in the night. *This must be the worst part of the race.*

As I reach the top, the wind whips me over the crest 1,200m above my starting point. Below are the tiny lights of the next village, and again the solitary fluorescent marker to aim for, then another, and another, as I made my way down the suicidally steep mountain. The leg muscles have now been truly softened up and the real damage is being done on this section, *which is undoubtedly the worst part of the race!* The footing is loose rock which requires a skiing action for the descent. Only one Comrades to go!

Victory over the mountain provides a spur as I set off. Karin has been unable to get to the last seconding point, prompting an imagining of all the possible calamities likely to befall her in the unfamiliar left-hand-drive car! Two headlights dazzle me, almost forcing me off the road, a sudden braking and relief that all is well, as she heads for our next rendezvous.

Slowly darkness lifts, as the realisation dawns that there have to be more climbs to get out of this valley. Hills that no one spoke of – small in stature compared with the overnight challenge, but massive in terms of the energy required to survive the encounter with them. Runners come back to me and gradually I climb through the rankings. The rise of the sun brings out the press and TV in search of the valiant runners. The heat seems to melt even the beads of sweat. I hide behind my dark glasses in search of that final downhill I was told would mark the beginning of the end.

At last I reach the crest and there below is Sparta. My eyes search for the centre of the town, for the monument or some other indication of the finish, as muscles jar with every downward step. The muscles are completely empty now; they scream that they have no more to give, but give they must! Crossing the steel girder bridge I am joined by a young man and girl. They carry olive branches and their stride pulls me along. They are my escorts to take me through the city to the finish. We twist and turn through the streets, a police car holding back any traffic from behind as applauding spectators stop their daily work to welcome me. Drivers leaving the city suddenly stop and wave or blow their horns – but where is this statue? Where is the base of the statue of the Spartan king that I must touch to stop this constant ache? Another corner and a crowd blocking the end of the road . . . I lift my eyes and see the sword and shield of the bronzed king . . . the pain is immediately soothed away by a joy that lifts my stride for one last 100m. The three steps are no obstacle, one stride takes me up, and with arm raised I tap my palm against the base. Victory is mine! The messages can be delivered to the mayor of Sparta who is there, the first to greet me. He crowns me with a laurel wreath and two toga-clad women offer the traditional drink of water from an ancient bowl. This is what we ran 250km for. It is only then that I hear that I have come sixth!

Sparta honours the 'messengers' that night in an ancient open auditorium. It is the tenth running of the race and top officials are invited to the splendid ceremony. The speeches are all translated into English, and my message from the State President is the only message that has been selected to be read out that night. It is a moving moment for Karin and me.

The following night, back in Athens, an even bigger ceremony takes place in the open auditorium in the national gardens. Ambassadors and embassy staff from all the participating countries attend. The athletes who have completed the race are fêted. Many expatriates came over to congratulate me, and I am passed a small packet of photographs from a Greek South African journalist who has followed the route. Owing to South African politics, this is the first time I have been able to compete, and it has been worth the eight-year wait!

APPENDIX ONE: TRAINING SCHEDULES FOR 10KM, THE MARATHON AND LONDON TO BRIGHTON

Due to the international flavour of the book, schedules are given in kilometres. The conversion to miles is: 1.6 km = 1 mile; thus every 4 km = 2.5 miles; 8 km = 5 miles; 16 km = 10 miles, etc.

The following pages give schedules for different target times for the 10km, marathon and 50 mile/100km distances. It is important to read the section headed 'Features of the schedules' later in this section whether you are training for an ultra or not, because the same notation as for the ultra is used in the other schedules too. You will not get the best results from the schedules unless you do this. London to Brighton runners must read all the notes very carefully.

How to use the training schedules for the London to Brighton
(or other 50 mile to 100km ultra)

These schedules are designed primarily for the use of runners who will not be going for silver, that is, for the majority of the field, who expect to finish in between 7:30 and the 11:00 cut-off. It is possible to modify the schedule for those runners who feel that they may be borderline cases for silver, but they should be capable of running a marathon in uder 3:10 and 10km in 0:40.

There are essentially three schedule options, each designed for a different type of runner. Your choice of schedule will depend on: your natural ability; the priority that you give running and training; the amount of time that you have available; and your background as a runner.

Each schedule details a training system for a different goal in the London to Brighton. In addition, remember to keep a daily record of your own training distances and your body's reactions. It is important that you keep this kind of record, as you should know by now. Your waking pulse will indicate whether you are recovering from your previous session (or other stressful situations, such as a late social night or pressure of work) in time for the next bout of training.

The schedules have been designed to accommodate a qualifying race and a shorter ultra in the build-up to the main target.

Right at the outset you must appreciate that it is necessary to restrict the amount of racing that you do in your training period if an optimum time is your goal in the London to Brighton. Thus the following options have been built into the schedules:

(a) Using an ultra marathon (56km) as a qualifier for London to Brighton, and then running a short ultra (50km to 56km) in August.

(b) Using a standard marathon as a qualifier in mid-March, again with a short ultra (35 miles) in August.

Other races and time trials over distances ranging from 8km to 21km have also been allowed for, with specific guidelines as to how hard these should be run. Only the qualifying race, the 15km race on the first or second weekend of September, and the listed 8km to 10km time trials should be raced. Participation in other races should occur at lesser exertion levels or not at all.

Obviously, training would be more sociable if the weekly races could be used as part of the weekly long runs, but only a few runners have the necessary willpower to run these at a pace sufficiently slow to avoid detriment to their training. It is up to you to decide whether you really want to achieve your optimum at London to Brighton, or produce average performances in a number of races.

I have tried to make the schedules suitable for the whole country, so you will have to accept a certain degree of flexibility when planning long runs, races and so on, since these are held on Saturdays in some areas and on Sundays in others.

It is acceptable to swap around the specified training sessions in any week to suit your specific needs, provided that the basic principles are not altered. In particular it is important that hard sessions are followed by easy days and that no more than two moderately hard days follow each other without a recovery day. (Sessions may be defined as hard either from a speed or a distance point of view.)

Which London to Brighton schedule is for you?
Schedule A is for you if you:

* have never run London to Brighton before and do not have a distance background;
* are able to complete only between 50km and 85km a week in peak training;
* are able to train only five days a week;
* have personal bests comparable to any of the following: 10km slower than 51:15; a half-marathon in over 2:00; a marathon in over 4:00.

In January you should be covering about 35km to 50km.

Completion of this training will result in a London to Brighton finish time of between 09:30 and 11:00.

Schedule B is for you if you:

* are able to train six days a week;
* have the time to put in between 70km and 100km training a week;
* aim to finish London to Brighton in between 08:00 and 09:30;
* have not done any track training in the last six months;
* have personal bests of the order of 10km in between 0:45 and 0:51; 21km in between 1:40 and 2:00; a marathon in 3:30 to 4:00.

You may have run London to Brighton before but are looking to improve on previous years' times.

Schedule C is for you if you:

* are able to put in six days' training a week with occasional days of double session during peak training;
* have at least a full year's running behind you;
* can handle a maximum of 110km training a week;
* at present train about 50km to 60km a week and can do so in January;
* have had some track speed training experience in the last six months;
* have personal bests in the region of 10km in between 0:40 and 0:45; half-marathon times of 1:25 to 1:40; a marathon time in between 3:10 and 3:30.

Your target is likely to be to finish London to Brighton in between 07:30 and 08:30.

If you can run between 2:55 and 3:10 for the marathon (0:39 to 0:40 over 20km) then you are probably a borderline case for a silver medal and you may wish to modify this schedule in order to break the 7:30 barrier on the day.

Features of all the schedules
The typical week
As you consult the schedules, you will note that in general the week is built up with at least one 'speed' session, a medium-length midweek run and a long run at the weekend. The remaining days tend to be recovery or easy running. Hard days are followed by easy days.

The long runs at the weekends alternate in length so that they too offer recovery.

Occasionally they are replaced by two medium-length runs back to back which will assist in development of the necessary endurance without requiring the same amount of recovery.

Fartlek

All schedules make some use of fartlek as a means of developing speed. Speed is an essential element of training. Running only long, slow distance develops a long, slow runner!

The session normally involves jogging 2km to 3km easy as a warm-up, which is followed by some stretching. The next few kilometres are then run by alternating faster periods with periods of easy running until the required session is completed. This is indicated in the charts in the following format: Fartlek 8km 5 x 1, 3. This means a total distance of 8km made up of 2km to 3km warm-up, followed by five faster runs each lasting a minute, each followed by three minutes' easy running, finished off with 2km to 3km of easy running. The speed of the fast sections should be about your best 5km race pace.

Hills

The hill sessions are an excellent way to introduce runners to the more demanding track sessions. They are also an ideal and specific way of improving leg strength and hill style.

There are many ways to vary these sessions, depending on where the emphasis is required. Short, steep hills concentrate more on strength, while longer, shallower hills primarily develop muscle endurance and hill style.

In these schedules I have compromised, using 200m long hills, and these session should be run at a pace about 10 seconds per kilometre faster than your best 5km time. The hills should therefore not be too steep, probably in the region of a 10 per cent incline.

Runners who have previously undertaken training on hills may wish to adjust the hill sessions in order to work on areas of weakness, but novices will find the given schedules a good introduction to hills.

As with all hard sessions, the hill repeats should be preceded by an easy 2km to 3km jog and stretching. Similarly, an easy 2km to 3km jog should be used as a cool-down afterwards.

Track

Track session are specified only for those runners using Schedule C. Since such sessions are stressful, it is advisable that runners have a sound background prior to commencing such training.

The speed of the track session will vary throughout the schedule but, as a guide, the 1km repeats should be done at approximately your best 15km pace, and the 400m repeats at your best 5km pace. Unless otherwise indicated, you should keep moving during recovery periods either by walking or by doing some very easy jogging for the stipulated duration.

Again, a warm-up and cool-down should be included in the session. In the schedule the session is indicated thus: track 8km, 10 x 400m, 1 R. This means that the total session, including warm-up and cool-down, will be approximately 8km long. After the warm-up and stretching, 400m is run at 5km pace, with a one-minute recovery prior to the next 400m. This is repeated until 10 x 400m are completed, and then a cool-down follows.

Many runners try to run the 400m repeats as fast as possible. This is not the objective. This would create a race situation, which breaks down the runner rather than building him or her up. Stick to approximately the prescribed pace.

Weight training
It is preferable to supplement this schedule with one or two sessions of weight training per week. However, always remember that this should not replace the specified running in each schedule.

A typical general weight-training schedule has been included in the chapter on supplementary exercises, and all exercises would generally involve doing three sets of 15 repetitions.

Weight training can be done at local gyms or on a home gym.

During August, when training for London to Brighton is the heaviest, only one session per week is required, and weights should be stopped in early September.

Days on which weight training could be undertaken are indicated with a 'W'. However, it is not intended that runners do weights on all of these days; rather that they choose the ones that are most convenient to them to make up the required number of sessions per week.

A. TRAINING SCHEDULES FOR 10 KM AND THE MARATHON

10 KM IN 50 MINUTES

Week 1

Day 1   Rest
2   Fartlek 6km
    (3 x 45 secs hard)
    (3 mins easy)
3   3–4km easy
4   5–7km + 5:30 min/km
5   Fartlek 6km *(as above)*
6   3–4km easy
7   6–8km LSD
    Total 35km

Week 2

Day 1   Rest
2   Fartlek 6–7km
    (3 x 1 min hard, 3 min easy)
3   4–5km easy
4   5–7km mod
5   Track *(5 x 200 60 secs, rest 2 mins)*
6   Rest
7   8–10 LSD
    Total 35km

Week 3

Day 1   Rest
2   Track *(3 x 400 1:58, rest 3½ then 2 x 200 in 55, rest 2 mins)*
3   4–5km easy
4   6–8km mod
5   Track *(5 x 400 1:58, rest 3½)*
6   4–5km easy
7   8–10km LSD
    Total 38km

Week 4

Day 1   Rest
2   Track *(6 x 400 +/- 1:55, rest 3)*
3   5km easy
4   6–8km mod
5   Track *(1 x 400 1:52, rest 2 mins. 1 x 200 53, rest 3½)*
    3 Reps
6   Rest
7   10–12km LSD
    Total 36km

Week 5

Day 1   Rest
   2   Track (*6 x 400 +/- 1:52,*
       rest 3 min, jog 300)
   3   5km easy
   4   6–8km +/- 5:20/km
   5   Track (*3 x 800 in 3:50*)
       Rest 4 +/- (*jog 500*)
   6   5km easy
   7   10–12km LSD
     Total 42km

Week 6

Day 1   Rest
   2   Fartlek 8km (*4 x 1 min hard, 3*
       easy)
   3   5km easy (+/- *27–28 mins*)
   4   5–6km (*26–32 mins*)
   5   Rest
   6   3–4km easy (+/- *25 mins*)
       stretching
   7   10km easy
     Total 33km

10KM IN 45 MINUTES

Week 1

Day 1   Rest
   2   Fartlek 6–8km (*3 x 1 min*
       hard, 3 easy)
   3   4–5km easy
   4   7–8km mod 4:45–5:00
   5   Fartlek 6–8km (*as above*)
   6   4–5km easy
   7   8–10km LSD
     Total 44km

Week 2

Day 1   Rest
   2   Fartlek 6km 2 x (*1 hard, 2*
       easy, ½ hard, 1 easy)
   3   4–5km easy
   4   7–8km mod 4:45–5:00
   5   Fartlek 6–8km (*3 x 1½ hard,*
       3½ easy)
   6   4–5 easy
   7   10km LSD
     Total 44km

Week 3

Day 1   Rest
   2   Track (*4 x 400 in 1:40,*
       rest 2 mins)
   3   4–5km
   4   7–8km mod 4:40–4:50
   5   Track (*3 x 800 in 3:30,*
       rest 4 mins)
   6   4–5km easy
   7   8–10km
     Total 46km

Week 4

Day 1   Rest
   2   Track (*5 x 400 in 1:40, rest 2*
       mins)
   3   4–5km easy
   4   8km mod 4:35–4:45
   5   Track (*3 x 1000 in 4:20, rest 5*
       mins)
   6   4–5km easy
   7   10–12km LSD
     Total 48km

Week 5

Day 1 Rest

2 Track (*3 x 600 in 2:35 rest,*
3 mins)

3 4–5km easy

4 8km mod 4:35–4:45

5 4–5km easy

6 Track (*1 x 1000 4:30, rest 2*
mins. 1 x 800 in 3:30, rest 2. 1
x 600 2:35, rest 2.
2 x 200 in 48, rest 1)

7 8–10km LSD
Total 47km

Week 6

Day 1 Rest

2 Track (*6 x 200 in 48, rest 1:40*)

3 4–5km easy

4 8km 4:35–4:45

5 4–5km easy

6 Track (*4 x 400 in 1:36, rest 2½*)

7 11–13km LSD
Total 47km

Week 7

Day 1 Rest

2 Track (*6 x 200 in 48, rest 1:50*)

3 4–5km easy

4 6km mod 4:35

5 Rest

6 Easy 3–4km

7 Race 10km in 45 mins
Total 33km

10KM IN 40 MINUTES

Week 1

Day 1 Rest

2 Fartlek (*5 x 1 min hard, 3 easy*)

3 6–8km easy

4 8–10km mod 4:20

5 Fartlek (*5 x 1 min hard, 3 easy*)

6 6–8km easy

7 10–12km LSD
Total 54km

Week 2

Day 1 Rest

2 Hills 5 x 200, (*double*
effort recovery)

3 6–8km easy

4 8–10km mod 4:20

5 6–8km easy

6 Fartlek (*6 x 1 min hard, 3 easy*)

7 10–12km LSD
Total 55km

Week 3

Day 1 Rest

2 Hills 6 x 200 (*full 2 x effort*
recovery)

3 6–8km easy

4 8–10km mod 4:20

5 6–8km easy

6 Track (*5 x 400 1:30, rest 2 mins*)

7 12km LSD
Total 60km

Week 4

Day 1   Rest
  2   Hills 7 x 200 (*full 2 x effort recovery*)
  3   6–8km easy
  4   8–10km mod 4:15 min/km
  5   6–8km easy
  6   +/- 5km time trial +/- 19 mins (*NOT FLAT OUT*)
  7   14km LSD
  Total 60km

Week 5

Day 1   Rest
  2   Track (*6 x 200 43, rest 1½ mins*)
  3   6–8km easy
  4   8–10km mod 4:15 min/km
  5   6–8km easy
  6   Track (*4 x 400, rest 1 min. 1 x 200, rest 3*) x 3
  7   11km LSD
  Total 54km

Week 6

Day 1   Rest
  2   Track (*6 x 200 43, rest 1½*)
  3   6–8km easy
  4   8–10km mod 4:15 min/km
  5   6–8km easy
  6   Track (*5 x 400 1:28, rest 2 mins*)
  7   15km LSD
  Total 58km

Week 7

Day 1   Rest
  2   6km 4:10 min/km
  3   Track (*2 x 400 1:30, rest 3. 3 x 200 43, rest 1½*)
  4   Rest
  5   4–5km easy/strides
  6   Race 10km
  7   11–13km LSD
  Total 27km

SUB 4:15 MARATHON

You should be capable of +/- 40km/week for the last 6–8 weeks.

Week 1

Day 1   Rest
  2   Fartlek (*3–4 x ½ min hard, 2 easy*)
  3   4–5km easy
  4   8–10km mod 6:10 min/km
  5   4–5km easy
  6   Rest
  7   18–20km
  Total 45km

Week 2

Day 1   Rest
  2   Fartlek (*4–6km x ½ min hard, 2 easy*)
  3   4–5km easy
  4   10km mod
  5   Fartlek 4–5km (*2–3 x 1 min*)
  6   Rest
  7   21–25km
  Total 50km

Week 3

Day 1   Rest
  2   Fartlek (*4–6 x ½ min hard, 2 easy*)
  3   4–5km easy
  4   12–14km LSD
  5   4–5km easy
  6   Rest
  7   10km race +/- 55 mins
  Total 40km

Week 4

Day 1   Rest

     2   Fartlek (*6–8km min hard, 2 easy*)

     3   5–6km easy

     4   10km mod 6:05 min/km

     5   5–6km easy

     6   Rest

     7   18–21km

       Total 49km

Week 5

Day 1   Rest

     2   Fartlek (*3 x 1 min hard, 4 easy.*
       3 x ½ min hard, 2 easy)

     3   5–6km easy

     4   8–10km mod

     5   5–6km easy

     6   Rest

     7   28–30km LSD

       Total 59km

Week 6

Day 1   Rest

     2   5–6km easy

     3   Fartlek (*4–6 x ½ min hard, 2
       easy*)

     4   8km +/- 50–51 mins

     5   5–6km easy

     6   Rest

     7   10km race +/- 52–53 mins

       Total 37km

Week 8

Day 1   Rest

     2   Easy Fartlek +/- 6km
       (*4 x ½ min bursts*)

     3   Easy 6km

     4   5–7km

     5   Rest

     6   Rest

     7   Race 42km

       Total 60km

SUB 3:30 MARATHON

Should be capable of +50km/week over the last 6–8 weeks

Week 1

Day 1   Rest

     2   Fartlek (*+8km with 3–5 x
       1 min hard, 3 easy*)

     3   6–8km easy

     4   Hills 3–4 x 200
       (*double recovery of effort*)

     5   6–8km easy

     6   15–20km LSD

     7   12–15km LSD

       Total 64km

Week 2

Day 1   Rest

     2   Fartlek (*8–10km with
       3 x 1 min hard, 3 easy.
       4 x ½ min hard, 1 easy*)

     3   6–8km easy

     4   +5km TT

     5   6–8km easy

     6   18–22km LSD

     7   10–12km LSD

       Total 63km

Week 3

Day 1   Rest

     2   Fartlek (*8–10km with
       4 x 1 min hard, 3 easy.
       6 x ½ min hard, 1 easy*)

     3   6–8km easy

     4   10km mod +5:10/km

     5   6–8km easy

     6   Fartlek (*8km 3 x 1½ hard,
       4½ easy*)

     7   20–25km LSD

       Total 64km

Week 4

Day 1   Rest
2   Fartlek (+*10km with*
    5 x 1 min hard, 3 easy.
    6 x ½ min hard, 1 easy)
3   6–8km easy
4   10–12km mod
5   6–8km easy
6   Fartlek (*8km with*
    3 x ½ hard, 4½ easy)
7   20–25km easy
    Total 66km

Week 5

Day 1   Rest
2   Fartlek (*8 x ½ min hard,*
    2 easy)
3   5–8km easy
4   10km mod +5:05
5   Fartlek (*3 x 1 min hard*)
6   5–6km easy
7   28–32km
    Total 68km

Week 6

Day 1   Rest
2   Fartlek (*1 min hard, 2 easy.*
    2 mins hard, 4 easy etc – up to 4
    mins hard, 8 easy)
3   6–8km easy
4   8–10km mod 5:05 min/km
5   6–8km easy
6   Fartlek (*8km*
    4 x 1 min hard, 3 easy)
7   20–25km LSD
    Total 67km

Week 7

Day 1   Rest
2   8–10km TT
3   5–7km easy
4   Fartlek (*6–8km with*
    4 x 1 min hard, 3 easy)
5   5–7km easy
6   10–12km mod
    +/- 5:00 min/km
7   Rest
    Total 45km

Week 8

Day 1   18–20km
2   5–7km easy
3   Easy fartlek (*½ min 'bursts'*)
4   Rest
5   Easy 4–5km
6   Rest
7   Race
    Total 70km

SUB 3:00 MARATHON

Should be able to do +60km/week for
the past 8 weeks

Week 1

Day 1   Rest
2   Hills 3–5 x 200 (*double*
    recovery as effort)
3   6–8km easy
4   12–15km mod
5   6–8km easy
6   Fartlek (*8–10km with*
    3–5 x 1 min hard, 3 easy)
7   18–20km LSD
    Total 69km

Week 2

Day 1 Rest
   2 Hills 4–6 x 200 (*double*
     recovery)
   3 8km easy
   4 5km TT (*not flat out +/- 98%*)
   5 8km easy
   6 Hills 3–4 x 300
   7 20–25km LSD
     Total 67km

Week 3

Day 1 Rest
   2 Track (*3–4 x 1km in 4:00,*
     rest 5 mins)
   3 6–8km easy
   4 12–15km mod
     +/- 4:20 min/km
   5 6–8km easy
   6 20km LSD
   7 15–20km LSD
     Total 76km

Week 4

Day 1 Rest
   2 Track (*4 x 800 in 3:10,*
     rest 4 mins)
   3 8km easy
   4 12–15km mod
   5 Hills 4–6 x 200
   6 6–8km easy
   7 30–32km LSD
     Total 80km

Week 5

Day 1 Rest
   2 Track (*5 x 800 in 3:10, rest 4*)
   3 8km easy
   4 12–15km mod
   5 Track (*3 x 400 1:30 rests,*
     3 x 200 in 43, rest ½)
   7 20–25km LSD
     Total 77km

Week 6

Day 1 Rest
   2 Track (*6–8 x 400 +/- 1:30 rests*)
   3 8km easy
   4 12km mod 4:15 min/km
   5 Track (*3 x 400 1:30, rest 3.*
     3 x 200, rest ½)
   6 6–8km easy
   7 32–36km
     Total 72km

Week 7

Day 1 Rest
   2 8 or 10km TT (+/- 98%)
   3 6–8km easy
   4 Track (*6–8 x 400 in 1:30,*
     rest 3)
   5 6–8km easy
   6 15km mod
   7 6–8km LSD
     Total 60km

Week 8

Day 1 Rest
   2 6–8km easy
   3 Fartlek +/- 8km (*informal but*
     easy – don't tax yourself)
   4 Rest
   5 4–5km easy
   6 Rest
   7 Race 42km
     Total 74km

B. TRAINING SCHEDULES FOR LONDON TO BRIGHTON

WARNING!
EXPERIENCED
RUNNERS ONLY

Day	A	B	C
1	Rest	Rest	Rest
2	5km	10km	8–10km mod
3	10km	8km	Hills 3–5 x 200 (double recovery as effort)

WEEK 1 (11 May)

	A	B	C
1	Rest	Rest	12–14km mod
2	5km	8km	5–8km easy
3	10km	10km	5 x 400 rest 1½
4	5km	5km	8–10km mod
5	Rest	Rest	2 x 2000 + 5mins 1 x 1000 @ 10 km pace
6	5km	15km	5km easy
7	12km	5km	4 x 800 – rest 3 mins

WEEK 2 (18 May)

	A	B	C
1	5km	Rest	Rest
2	Rest	8km	15-20km LSD
3	7km	5km	5km easy
4	10km	12km	10 x 400 r 1 min @ 5–10 km pace
5	Rest	Rest	10km mod
6	7km	10km	4–5km @ 10 km pace (as TT)
7	12km	10km	5–8km easy

WEEK 3 (25 May)

	A	B	C
1	Rest	Rest	15–20km LSD
2	5km	5km	12–15km LSD
3	10km	10km	Rest
4	7km	8km	5–7 x 200 Hills
5	Rest	Rest	10–12km mod
6	5km	17km	4 x 800 rest 2½ mins
7	15km	5km	6–8km easy

WEEK 4 (1 June)

	A	B	C
1	5km	Rest	18–24km LSD
2	Rest	5km	5–8km easy
3	10km (incl 5km TT)	12km (incl 5km TT)	2 x 2000 @ 10 km pace 5 mins rest
4	5km	5km	8–10km mod
5	Rest	Rest	8km easy
6	8km	12km	Rest
7	10km	12km	10km @ proposed 21km pace

WEEK 5 (8 June)

	A	B	C
1	Rest	Rest	8km easy
2	8km–W	8km–W	6–8 x 300 Hills
3	12km	12km mod	10–12km mod
4	8km	8km	4–5km @ 10 km pace as TT)
5	Rest–W	Rest–W	8km easy x 4
6	10km	10km	(2 x 400 r 45)
7	17km	17km	20–26km LSD

WEEK 6 (15 June)

1	Rest	Rest	8–10km
2	8km–W	8km–W	Rest
3	15km	15km mod	3–5 x 1000 rest 3 mins @ 8km pace
4	Fartlek 8km (4 x ½ hard, 3 easy)	Fartlek 8km (4 x ½ hard, 3 easy)	5–8km easy
5	Rest–W	Rest–W	1 x 1000 r 2½ 1 x 2000 r 5 1 x 3000 (all @ 10 km pace)
6	8km	8km	10–12km
7	21km LSD	21km LSD	18–22km

WEEK 7 (22 June)

1	Rest	Rest	8km easy
2	8km–W	Fartlek 8km (3 x 1 hard, 3 easy)	8–10 x 200 hills
3	6km	15km mod–W	Rest
4	Fartlek 8km (4 x ½ hard, 3 easy)	10km	8–12km
5	Rest	Fartlek (3 x 2 hard, 5 easy)	8–10km
6	8km easy–W	10km easy–W	6–8 x 400 r 2 mins
7	8km	21km LSD	15–18km LSD

WEEK 8 (29 June)

1	Rest	Rest	4 x 400 (complete recovery @ 1500 pace)
2	10km (incl 5km TT)	10km (incl 5km TT)	3 x 400 (complete recovery @ 1500 pace)
3	16km	8km–W	2 x 400 (complete recovery @ 1500 pace)
4	Fartlek 8km (3x1H 5E)	Fartlek 8km (3x2H 5E)	Rest
5	Rest-W	8km	1 x 400 (complete recovery @ 1500 pace)
6	21km LSD		
7	32km LSD		21.1km race

WEEK 9 (6 July)

1	Rest–W	Rest–W	Rest
2	Fartlek 8km (5x1H 2½E)	Fartlek 8km (5x1H 2E)	8km easy
3	17km–W	18km–W	15km–W
4	8km	10km	8km easy
5	Rest–W	8km	Hills 8km 5 x 200 m
6	30km LSD	15km total– 10km hard, 5km easy	15km total– 3 x 3km @ 15km pace, 6km easy
7	8km easy	25km run in afternoon	PM: 25km

WEEK 10 (13 July)

1	Rest	Rest	Rest
2	Fartlek 8km (5x1H 2E)	Fartlek 8km (4x1H 1½E)	Track 10km (6 x 400 at 10km race pace)
3	17km–W	20km–W	20km–W
4	8km	8km	8km
5	Rest–W	Fartlek 8km (3 x 2H 5E)	Hills 8km (5 x 300)
6	21km LSD	10km–W	15km–W
7	10km	25km	25km

WEEK 11 (20 July)

1	Rest	Rest	Rest
2	Fartlek 8km	Fartlek 8km	Track 10km (5 x 400 at 5km pace, 1 rest)
3	12km–W	15km	10km at 21 km race pace
4	5km easy	5km easy	5km track (2 x 400 at 5km pace, 1 rest)
5	Rest	Rest	Rest
6	42km qualifier or rest	42km qualifier or rest	40km training if already qualified or 10–15 easy

WEEK 12 (27 July) RECOVERY WEEK

1	Rest–W	Rest–W	Rest–W
2	5km easy	5km easy	5km easy
3	8km easy	8km easy	10km easy
4	8km easy	8km easy	10km easy
5	Rest–W	Rest–W	Fartlek 10km (3x1H 3E)
6	10km	10km	10km–W
7	15km	15km	15–20km

WEEK 13 (3 August)

1	Rest	Rest	Rest
2	Fartlek 8km	Fartlek 8km (5x1H ½E)	AM: 8km PM: 10km track, 5 x 1000 km 1½R 15 km pace
3	21km–W	20km–W	25km–W
4	8km	Hills 8km, 5 x 200 m	Hills 8km, 8 x 200 m
5	Rest–W	8km–W	8km–W
6	25km	25km	25km
7	15km	10km	10km

WEEK 14 (10 August)

1	Rest	Rest	Rest
2	Fartlek 8km (5x1H 2E)	Fartlek 8km (4x2H 3E)	AM: 8km PM: 10km track, 10 x 400 m 1½R. 5 km pace
3	20km–W	15km–W	20km–W
4	8km	Hills 8km, 4 x 200 m	Hills 8km, 5 x 300 m
5	Rest	8km or rest	8km or rest
6	50–60km LSD or rest	50–60km LSD or rest	50–60km LSD or rest
7	50km LSD or rest	50km or rest	50km or rest

WEEK 15 (17 August)

1	Rest	Rest	Rest
2	5km easy	8km easy	8km easy
3	8km easy	8km easy	8km easy
4	10km	15km	15km
5	Rest–W	Hills 8km, 4 x 200 m	Hills 8km, 4 x 200 m
6	10km	10km–W	10km–W
7	22km	26km	26km

WEEK 16 (24 August)

1	Rest	Rest	Rest
2	Fartlek 8km (5x1H 2E)	Fartlek 10km (5x1H ½E)	AM: 8km PM: 10km track, 5 x 1,000 m 1½R 15km pace
3	21km–W	15km–W	25km–W
4	8km	8km	8km
5	Rest–W	Hills 8km, 4 x 200 m	AM: 8km PM: Hills 8km, 5 x 300 m
6	15km	10km–W	15km–W
7	25km	32km	32km

WEEK 17 (31 August)

1	Rest	Rest	Rest
2	Fartlek 8km (5x1H 2E)	Fartlek 10km (6x1H 2E)	AM: 8km PM: 10km track (5 x 1,000 m 1½ R. 10km race 5 x 100 m 1½R)
3	25km–W	30km	30km
4	Fartlek 8km (3x2H 5E)	12km–W	10km–W
5	Rest	Hills 10 km, 4 x 300	AM: 8km PM: Hills 8km, (5 x 300 m)
6	10km easy	10km easy	15km easy
7	15km race, 20 for day	15km race, 20 for day	15km race, 20 for day

WEEK 18 (7 September)

1	Rest	Rest	Rest
2	Fartlek 8km (5x1H 2½E)	15km	AM: 8km PM: 10km track (3 x 800 m R1½ 5 x 300 R1 10km pace
3	25km	30km	21km
4	10km	10km	AM: 8km PM: Hills 8km (8 x 200m)
5	Rest	Fartlek 10 km (5x1H 1½E)	10km
6	10km easy	10km	10km easy
7	21km at 80%	21km at 80%	21km at 80%

WEEK 19 (14 September)

1	Rest	Rest	Rest
2	8km	Hills 10km (6 x 200 m)	Track 8km (10 x 400 m 1R at 5km pace)
3	16km	25km	16km
4	Fartlek 8km (5x1H 1½E)	10km	Track 8km (4 x 1000 m 2R)
5	Rest	Fartlek 10km (5x1H 1½E)	8km
6	22km	12km	12km
7	22km	28km	30km

WEEK 20 (21 September)

1	Rest	Rest	Rest
2	Fartlek 8km (5x1H 3E)	Fartlek 8km (5x1H 2E)	12km
3	18km	17km	Track 8km (4 x 1000 m 3R)
4	8km	10km easy	20km
5	Rest	Fartlek (4x1H 3E)	Track 5 x 400 m at 3km pace
6	5–10km easy	Fartlek (3x1H 3E)	Track 5 x 400
7	Fartlek 5km (3x1H 2E)	Fartlek (2x1H 2E)	Track 4 x 400

WEEK 21 (28 September)

1	8km easy	Fartlek (2x½H 2E)	Track 3 x 400
2	3–5km easy	Rest	Track 2 x 400
3	Rest	Fartlek (2x½H 2E)	Rest
4	3–5km easy	Rest	Track 2 x 400
5	Rest	Fartlek (2x1H 2E)	Rest
6	3–5km easy	Fartlek (2x½H 2E)	Track 1 x 400
7	Rest	Rest	Rest

OCTOBER 4

Race	Race	Race

Note:

This schedule was designed for a specific year and will need to be adjusted for the year in which you are training.

Symbols used

AM:	morning run
PM:	evening or afternoon run
W:	weight training
TT:	time-trial
H/E:	hard/easy
R:	recovery
LSD:	long, slow distance

APPENDIX TWO: INTERNATIONAL MARATHONS

JANUARY
Walt Disney World Marathon, USA
Osaka International Ladies' Marathon, Japan

FEBRUARY
Beppu-Oita Mainichi Marathon, Japan
Las Vegas International Marathon, USA
Marathon Popular de Valencia, Spain
Tokyo International Marathon, Japan
Tokyo – New York Friendship Marathon, Japan
Egyptian Marathon, Egypt
Caribbean Cement Jamaica Marathon, Jamaica
Ohme 30km Road Race, Japan
Tahiti-Moorea Blue Marathon, Tahiti
Old Mutual Capetown Marathon, South Africa
Marathon Ciudad de Sevilla, Spain
Cebu Tri-City International 25km, Philippines

MARCH
Lake Biwa Mainichi Marathon, Japan
Vigaranomaratona, Italy
China Coast Marathon, China
Kyoto City Half Marathon, Japan
Nagoya International Women's Marathon, Japan
EDP Meia Maratona de Lisboa, Portugal
Marathon Catalunya-Barcelona, Spain
Maui International Marathon, USA
Graz-Murpromenaden Marathon and Half Marathon, Australia
Roma City Marathon, Italy
City-Pier-City Half Marathon, the Netherlands
Dong-A International Marathon, Korea
Los Angeles Marathon, USA
Malang International Marathon, Indonesia
Gallipoli International Half Marathon, Turkey

APRIL
Berlin Half Marathon, Germany
Two Oceans 56km, South Africa
Splendid International Half Marathon, Italy
Generale Bank Marathon Rotterdam, the Netherlands
Maraton Internacional de Santiago, Chile
Shell hanse-Marathon Hamburg, Germany
BAA Boston Marathon, USA
Belgrade Stark Marathon, Yugoslavia
Big Sur International Marathon, USA
Flora London Marathon, Great Britain
Marathon Popular de Madrid, Spain
Maraton Wroclaw, Poland
Paris International Marathon, France
Lipton's Ice Tea Antwerp Marathon, Belgium

MAY
Fletcher Challenge Marathon, New Zealand
Turin Marathon, Italy
Vancouver International Marathon, Canada
25km von Berlin, Germany
Green Bursa Half Marathon, Turkey
Copenhagen Marathon, Denmark
Göteborg Half Marathon, Sweden
Prague International Marathon, Czech Republic
Vienna City Marathon, Austria
Porto Alegre Marathon, Brazil

JUNE
Stockholm Marathon, Sweden
International Enschede Marathon Twente, the Netherlands
Comrades Marathon, South Africa
Corrida de São João, Portugal
Veterans' Grand Prix, Brugge, Belgium
São Paulo Marathon, Brazil

JULY
Midnight Sun Marathon, Norway
Guldensporenmarathon, Belgium
Paavo Nurmi Marathon, Finland
Marvejols – Mende, France
Sapporo International Half Marathon, Japan
International Road Race of Castelbuona, 11km, Italy
Swiss Alpine Marathon 67km, Davos, Switzerland
Blumenau Marathon, Brazil

AUGUST
Siberian International Marathon, Russia
Mount Meru International Marathon, Tanzania
IAAF World Marathon Championships, Athens, Greece
Helsinki City Marathon, Finland
Great Scottish Run, Glasgow, Great Britain
Reykjavik Marathon, Iceland
100km de Cleder, France
Brazil Half Marathon, Rio de Janeiro, Brazil
Erewash 10 Mile Classic, Great Britain
Maraton Internacional de la Ciudad de Mexico, Mexico
Hokkaido Marathon, Japan
Moscow Peace Marathon, Russia

SEPTEMBER
International Jungfrau Marathon, Switzerland
Buenos Aires City Half Marathon, Argentina
Nike Budapest Half Marathon, Hungary
100km World Challenge, Winschoten, the Netherlands
Philips International 15km Road Race, Pila, Poland
Bükk International Mountain Marathon, Hungary
Singha Gold River Kwai International Half Marathon, Thailand
Tallin Half Marathon, Estonia
10km de Tagarro, Portugal
Berlin Marathon, Germany
Kaiser's Plus Budapest Marathon, Hungary
Le Lion, France
Maraton Adidas de la Republica Argentina, Argentina
Paris – Versailles 16km, France
Portland Marathon, USA
Route du Vin Half Marathon, Luxembourg

OCTOBER
IAAF World Half Marathon Championships, Slovakia
Kosice Peace Marathon, Slovakia
Santa Cruz de Bezena 100km, Spain
Smarna Gora Mountain Race, Slovenia
Lidingöloppet, Sweden

Vardinoyannios Marathon, Greece
Bucharest International Marathon, Romania
Beijing International Marathon, China
Istanbul Eurasia Marathon, Turkey
Le Marathon de Reims, France
Marathon de Asturias 'Valle de Nalón', Spain
Maratona D'Italia, Carpi, Italy
Royal Victoria Marathon, Canada
Zagreb Marathon, Croatia
LaSalle Banks Chicago Marathon & 5km, USA
Lausanne Marathon, Switzerland
River Shimanto 100km Kouchi, Japan
20km de Paris, France
Canadian International Marathon, Canada
Belgrade Stark Marathon/Race Through History, Yugoslavia
BMW Auckland International Marathon, New Zealand
Eta Marathon Frankfurt, Germany
Marseille – Cassis, France
Spa Euro Marathon Echternach, Luxembourg
US Marine Corps Marathon, USA
Venice Marathon for UNICEF, Italy

NOVEMBER
Chosunilbo Chunchon International Marathon, Korea
Delta Lloyd Amsterdam Marathon, the Netherlands
New York City Marathon, USA
Sportsmans Travel International Malta Challenge Marathon, Malta
Marathon de Habana, Cuba
Amagasaki International Marathon for the UNICEF Cup, Japan
Discoveries Marathon, Lisbon, Portugal
Tsukuba Marathon, Japan
Seattle Marathon & Half Marathon, USA
Firenze Marathon, Italy
Old Mutual Soweto Marathon, South Africa
Tokyo Women's Marathon, Japan

DECEMBER
Course de l'Escalade, Geneva, Switzerland
Marathon Internacional Costa Rica, Costa Rica

Fukuoka International Open Marathon
Championship, Japan
Macau International Half Marathon,
Macau
Marathon International Costa de Calvia,
Spain
Honolulu Marathon, USA
Angkor-Wat Half Marathon, Cambodia

Zürcher Silvesterlauf, Switzerland
Delhi International 10km, India
Corrida Pedestre Internationale de
Houilles, France
International São Silvestre Road Race,
Brazil
São Silvestre da Amadora, Portugal

APPENDIX THREE: USEFUL ADDRESSES

UK Sports Council, Walkden House, 10 Melton Street, London NW1 2EB; Tel/Fax 0171 380 8000; drugs information line 0171 380 8030

English Sports Council, 16 Upper Woburn Place, London WC1H 0QP; Tel 0171 273 1500; Fax 0171 383 5740

N. Ireland Sports Council, House of Sport, Upper Malone Road, Belfast BT9 5LA; Tel 01232 381222; Fax 01232 666073

Scottish Sports Council, Caledonia House, South Gyle, Edinburgh EH12 9DQ; Tel 0131 317 7200; Fax 0131 317 7202

Sports Council for Wales, Sophia Gardens, Cardiff, South Glamorgan CF1 9SW; Tel 01222 397571; Fax 01222 222431

AAA: English Cross-Country Association, c/o I. Byett, 273 Cranbourne Lane, Basingstoke, Hants RG21 3NX; Tel 01256 28401

AAA: Road Running, c/o E.C. Butcher, 26 Ryecroft Avenue, Deeping St James, Peterborough, Cambs PE6 8NT; Tel 01778 345062

AAA: Track and Field, c/o R. Tilling, 53 Burnham Court, Muscovy Road, Erdington, Birmingham B23 7YW; Tel 0121 681 4612

Midland Counties Athletic Association, Edgbaston House, 3 Duchess Place, Hagley Road, Birmingham B16 8NM; Tel 0121 452 1500; Fax 0121 455 9792

North of England Athletic Association, Suite 106, Emco House, 5/7 New York Road, Leeds LS2 7PJ; Tel 0113 246 1835; Fax 0113 234 3464

South of England Athletic Association, Suite 36, City of London Fruit Exchange, Brushfield Street, London E1 6EU; Tel 0171 247 2963; Fax 0171 247 3439

Northern Ireland Amateur Athletic Association, Athletics House, Old Coach Road, Belfast BT9 5PR; Tel 01232 602707; Fax 01232 309939

Scottish Athletics Federation, Caledonia House, Redheughs Rigg, South Gyle, Edinburgh EH12 9DQ; Tel 0131 317 7320; Fax 0131 317 7321

Athletics Association of Wales, Morfa Stadium, Llandore, Swansea SA1 7DF; Tel 01792 456237; Fax 01792 474916

Regional Coach Education

Scotland: Mr J. Keddie, 8 Muirkirk Drive, Earnock, Hamilton, Lanarkshire ML3 3EX; Tel 01698 301280

England – North (Northern Division): Mr C. Gould, 59 Cavendish Court, Birdon's Green, Brandon, Co. Durham DH7 8UL; Tel 0191 378 9616

England – North (Western Region): S. Sampey, 23 Pimlico Road, Clitheroe, Lancashire BB7 2AG; Tel/Fax 01200 27762

England – North (Eastern Region): Mrs A. Warburton, 60 Tinshill Road, Cookridge, Leeds LS16 7DS; Tel 01132 936195

England – Midlands: Mrs C. Franks, 23 Salisbury Avenue, Cheltenham Spa, Gloucestershire GL51 5BT; Tel 01242 528548

England – South (North of the Thames): Mr R. Kinge, 1 Bluebell Close, Scarning, Dereham, Norfolk NR19 2UQ; Tel 01362 697173

England – South (South-East Region): Mrs C. Shuttleworth, 11a Prince Edward's Road, Lewes, East Sussex BN7 1BJ; Tel 01273 477322

England – South (Western Region): Mr R. Blank, 13 School Close, Woodford, Plympton, Devon PL7 4HP; Tel 01752 336829

Wales: Coach Education Manager, AA of Wales, Morfa Stadium, Llandore, Swansea SA1 7DF; Tel 01792 463177

Northern Ireland: Mr S. Enright, 10a Kilbright Road, Carrowdore, Newtownards, Co. Down BT22 2JD; Tel 01247 861558

Schools Associations

English Schools AA (Hon. Sec. D.R. Littlewood), 26 Newborough Green, New Malden, Surrey KT3 5HS; Tel 0181 949 1506

Scottish Schools AA (Hon. Sec. A. Jack), 11 Muirfield Street, Kirkcaldy, Fife KY2 6SY; Tel 01592 260168

Ulster Schools AA (Hon. Sec. G. Moffett), c/o Belfast Road Academy, Cliftonville Road, Belfast BT14 6JL; Tel 01232 740423

Welsh Schools AA (Hon. Sec. G. Coldwell), 21 John Street, Neyland, Milford Haven, Dyfed SA18 3BZ; Tel 01269 850390

APPENDIX FOUR: DRUGS CONTAINING BANNED SUBSTANCES

Below are examples of substances currently permitted or prohibited by the International Olympic Committee. If in doubt about what is legal or not, consult the doping control officer at your local athletics club. Remember that many items available over the counter contain banned substances. The responsibility to check what may be used lies with the athlete.

Listing according to drug types

Stimulants, e.g. amphetamine, bromantan, caffeine (above 12mcg/ml), cocaine, ephedrine, certain beta 2 agonists.

Narcotics, e.g. diamorphine (heroin), morphine, methadone, pethidine.

Anabolic agents, e.g. methandienone, nandrolone, stanozolol, testosterone, clenbuterol, DHEA.

Diuretics, e.g. acetazolamide, frusemide, hydrochlorothiazide, triamterine.

Peptide & Glycoprotein Hormones & Analogues, e.g. growth hormone, corticotrophin, chorionic gonadotrophin, erythropoletin

Alcohol & Marijuana not prohibited, but may be restricted

Local Anaesthetics route of administration restricted to local or intra-articular injection

Corticosteroids route of administration restricted to topical, inhalation, local or intra-articular injection

Beta-blockers not prohibited, but may be restricted

Listing according to condition being treated

Asthma: *Allowed* – salbutamol*, terbutaline*, salmeterol*, beclomethasone*, fluticasone*, theophylline* (*by inhalation only) sodium cromoglycate.
Banned – products containing sympathomimetics, e.g. ephedrine, isoprenaline, fenoterol, rimiterol, orciprenaline.

Cold/Cough: *Allowed* – all antibiotics, steam & menthol inhalations, permitted antihistamines, terfenadine, astemizole, pholcodine, guaiphenesin, dextromethorphan, paracetamol.
Banned – products containing sympathomimetics, e.g. ephedrine, pseudoephedrine, phenylpropanolamine.

Diarrhoea: *Allowed* – diphenoxylate, lopermide, products containing electrolytes (e.g. Dioralyte, Rehidrat).
Banned – products containing opioids (e.g. morphine)

Hay Fever: *Allowed* – antihistamines, nasal sprays containing a corticosteroid or xylometazoline, eyedrops containing sodium cromoglycate.
Banned – products containing ephedrine, pseudoephedrine.

Pain: *Allowed* – aspirin, codeine, dihydrocodeine, ibuprofen, paracetamol, all non-steroidal anti-inflammatories, dextropropoxyphene.
Banned – products containing opioids, caffeine.

Vomiting: *Allowed* – domperidone, metoclopramide.